American Aloha

American Aloha

Cultural Tourism and the Negotiation of Tradition

Heather A. Diamond

University of Hawai'i Press
Honolulu

Printed in the United States of America
Paperback edition 2011
16 15 14 13 12 11 6 5 4 3 2 1

Library of Congress Cataloging-in-Publication Data

Diamond, Heather A.
American aloha : cultural tourism and the negotiation of tradition / Heather A. Diamond.
p. cm.
Includes bibliographical references and index.
ISBN 978-0-8248-3171-4 (hardcover : alk. paper)
ISBN 978-0-8248-3616-0 (alk. paper)
1. Folklore—Hawaii. 2. Hawaii—Social life and customs. 3. Folk festivals—United States—Public opinion. 4. Public opinion—United States. 5. Festival of American Folklife (13th : 1989 : Washington, D.C.) 6. Smithsonian Folklife Festival. I. Title.
GR110.H38D53 2008
398.209969—dc22
2008001824

University of Hawaiʻi Press books are printed on acid-free paper and meet the guidelines for permanence and durability of the Council on Library Resources.

Designed by University of Hawaiʻi Press production staff

Printed by The Maple-Vail Book Manufacturing Group

Contents

Preface / vii
Note on Names / xi
Acknowledgments / xiii
Abbreviations / xv

Introduction / 1
Chapter 1. Cultural Intervention in America's Eden / 12
Chapter 2. Finding and Defining Traditional Hawai'i / 61
Chapter 3. Interpreting an Authentic "Sense of Place" / 98
Chapter 4. Performing "The Other Side of the Island" / 134
Chapter 5. Beyond the Festival Afterglow / 175

Conclusion / 213
Notes / 219
Glossary / 239
References / 241
Index / 251

Preface

My research on the 1989 Hawai'i program at the Smithsonian began, as do many endeavors in Hawai'i, with "talk story." At the time, I was a recent transplant to the islands, and I was working as a volunteer archivist in the Folk Arts division of the Hawai'i State Foundation for Culture and the Arts (HSFCA). As I sifted through records of many impressive HSFCA projects, I ran across the program book for the 1989 Hawai'i program at the Festival of American Folklife (FAF; now Smithsonian Folklife Festival, or SFF). Based on my reading of the FAF program book, it seemed to me that a folklife festival involved an incredible amount of money and work for an event that lasted only ten days, and I (never having put on a folklife festival) naively decided that a festival was a showy, but transitory and inefficient, way to support traditional arts and artists. I made this assessment primarily in contrast to the behind-the-scenes sponsorship of the HSFCA Folk Arts Master and Apprentice Program, which funds the perpetuation of traditional cultural practices and to which I accorded more long-range impact. As I skimmed the program book for the 1989 FAF, I noticed that many of the same traditional arts practitioners—musicians, lei makers, dancers, saddle makers, and so on—who had been in the Master and Apprentice Program had also represented Hawai'i in Washington, D.C. The idea of celebrating Hawai'i's thirtieth anniversary of statehood with a display of Hawaiian culture on the National Mall struck me as ironic given the presence of an active sovereignty movement.

I took the program book home with me for a closer look and discovered familiar names on the staff page. People I knew through the ethnomusicology department of the University of Hawai'i at Mānoa had been involved as staff. When I asked them about their experiences, a rich vein of intriguing anecdotes surfaced—memories that were remarkably vivid even after fourteen years. It was then that I began to suspect that there was more to a folklife festival than meets a casual festivalgoer's eye. My subsequent investigation into the making of the Hawai'i program in 1989 not only revealed the complexity of the festival-making process and the existence of festival culture, but also illuminated the complexity of cultural identities in Hawai'i and how they are often construed in opposition to identity politics in the continental United States, or "the mainland," as it is called in Hawai'i. Despite having been a student and a teacher of multicultural literature and culture on the mainland for many years, I had to learn from scratch how multiculturalism is constructed in Hawai'i.

That I live in Hawai'i but am not from Hawai'i is a position that provides a unique view. Being both a *haole* (Caucasian) and settler in Hawai'i, a place with a long history of socioeconomic exploitation by outsiders, I am often aware of being in the position of perpetual outsider. This position bears both limitations and advantages. With regards to this research, my positionality had useful parallels with the positions of some festival workers and many festival viewers. Like many of the visitors to the Hawai'i program in Washington, D.C., in 1989, my previous notions of Hawai'i had been filtered through romanticized stereotypes based on tourist industry and media hype. My own process of discovery was instructive in understanding how many visitors to the National Mall were surprised by a representation of Hawai'i that was not in accord with expectations shaped by Tin Pan Alley and Waikiki tourism. For festival visitors and for the mostly *haole* culture workers from the Smithsonian who brokered the Hawai'i program, the 1989 Festival became an invaluable tool for learning more about Hawai'i history and culture, a threshold to "the other side of the island," as once festivalgoer put it. Although I did not attend the 1989 FAF, through my research into the nuts and bolts of its festival-making process, I, too, like program visitors, heard many local voices to which I would not otherwise have been privy.

In my efforts to contextualize and get below the official narratives of the Hawai'i program, I turned to a variety of sources. To understand the intertwined histories of tourism and state sponsorship for traditional arts in Hawai'i, I perused the Bishop Museum Archives, where I found old photographs of Mossman's Leilani Village and World's Fair pamphlets. At the Hawai'i State Archives I discovered correspondence on the Folklore Commission established by the territorial government in 1926 and the subsequent hiring of Helen Roberts to document vanishing Hawaiian songs and chants. Hamilton Library at the University of Hawai'i turned up all the 1989 Festival logs and stage recordings and kindly transferred the recordings from aging and forgotten audiocassettes to 150 CD-ROMs. At the Hawai'i State Foundation for the Arts, I found the stage recordings for the 1990 restaging.

My view of the Festival is presented as a chronology that contextualizes and recaptures the festival-making process. I first attended the Festival in 2002, and being there both sharpened and dulled my critical proclivities. The Festival is an impressive production, and its proximity to national monuments of government, social science, and art make it appear as the ultimate radical juxtaposition. The experience of physically being at the festival is, well, *festive.* In December 2002 I met with Richard Kennedy, deputy director of the Festival, and Diana Parker, the Festival director. I also spent time in the Ralph Rinzler Archives and Collections at the Center for Folklife and Cultural Heritage (CFCH) to get a sense of the Hawai'i program from visual records. Then in 2003 I returned to the CFCH and worked on the Festival as staff during the Mali, Scotland, and Appalachia programs. This time I hit pay dirt when Richard Kennedy, who had curated the Hawai'i program, granted me access to his personal files from that program's curatorial process. Kennedy's files and the CFCH archives contained all of the records on the creation of the Hawai'i program, from correspondence to purchase orders, from Hawai'i to Washington, D.C. Lynn Martin, who had masterminded much of the Hawai'i end of the Festival (and is now working for the state of New Hampshire), talked to me via phone and e-mail, and while I helped her during a whirlwind archiving spree in Honolulu. It is, for the most part, from these sources and Festival observation that I have reconstructed the administrative end of the Hawai'i program. At this point, I thought I had the whole picture. I was wrong.

Understanding the cultural work that a festival does requires that the lived experience of participants accompany documentation of festival planning and performance. The many anecdotes I heard about the Festival told me that there was much about the Festival that was not in the files. Consequently, interviews, conversations, and even chance encounters became an important component of the research. In Honolulu, I interviewed several Hawai'i program fieldworkers and advisors. Then I began interviewing former participants in the program. This was not as easy as it sounds. In local terms I am a mainland *haole,* even if I do live in Hawai'i. This, on top of my being a university affiliate, meant that I did not have easy access to some communities where there are good reasons to be suspicious about the motives of outsiders who want information. I was most successful when Linda Moriarty facilitated connections for me. This process also told me how brilliant Richard Kennedy had been to hire Moriarty as his local coordinator. A "local" connection opens doors that even the Smithsonian cannot open. However, I did talk-story with a variety of people about their Festival memories, and they brought the Festival experience alive in ways that no amount of archival work could have done.

When interviewing presenters and participants, I was interested in how the subjects of the program interacted with the overall concept. How did Hawai'i participants respond to the site design, the program's ethnic categories and themes, neighboring programs, and visitors? Festival memories allowed me to see that even performance was layered and that there were sites, resistances, and epiphanies beyond the official records. Participants also hinted at how Festival memories have become part of a meaning-making loop for themselves. I have tried to do them justice and represent their stories accurately. Any mistakes in the recounting are mine alone.

Being a relative outsider in Hawai'i helped me to understand some of the motives and issues of researchers and public culture workers who, like myself, admire, try to understand, and represent the folklife of others. As a resident of Hawai'i, my aim is to present the Hawai'i program at the national festival from a Hawai'i-centric position and to consider the ethos and effects of cultural mediation by outsiders. By examining the role of institutionally based cultural intervention in Hawai'i through a specific case study, this book sheds light on the larger issues and ramifications of culture workers and public culture scholars who turn their efforts to the representation of cultures other than their own.

My interpretation has necessarily been fragmentary—a construction of the events after the fact. It does not preclude other readings, nor would I presume to consider it comprehensive. There are many other directions that a study of this program could have taken. Because I am not a professional culture worker, it would have been presumptuous of me to attempt to address Hawai'i folklife in this study. I have instead looked to the frames, layers, and edges of the festival-making process. In fact, I hope to show that, contrary to the Hawai'i program's cohesive message, that Hawai'i on the Mall was actually a "crucible of culture" in which multiple stories can be discerned (Stanley 1998, 12).

Note on Names

SOME CONFUSION over names is unavoidable in this account. At the time of the Hawai'i program the Center for Folklife and Cultural Heritage (CFCH) was called the Office of Folklife Programs (OFP). That title later became the Center for Folklife and Cultural Studies. In 1989 the Festival was known as the Festival of American Folklife (FAF), and the administrative agency at the time of the Hawai'i program was the OFP. When speaking of the past, I have used the names that were current at the time, but sources will reflect current names for archives. For convenience, I use acronyms for agency names after the first reference, and a list of abbreviations is provided in the front matter of this book. Additionally, a glossary of frequently used Hawaiian words is found in the back matter. In many cases, I use "Festival" when referring specifically to the SFF and "festival" for general references.

I have used the term "Native Hawaiian" throughout to refer to the indigenous people of Hawai'i. This name did not come into currency until the 1970s, and although "Hawaiian" is now used in Hawai'i to refer exclusively to indigenous people and not all residents of the state of Hawai'i, I have chosen to use Native Hawaiian to avoid confusion for readers. In accord with contemporary standardization of Hawaiian language, I have used diacritical marks except where they did not appear in the original. I have chosen to italicize all non-English words except proper names and in titles, including some words like *hula* that are the result of cultural crossings.

Acknowledgments

THIS PROJECT was made possible through the help of people and institutions that offered support for which I am deeply indebted. My research was supported by fellowships from the East-West Center and the Smithsonian Center for Folklife and Cultural Heritage and by grants from the East-West Center Association, the University of Hawai'i Arts and Sciences Advisory Council, and the Hawai'i Committee for the Humanities. Mari Yoshihara provided endless support and encouragement as well as a critical eye and expert editing. Mark Helbling and Robert Perkinson added their valuable critiques early on, as did David Hanlon and Geoff White, who inspired me to push it further. The Center for Folklife and Cultural Heritage at the Smithsonian, Carl Heffner, Ray Tanaka, Lynn Martin Graton, and the Hawai'i State Foundation for Culture and the Arts all graciously granted permission to use photographs.

I have deep admiration for all of the people who researched, constructed, staged, and performed in the 1989 program. I am very grateful to Richard Kennedy, who generously opened his files on the Hawai'i program and shared his curatorial experiences and a corner of his office during the summer of 2003, and to Lynn Martin Graton, who made time to answer all my questions and share her insights. In Hawai'i, Ricardo Trimillos, Linda Moriarty, and Jay Junker took time to air their festival stories and perceptions, and Linda kindly made connections for me with several festival participants. Thanks to the festival participants who granted me interviews and who invited me into their homes and workplaces and even a wedding. I add my deepest appreciation to them for taking time to reminisce and for trusting a stranger with their stories.

Michael Schuster and Keoni Fujitani opened doors at the Hawai'i State Foundation for Culture and the Arts (HSFCA) and made time to talk-story about the business of culture brokering. Jay Straker and Emily Satterwhite greatly expanded my view on the Festival through intense conversations at the 2003 festival. My thanks to Rochelle Fonoti, Nao Ikenaga, Kalindi Vora, Sunhee Koo, and Kyle Ikeda, all of whom patiently read and commented on various stages of this manuscript. Thanks also to Masako Ikeda and Ann Ludeman at UH Press for their support, to Kristy Ringor, who helped with research for chapter 5, and to Susan Biggs Corrado for her expert copyediting.

To put the people in the background last seems deceptive since they are my mainstays. Carl Lindahl nurtured my appreciation for folklore and set a standard for ethical, insightful scholarship to which I continue to aspire. Sandra, Cheryl, Lisa, Francie, and Kathleen helped keep me sane. My grandparents, Izzy and Xenia Diamond, and my parents, Ed and Arlene Diamond, taught me to love books and the details of everyday culture—a gift I have taken for granted. My smart daughter, Sorrel McCarthy, inspires and amazes me with her passion for learning and her determination to foster a love of ideas in her children.

Finally, but most importantly, I am grateful to my amazing husband, Frederick Lau. He tagged along to interviews, solved countless computer and emotional crises, read revisions, supported this project from beginning to end, made me laugh, and still managed to get his own work done.

Mahalo nui loa to all.

Abbreviations

CFCH	Center for Folklife and Cultural Heritage (formerly OFP)
EWC	East-West Center
FAF	Festival of American Folklife
HPC	Hawai'i Promotion Committee
HSFCA	Hawai'i State Foundation for Culture and the Arts
HSS	Hawai'i State Society
HTB	Hawai'i Tourist Bureau (formerly HPC)
HVB	Hawai'i Visitors Bureau (formerly HTB)
LDS	Church of Jesus Christ of Latter-Day Saints (Mormon Church)
NEA	National Endowment for the Arts
NHF	National Heritage Fellowship
OFP	Office of Folklife Programs
OHA	Office of Hawaiian Affairs
SFF	Smithsonian Folklife Festival (formerly FAF)
UH	University of Hawai'i

Introduction

During the last week of June and first week of July 1989, a visitor to the National Mall in Washington, D.C., could have been transported to some intriguing destinations, including the Caribbean, the Great Plains, the Mississippi Delta, and the American Pacific. That year, the thirteenth annual Festival of American Folklife (FAF; renamed the Smithsonian Folklife Festival in 1998) juxtaposed four programs: French traditions in America, the Caribbean, Plains Indians, and Hawai'i. The French and Caribbean programs honored the two-hundredth anniversary of the French Revolution and the Declaration of the Rights of Man. The Hawai'i program marked the thirtieth anniversary of Hawai'i's transition from a U.S. territory to the fiftieth state. Twice the size of the other programs, the Hawai'i site was located across the Mall from the Plains Indians and French sites. In between stretched a buffalo pen and a lacrosse field as well as booths in which recordings and crafts relevant to all the programs could be purchased.

The Hawai'i program was alluring and memorable. Festivalgoers wandering through might have watched a *hula* performance; listened in on a miked discussion about tourism or *'ukulele* music styles on the porch of the store; salivated over island foods being prepared; talked to craftspeople making feather *lei,* a canoe, or a quilt; learned about Hawaiian *paniolo* (cowboys); caught some Hawaiian slack-key or Puerto Rican *katchi katchi* music; and watched a Korean masked dance. Depending on when they arrived, festivalgoers might have been lucky enough to catch a glimpse of the magnificently flower- and fabric-bedecked *pā'ū* riders in the opening parade or gotten a mouthwatering whiff of roast pig as a group of men unearthed an *imu* (underground pit). On any given festival day around 3:00 P.M., they might have joined in with various Hawai'i residents and Festival visitors answering the call to participate in a Japanese *bon* dance. All that was missing was the ocean, and there were net-throwing demonstrations and canoe building to evoke even that.

The SFF is staged annually in America's most public physical site—the Washington, D.C., Mall—by the Smithsonian Center for Folklife and Cultural Heritage (CFCH; formerly the Office of Folklife Programs) in conjunction with the National Park Service. The Festival was originally the idea of James Morris, director of Museum Services and later of the Division of Performing Arts, and was developed under its first director, Ralph Rinzler, with the strong support of Smithsonian Institution secretary S. Dillon Ripley.[1] Each summer, the Festival presents folklife to throngs of domestic and international visitors on the National Mall in Washington, D.C., for ten days during a two-week period that extends over the July 4th holiday. It is free to the public and claims to host approximately a million domestic and international visitors each year. Most years the SFF juxtaposes three or four simultaneous programs.

According to CFCH director Richard Kurin, the Festival was founded as an addition and alternative to the national museums, as "a way of telling the story of the diverse peoples who populated the nation but whose cultural achievements were not represented in the museums or their collections" (Kurin 1998, 54). On the other hand, the SFF is, in large part, constructed and operated according to museum precepts. Since its inception in 1967, the SFF has problematized static notions of tradition and heritage by defining folklife as dynamic, inclusive, and contemporary. As its rhetoric reveals, the SFF is at heart a scholarly endeavor created by professional folklorists with a social agenda. Its goals, as stated on the SFF website, are to celebrate cultural diversity and to advocate cultural conservation (SFF 2005). It does much of this work through fieldwork-based research that identifies culture bearers and offers public presentations and interpretations of their cultural contributions. The diversity it constructs is shaped by the complexity of folklore studies precepts and not solely on the ethnic categories invoked in most American multicultural venues; rather, the SFF's vision of diversity juxtaposes communities—occupational, regional, and ethnic—that are marked by shared values, beliefs, experiences, practices, and so forth. These SFF "communities" are most often represented through aspects of their expressive culture, specifically music, dance, foodways, and material culture. Occupational and ethnic groups have generally been organized and framed according to state and/or region while thematic programs, such as those on cultural conservation, have served to establish common threads between cultural groups. Using multiple modalities to achieve its educational goals, the SFF defies convenient categorization and invites, yet baffles, theorizing. It contains aspects of the zoo, museum, theme park, carnival, concert, community center, and traveling theater. Presented on national sacred ground and incorporating sacred ritual, it often takes on a hallowed and reverential aura. It might be argued that what it least resembles is an actual festival, if one were to define festivals as "collective phenomena" serving "purposes [that] are rooted in group life" (Stoeltje 1992, 261).

The SFF blurs the boundaries of both museum and tourism presentations that rely on clear demarcations between viewers and viewed. It uses a conversational model that is grounded in a concept of hosts and guests while avoiding the rhetoric of tourism. Performers, in the role of hosts, are referred to as "participants," while tourists are called "visitors." An idealistic, innovative, populist-based experiment in cultural democracy, the SFF brings culture from the margins to the nation's symbolic center, where it sets the stage for dialogue between the visitor and the cultural practitioner presumably coming from, and therefore representing, different walks of life. Its exhibition space is designed with permeable boundaries that encourage interchange between participants and visitors. In Washington, D.C., it also seeks to enable conversations among the national museums, politicians, and communities. Notwithstanding these efforts to break down the barriers and hierarchies of museum representation, the Festival is also laden with museum interpretation in the form of themes, site design, presenters, signage, program books, and media coverage.

The SFF comprises many of the contradictions inherent in American cultural ideals and politics. Organizers claim a lineage based in American populism and New Deal projects and objectives (Bronner 2002, 42–45). They view its concept and production as an intervention in cultural homogenization and as a subversive enactment of American democratic ideals designed to "scare away [the] evil" of cultural intolerance (Kurin 1998, 48–51). At the same time, it is subject to corporate funding, local governments, special interest groups, and the whims of changing administrations as they impact arts and museum funding. These tensions permeate the Festival. The SFF expresses the highest ideals of cultural diversity and tolerance, and many cultural groups and practices that are otherwise undervalued are valorized at the SFF. However, if visitors do not get below the celebratory surface, American (and international) pluralism can be absorbed as a benign, cohesive, and de-politicized fact that belies the actual histories and socioeconomic circumstances of many of the represented groups. The Hawai'i program's construction and performance teetered on this dilemma.

The central focus of this book is a critical view of the poetics and politics of festival making as seen through an ethnographic history of the 1989 Hawai'i program at the Smithsonian Folklife Festival in Washington, D.C. By making the underpinnings of this event transparent, this account sheds light on the linked themes of public sector folklore culture brokering, cultural tourism, ideas about multiculturalism, the role of tradition in national image making, and the impact of cultural intervention on local communities. What does the fact that the largest national tourist event in the United States is devoted to educating the public about traditional culture say about the construction of a national image and the valuation of tradition in the national imagination? On another level, this study highlights the process behind an event that is generally viewed as simply a performance. It looks at who orchestrates this annual event, how it is constructed, what happens behind the scenes, how participants engage the frames of performance, and the long-term effects of such a production. Finally, this book raises important questions about the stakes surrounding the politics of tradition and multiculturalism and emphasizes the importance of looking critically at how peoples and places are represented through cultural agencies.

By turning a critical lens on the processes of cultural intervention, this study delves into the role of "culture brokers" and the impact of "cultural intervention" in the politics of representation. Folklife festivals are cultural interventions in that they shape and mediate culture, and they are staged by culture brokers—public sector culture workers who operate between ethnographic subjects, sponsoring agencies, the media, and the public. Ironically, the business of successful culture brokering depends on invisibility as opposed to transparency, and this may be why most of the material available on culture brokering is generated by culture brokers themselves (e.g., see Kurin 1998; Baron and Spitzer 1992; Sommers 1994; Baumann 1992). That the efficacy of folklife festivals as a tool of cultural conservation and public awareness is contested is clear from the self-reflexive writings of culture brokers. For example, in 1980 two folklorists who were actively involved in staging folklife festivals published an article titled "Six Reasons Not to Produce a Folklife Festival" in which they stated that "folklife festivals (which require enormous amounts of money to produce) do not create the widespread public knowledge and sensitivity that they are intended to create, and thus do not work to solve the social and cultural problems they are intended to solve" (Camp and Lloyd 1980). Richard Kurin, director of the CFCH, replied to these and other critics in his 1998 book, *Smithsonian Folklife Festival: Culture Of, By, and For the People.* These interchanges have created a lively debate, but one conducted mostly among insiders who are invested in the business of culture brokering. They testify that fieldwork, ethnography, and representation methods have evolved to incorporate self-reflexivity and professional ethics, but some scholars insist that this is not enough to ensure that folklife festivals actually accomplish what they claim to do.

Critics of cultural intervention practices in general have interrogated the ethics of fieldwork practices of the past, demonstrating that cultural intervention has not always had happy consequences and has often served the interests of sponsoring institutions over those of culture bearers and their communities (Whisnant 1983; Filene 2000). By looking at long-term outcomes, these views of the past reveal that there are sociopolitical factors implicated in cultural intervention and public representation of folklife that cannot easily be addressed through improved fieldwork ethics and more sensitive interpretation. What they emphasize in particular is that when culture brokers have dealt with culture in isolation from politics, both cultural expressions and communities have been misrepresented. They also suggest that drawing public attention to folklife can result in ethnographic subjects being in a position of increased vulnerability to various forms of appropriation and exploitation, from aestheticization to commodification.

Culture brokering, especially at the national level, is not disconnected from hegemonic institutions and nationalism. Robert Cantwell has argued that "a folklife festival . . . reframes folk culture as an element of a legitimate, polite, or elite culture typically under the auspices of institutions representing those interests" (1992, 263). In 1989, the year of the Hawai'i program, a pitched battle was being fought in Congress over National Endowment for the Arts (NEA) funding for allegedly blasphemous and obscene art. Despite its genesis as a disruption of the museums and a challenge to cultural homogeneity, in contrast to debates over provocative artworks challenging the status quo, the SFF appeared a virtuous (read: conservative and politically safe) endeavor. After all, its emphasis was on cultural conservation within a frame of national unity.

Folklife festivals are embedded in politics, and the liberal goals of the SFF to subvert cultural elitism and hegemony are always in danger of being co-opted by conservative causes that see tradition as a stable alternative to real political change. In an edited volume on cultural conservation published in 1988, David Whisnant was the lone critic calling for culture brokers to pay attention to the dangers of state appropriations of tradition. He advocated "tougher politics" to counter public sector folklore's tendency to flatten and gloss over socioeconomic disparity and political conflict and warned that "it appears to be a characteristic of modern times that the imperial flag is so regularly and so firmly planted in the midst of the territory called tradition" (1988, 244–245). He echoed earlier observations that traditions cannot only be invented, but are often appropriated in the service of a dominant narrative (Hobsbawm and Ranger 1984).

The Festival represents "tradition." In a mercurial global culturescape dominated by media and movement, tradition is often either posed against the modern (by modernists) or invoked as a stay against change, a constant in a shifting world (by traditionalists). From a modernist perspective, the terms "tradition" and "traditional" are often used dismissively to connote resistance to innovation (Williams 1983, 319). Contrarily, these same terms are often used nostalgically and reverentially by those who see society changing for the worse and who romanticize tradition as an alternative (Bauman 1992, 31). Although "tradition" is still commonly used to imply static, unchanging, conservative, and even outdated cultural relics, folklorists have come to understand tradition as something much more fluid, as both cultural product and the processes through which it is created, transmitted, altered, and put to use. In folklore parlance, ideas about tradition have evolved away from a "view of tradition as a cultural inheritance rooted in the past" and toward an understanding of "tradition as symbolically constituted in the present" (Bauman 1992, 31). These conflicting views were a critical part of the negotiations in the 1989 Hawai'i program.

So why foreground tradition in a national festival? In part, the Festival puts the Smithsonian's abuses of the past to right. The history of ethnographic spectacle in the United States implicates the powerful Smithsonian in a number of endeavors that showcased the traditional practices of people considered cultural outsiders in ways that emphasized Anglo-Saxonist and social Darwinist ideologies. For example, the Smithsonian Bureau of Ethnography was involved in turn-of-the-century World's Fair exhibitions where Native Americans and residents of the Philippines were exhibited and studied as ethnographic specimens, and "tradition" was used to demonstrate degrees of savagery to barbarism. The SFF cleanses this past by presenting a paradigm of cultural democracy and pluralism in which multiple belief systems and cultural practices are publicly recognized as significant and beautiful, and community stories are told as valuable parts of the national story.

Significantly, the SFF is the brainchild of professional scholars who study tradition. "In the approximately 150 years since the discipline began, folklore has been based in the study of tradition" (Sims and Stephens 2005, 64). Because traditions create and confirm identity for small communities, it makes sense by extension that traditional culture has been construed as an important component in national identity. Traditional culture—such as heroic legends, foodways, holidays, and material culture—has historically been the raw material of an American national image (Bronner 2002, 3–78). While academic views have changed from an emphasis on locating/creating a unifying American folklore to an appreciation of the diversity of folklore in America, and academic, national, and vernacular definitions and evaluations might disagree on what it is and its value, discussions of tradition have remained central to paradigms of American culture.

The politics of tradition and authenticity take a different spin in the Pacific, where they converge in post-colonial debates over ownership of culture, authenticity, identity, and sovereignty. In Hawai'i, many of these issues have crystallized around ethnography and tourism sites in which representation of culture has historically been done by outsiders. Following the leads of Maoris in New Zealand and Native Americans in the continental United States, Native Hawaiian activists have asserted their right to interpret their culture from an insider perspective alongside their ownership of cultural properties tangible and intangible. In some cases this has led to heated internal and external disputes over authenticity and cultural invention (Jolly 2000, 274–329; Trask 2000, 255–263; Keesing 2000, 232–254).[2] The year 1989 was an important midpoint in this politicization process: an active Native Hawaiian movement was in progress, Hawai'i had a Native Hawaiian governor, and 1988 had been declared the Year of the Hawaiian. The Hawaiian sovereignty movement gained momentum immediately after the Hawai'i program and its local restaging in 1990. It made headlines and major news coverage in 1993 when a conglomerate of Hawaiian organizations staged a public reenactment of the overthrow of the Hawaiian monarchy on the grounds of the former royal residence in Honolulu.

Despite the Festival's flexibility and adaptability, the presentation of Hawai'i posed unique questions and logistical problems. Hawai'i is both within and outside mainland America—geographically and culturally.[3] It is strategically situated midway between the continental United States and Asia. It has an independent past as a sovereign nation and an incorporated presence as the fiftieth state. Its multiculturalism is distinct from that of the mainland due to a continuous occupation by its indigenous population, its location as a mid-Pacific crossroads, its colonial legacy, and the distinctive histories of immigration and commerce in the islands (Kent 1983). Many immigrant groups from Asia and elsewhere in the Pacific retain strong transnational identifications and affiliations and, as a result, hold definitions of tradition that conflict with the academic and continental rhetoric of the CFCH. It should be no surprise that Pacific and continental U.S. multicultural paradigms collided in the Hawai‘i program.

In addition to its cloudy political history vis-à-vis the continental United States, Hawai‘i holds a unique position in terms of the American imagination. Hawai‘i has functioned as a gendered, eroticized, and primitivized playground for continental America (Desmond 1999).[4] Hawaiian cultural products—music, dance, dress, food, and language—have been exported to other destinations where they have been enjoyed, desired, appropriated, misinterpreted, and consumed. Both Hawai‘i the tourist destination and Hawaiiana are the stuff of imagination and desire. Ironically, presenting Hawai‘i in the Folklife Festival's terms of traditionality required unpackaging the imagined Hawai‘i to assert and reinvent a more "authentic" version of the "real Hawai‘i." In other words, rather than conceptually packaging Hawai‘i to import tourists, state and national culture workers aimed to divest Hawai‘i of its slick, manufactured image, reinvent it according to its self-definitions, and pack this new/old version for export to the mainland. Additionally, these efforts had to accord with state and national parameters while navigating the potentially volatile 1980s politics of cultural identity in Hawai‘i.

This book first contextualizes the Hawai‘i program within the history of cultural intervention in Hawai‘i. The first chapter traces the history of institutional intervention in traditional arts in Hawai‘i. The Smithsonian project in 1988–1989 fit into ongoing negotiations over ethnographic authority. At the end of the monarchy, traditional arts were politicized and collected as a way of establishing a record of indigenous civilization in relation to nineteenth-century ideals held by European powers. Native arts were subsequently suppressed under the territorial government, only to be encouraged as tourist fare. Beginning in the 1920s religious institutions and national and local government have played a critical role in shaping ethnic identity by sponsoring ethnographic studies and cultural revivals. Since the 1960s collaborations between the HSFCA and the NEA have established programs for cultural conservation based on assessments of traditional culture as both valuable and endangered. While the usual purpose of officially sponsored cultural intervention has been cultural revitalization, the attendant codification of traditional culture can also reshape community self-images and relations in unintended ways. In the 1988 planning meetings between the Festival directors, the HSFCA, and community scholars, debates over variant histories and cultural authority were resolved in the interests of presenting a unified Festival view. Local politics was deliberately sidestepped, and the themes of cultural hybridity and creolization were chosen as a way to transcend ethnic tensions.[5]

Subsequent chapters cover the chronology of the Hawai‘i program process: planning, fieldwork, performance, and legacy. Chapter 2 examines the construction of ethnicity and multiculturalism through definitions of tradition. Between October and December 1988, twenty-seven local fieldworkers were selected, briefed, and dispatched to survey and report on Hawai‘i folklife. My account of the fieldwork process points to some of the disjunctions between Hawai‘i and mainland cultural paradigms. The records indicate that the question of "who can speak" for a community by way of a cultural practice was inflected by predetermined notions of authenticity and traditionality, as well as on notions of officially sanctioned authority.[6] The HSFCA followed its previous categorizations to divide ethnic groups into Polynesian, Asian, and Other categories. In application, ethnic definitions slipped between racial, cultural, and national categories. In the final selection, nine ethnic groups were chosen based on "cultural value" and contributions to island culture and linked through a historical master narrative.

Chapter 3 outlines how "authenticity" was mediated through the rhetorical and spatial constructions of the program production. Festival performance is ephemeral, but performance occurs in a built environment. The careful deliberations that crafted the Hawai‘i program Festival environment underline the Smithsonian's concern for the educational mission of the Festival and indicate the potential for site design to influence Festival interactions and guide festivalgoers' perceptions. Through a variety of spatial and textual devices, the Hawai‘i program site design located Hawai‘i in relation to the rest of the nation, a geographical exercise many continental residents still cannot do. Using a design that encouraged permeable boundaries between visitors and program participants, the program design employed an interactive, dialogic model that made space for tradition bearers to speak. Ironically, the organizers' concerns with authenticity and overcompensation for touristic images had the effect of fixing culture in ways that encouraged performers to transgress the limitations of the site and festival cultural categorizations once the framework was inhabited.

While much analysis of festival/public culture concentrates on what is seen by the public, chapter 4 argues that this was not the only locus of meaning for participants and staff. In fact, much of what performers and staff found memorable about the Festival happened out of the public eye altogether. Spontaneity did erupt at the Festival, instigated by participants, but in the program's seams much more than onstage. The spatial and rhetorical constructions that directed the tourist gaze became the edges transgressed in performance. Whereas the fieldwork and production phases of the Festival had homogenized pluralism into an institutional counter-narrative of cultural harmony expressed as creolization and cultural resurgence, the Festival actually became multi-vocal only in the sum of its parts. In its totality—front, back, and offstage, as well as contexts—it embodied conflict, negotiation, and community in forms that eluded cooptation.

The final chapter presents the legacy of the Festival in its restaging, national and local offshoots, and memory and reflects on the local impact of national cultural intervention. In 1990 the Hawai'i program was restaged as a local production in Honolulu. The local version of the Smithsonian program, sponsored by the HSFCA, underwent several subtle changes to adapt it to its local context. These changes demonstrate a shift in audience assessment as well as program educational goals. There were also efforts to continue the collaboration with the Smithsonian in the form of an Asia/Pacific research center. The joint proposal was advanced as far as the Hawai'i State Legislature, but failed when the political and economic winds changed in both Washington, D.C., and the state of Hawai'i. Meanwhile, Native Hawaiian politics heated up in Hawai'i, culminating in a 1993 restaging, called the Onipa'a, of the monarchy's overthrow. A comparison of this grassroots spectacle to the orchestration of the Hawai'i program at the Festival reveals a very different narrativization of Hawai'i history and a different agenda for politicization of indigenous cultural practices. The Festival and the 1990 restaging reinforced the notion that geniality, hospitality, reciprocity, and inclusivity are qualities inherent in Hawai'i lifestyles. The Onipa'a, on the other hand, revealed that this cohesive picture of Hawai'i multiculturalism precluded separate agendas for Hawai'i's ethnic groups and masked grief, loss, and anger over the past.

Because the Festival is an instrument of healing and peace, organizers intentionally leave little room for conflict. As a tool of peaceful dialogue and intercultural understanding, it is an impressive undertaking. I applaud the devotion and professionalism of the CFCH staff and the willingness of culture brokers like Kurin and Kennedy to not only listen to criticism, but also to ask for it by encouraging research on past and current programs. Public sector folklorists do not agree on what a festival should do or be, but they are not unaware of the political implications of what they do. Culture brokers who operate at the national level know that they put their thumbprints on what they present, and they are willing to debate effects and directions. My intent in interpreting the Hawai'i program has been to contribute to this debate by using a folklife festival that was enacted in a "hot spot," as Kurin referred to Hawai'i, to illustrate how power relationships operated during a transitional period in the interpretation of culture.[7] By extension, this book then speaks to how power relationships continue to be enacted through public culture presentations that mediate the meaning of tradition.

Chapter 1

Cultural Intervention in America's Eden

> The state shall have the power to preserve and develop the cultural, creative, and traditional arts of its various ethnic groups.
>
> —Hawai'i State Constitution, Article IX, Section 9, Cultural Resources

The 1989 Festival of American Folklife (FAF) in Washington, D.C., began, as had its predecessors, with an opening ceremony attended by dignitaries, officials, and participants. Governor John Waihee, Hawai'i's first and only Native Hawaiian governor, set the tone for the Hawai'i program in his opening speech. Program staff members recall that it brought tears of pride to everyone involved. Waihee was a charismatic speaker, and the following portion of his speech was excerpted and preserved in a later SFF promotional film.

> Because we are more than wonderful weather or beautiful beaches or powerful volcanoes. We are a people. We are people from many different backgrounds in the middle of God's Pacific—based on our Native Hawaiian culture which bonds us together in a spirit of love and pride, building upon those that came later for a better life, reaching out so that their children's future would be secure. Our E Pluribus Unum. All of this is there for you to enjoy. To reinforce our nation's motto: E Pluribus Unum. Out of the many, one. You see, to you, from the community of communities to the nation of nations, we bring you our spirit of *aloha*.[1]

In his invitation to those gathered on the National Mall to experience Hawai'i through a sampling of its cultural plurality, Waihee challenged several Hawai'i stereotypes. Although acknowledging Hawai'i's fetishization as a resort location, he challenged the nature/culture conflations of tourist imaging in which indigenous people are iconicized to represent the islands as primitive and sensual, and he pluralized Hawai'i's ethnoscape by including the immigrant populations usually erased. He also challenged geocentrism by locating Hawai'i in the center of the Pacific rather than at the American periphery. His invitation and "spirit of *aloha*" were proffered from Hawai'i's people, temporarily inverting the appropriations of the corporate-controlled tourist industry. Waihee's message to the gathering reiterated the Festival's message to the nation that Hawai'i's culture and communities were worthy of recognition and of importance to the nation. Less obviously, this speech and the presence of Hawai'i at the Festival underscored the complexity of Hawai'i's relationship with the continental United States (what people in Hawai'i refer to as "the mainland"). In particular, he spoke in the language of Hawai'i's entanglement with tourism.

Tourism and tradition are bound together in the marketing of Hawai'i. Tourism is the industry on which the state's economic fortunes have turned since the shutdown and relocation of the sugar industry. On one end of the spectrum are claims that tourism has helped perpetuate traditional culture in the face of modernity. Both Elizabeth Buck and Jane Desmond, however, point out that the Hawai'i Visitors Bureau's (HVB) "Keep It Hawai'i" campaign in the 1990s is evidence that "Hawaiianness" has been eroded within and by tourism (Buck 1993; Desmond 1999). Critics see Hawai'i tourism as a form of neo-colonialism. In her book *From a Native Daughter*, published in 1999, Native Hawaiian activist and scholar Haunani-Kay Trask took a critical view of tourism's effect on Native Hawaiians that counters Waihee's benign message, saying,

> Of course, all this hype is necessary to hide the awful truth about tourism, the awful exploitative truth that the industry is the major cause of environmental degradation, low wages, land dispossession, and the highest cost of living in the United States. . . . The point, of course is that everything in Hawai'i can be yours, that is, you the tourist, the non-native, the visitor. The place, the people, the culture, even our identity as a "Native" people is for sale. (1999, 144)

For Trask and others who speak out against Hawai'i's dependence on tourist dollars, the marriage of tourism and tradition is a deal with the devil that perpetuates exploitation of native people and the environment. By extension, this view might be taken to suggest that the representation of Native Hawaiian culture in a national tourist event and the linked promotion of Hawai'i tourism through a national cultural festival are deeply problematic even if they changed the terms of how culture in Hawai'i is represented in public venues.

The imaging of Hawai'i has been critical because tourism relies on visual imagery. According to John Urry, "the gaze is constructed through signs and tourism involves the collection of signs" (1990, 3). The signification of Hawai'i as a space of "Edenic regeneration" (Desmond 1999, 3) through signifiers such as grass skirts, flower *lei, 'ukulele,* and *hula* is the result of a historical process enmeshed with the history of colonization and Americanization. Hawai'i's construction as an American playground developed over time and was as much a process of re-imagining it as it was a political transformation. Inversely, changing images of Hawai'i culture reveal another discourse in which collaborations and resistances have contested cultural appropriation and commodification.

In sponsoring the Festival, the Smithsonian takes a pragmatic view toward tourism, engineering an elaborate and costly folklife spectacle as an opportunity for educating the public, empowering communities, attracting governmental attention to folk arts, and promoting its programs. Thinking back about why the Office of Folklife Programs (OFP) chose to represent Hawai'i in the 1989 FAF, director Richard Kurin said, "There's no question in Hawai'i at that time that we felt this was a case where Hawai'i was one of those hot spots. Cultural hotspots—where by doing this we could be doing important work."[2] The state of Hawai'i was also pragmatic, seeing the Festival as an opportunity to present a more nuanced and accurate self-image and to promote the local economy, for which tourism is the number one industry. The Hawai'i program in 1989 that inserted Hawai'i into a national tourist event was partially underwritten by the HVB. While advocating cultural conservation, this collaboration between arts agencies and commercial interests, between national and local arts agencies, and between official and unofficial culture also crystallized an ongoing negotiation over definitions of tradition and authenticity.

Since at least the 1880s, local and federal institutions—governmental, religious, and academic—have intervened in Hawai'i's "traditional" culture through regulation, promotion, collection, exhibition, and redefinition. From the monarchy period, through the territorial period, and into statehood, "tradition" has been a medium for negotiations over cultural authority, ownership, and identity. In proposing to represent Hawai'i in national space, the Smithsonian stepped into a long-standing trajectory—a tradition of intervention that already existed as a gray zone between institutionally generated cultural conservation and appropriations. A clear view of the negotiations that followed requires a penetrating look at cultural continuity and change in the island past.

Politicizing Culture in the Kingdom of Hawai'i

Colonization in Hawai'i was greatly abetted by cultural domination. Explorers, merchants, and missionaries brought foreign cultural values into an environment in which culture—music, dance, agriculture, aquaculture, religion, cooking, craft—was integrated into daily life. Prior to contact, cultural practices in Hawaiian society were divided according to sacred and secular, male and female, *ali'i* (chiefly) and *maka'āinana* (commoner) aspects. *Hula* (dance) and *oli* (chant) had strong and intertwined sexual and sacred connotations. After contact with Euro-American cultural practices, the indigenous relationship to traditional culture grew more complex. Margaret Jolly points out, "From early contact, the presence of Europeans created a more intense self-consciousness about what was distinctly indigenous. This sometimes entailed a positive defense of tradition but often a rejection of it" (2000, 285). Calvinist missionaries and other foreigners stigmatized Native Hawaiian practices such as *hula,* as well as sexual mores and styles of dress, as "primitive" and "backwards," setting the stage for oppositional definitions of tradition that altered how native people viewed practices that had previously been unquestioned.

Between Captain Cook's voyages to what he named the Sandwich Islands in 1776–1779, and when American missionaries arrived in 1820, dramatic sociopolitical changes were triggered in Hawai'i by Western contact. Native Hawaiian *ali'i* responded to infiltration by Euro-American cultures and ideas by adopting, appropriating, and/or resisting them (Merry 2000).[3] King Kamehameha I centralized control of the islands with the aid of Western weapons in 1810. Kamehameha II and Ka'ahumanu, the Queen Regent, precipitated a number of changes in Hawaiian society and government by breaking the gendered *kapu* system upon the death of Kamehameha I in 1819. The resulting social upheaval, added to population devastations caused by disease and social disruptions caused by increased commerce (sexual, military, etc.) with foreigners, facilitated missionization of the islands in the 1820s (Buck

1993; Ferguson and Turnbull 1999).[4] In 1824 Ka'ahumanu became a convert to Calvinist Protestantism and soon (1830) incorporated Christian values into a codified set of laws for Hawai'i that regulated alcohol and *awa* (a mildly stimulating beverage) drinking, polygamy, and adultery, as well as worshiping the old gods and *hula,* which had been deemed lascivious and lewd by missionaries. Although Kamehameha III brought *hula* back for a short period, he, too, embraced the Christian aversion. The Hawaiian Evangelical Association issued a restriction on *hula* in 1859, effectively banishing it from public spaces by instituting a prohibitive system of fines for transgressors. Consequently, *hula* was devalued and relegated to rural areas (Silva 2000).[5] A period of cultural suppression and rapid acculturation ensued for the next four decades.

Under King David Kalākaua in the 1860s, Native Hawaiian cultural practices were revived and foregrounded as a symbol of Hawaiian nationalism. Dramatic shifts had occurred in the systems of labor and land distribution by this time, to the detriment of the Native Hawaiian people and the enrichment of missionary descendents and other entrepreneurs. As the power and influence of Americans in Hawai'i expanded, increasing pressure was put on the monarchy to pass power into the hands of pro-American anti-monarchists who had insinuated themselves into the court's inner circle. Daring disapproval from the *haole* (white foreign) elite, Kalākaua revived the tradition of court patronage for *hālau hula* (schools) and staged large public *hula* performances for his coronation ceremony in 1883 and his birthday Jubilee in 1886. Kalākaua had learned *oli* from his grandmother and from court chanters. According to George Kanahele, "His active pursuit of the ancient chants was perhaps the most important factor in the revival and perpetuation of the *oli* and *hula,* for he did this in the face of opposition and denigration by *haole* missionary-oriented groups of the day" (1979, 201). Kalākaua also compiled a volume of myths and legends. He used Native Hawaiian oral and performative culture to revalue Hawaiianness, create political solidarity, and enact national resistance to foreign domination (Kanahele 1979, 200–203).

After years of suppression and accelerated social change, the *hula* presented at Kalākaua's court had been altered from its earlier form and function. Adrienne Kaeppler asserts that the changes in public acceptability and religious sensibility during the initial decades of missionary influence had changed the character of the *hula,* which had been influenced by European dance and music. According to Kaeppler, the function of *hula* had shifted from sacred to secular, and by the time of the Royal Jubilee, *ali'i* had been substituted for deities in certain *mele* (songs).

> For the official coronation of Kalākaua and Kapi'olani in 1883, many *hula* performances were presented, in spite of the disapproval of Christian Hawaiians and non-Hawaiians. These performances featured chants and dances that honored Kalākaua. At least two chants that became *hula pahu* [sacred chants and rituals performed with a shark-skin drum]—Kaililua and Au'a 'ia—were among them. Since that time, Kaililua has been used to honor Kalākaua, symbolically legitimizing his rise to power in the Hawaiian way by invoking tradition and by implying that he was a descendent of the gods. (1993, 24)

It is possible that these changes may have been a result of seeing the *ali'i nui,* those deemed to have the most pure bloodlines according to Native Hawaiian systems of lineage, as imbued with such potent amounts of *mana* (spiritual energy) that they were akin to, and therefore substitutable for, deities. It is just as likely that the chants were deliberately altered and employed as political resistance by using them to praise Kalākaua in the face of outside interference with the powers of the monarchy.

Kalākaua was a Renaissance man who did not restrict his interest to traditional arts, and the degree to which he was exposed to Western arts indicates the extent to which those arts were used as a tool of colonialism. From the Royal School created by missionaries for their own and the children of *ali'i,* Kalākaua learned to play several Western instruments and to write Western-style music. He was also an enthusiast of orchestral music. However, as Sally Engle Merry points out, responses to colonialism can also take the form of adaptation and seeming compliance (2000, 220). Kalākaua was adept at appropriating and incorporating what he learned into hybrid performance arts. He played and promoted the Portuguese-derived *'ukulele* as a Hawaiian instrument, and he featured it alongside the *ipu* and the *pahu* in his Jubilee (Kanahele 1979, 200). The same argument can be made for Kalākaua's sister Lili'uokalani, who became Hawai'i's last monarch upon the death of her brother and who was also schooled in Western music. Kalākaua's "Hawai'i Pono'i," adopted as the state song in 1967, and Lili'uokalani's "Aloha 'Oe," which is sung at many official occasions, are important tributes to their skill at combining Hawaiian and Western sensibilities. Some scholars speculate about the resistances expressed in their bicultural music (Silva 2004).[6] Meanwhile, the fact that the Royal Hawaiian Band was renamed the Provisional Government Band after the American-backed overthrow of the monarchy and then the Territorial Band after annexation testifies to the politically dominant group's evaluation of performing arts as useful for self-imaging. That members of the transformed Royal Hawaiian Band were required to take pledges of loyalty to the new government acknowledges that subversion could easily inhabit the performing arts.[7]

International Exhibitions and National Designs

From the 1880s to 1915, international exhibition was another arena where the image of Hawai'i was altered according to whom was in power, and tradition was a medium of expression. Over the previous decades, the power of Hawai'i's monarchy had been severely limited due to Euro-American influence. Privatization of land, economic dependence on a corrupt plantation system that benefited the *haole*-dominated elite, an influx of mostly Asian immigrants for contract labor, the presence of American military, and corrupt Euro-American advisors in the court were all destabilizing factors. In January 1893 Hawai'i's monarchy was illegally overthrown in a bloodless coup executed by a group of American-backed businessmen. The provisional government was instituted, with Sanford Dole as president. Annexation took place in 1898, the establishment of the Territory of Hawai'i ensued in 1899, and in 1900 the Organic Act extended American law to the new territory. Throughout these changes, state and commercial manipulations of traditional culture intermingled in a tangle of interests that has continued into the present.

Changing views of Native Hawaiian traditions can be traced through a look at Hawai'i's representation in international exhibitions. In 1885 and 1889 Native Hawaiian fine handicrafts and antiquities were exhibited abroad at international exhibitions, and the manner of their display illustrates the power of captioning and contextualizing to characterize a people as well as revealing the views of exhibit organizers. A brochure from the Hawaiian exhibit of the 1885 World's Industrial and Cotton Centennial Exposition in New Orleans lists the items on display, along with photographs, botanicals, sugar, and pineapples, as including traditional craft items like featherwork, *kapa* (bark cloth), seed *lei* (garlands), and braided hats. In the Hawai'i exhibit, overseen by commissioners Samuel Parker (Minister of Foreign Affairs) and John Mott-Smith (Minister of the Interior), these items are presented as exotic curiosities, rendering Native Hawaiians as primitive to the American public and suggesting that the commissioners were in sympathy with American interests working toward control of the islands. Despite the fact that the displayed items included royal *kahili* (feather-topped standards) and feather capes, both symbols of royalty and believed by Native Hawaiians to contain royal *mana,* the brochure feminizes and devalues all of the items by referring to them as "mostly articles of fancy work, made from fibers and seeds, shells and feathers, found on the islands, and are specimens of feminine taste and in domestic wear, rather than articles of commercial value (Smithsonian Institution 1885). It is apparent that the commissioners displayed either these items or the cultural group producing them as relics of the past. In contrast, the commissioners appeared to be infinitely more civilized.

Inversely, a brochure for the Hawai'i exhibit in the 1889 Exposition Universelle in Paris presents similar items as evidence of Hawaiian civilization. The brochure states that it was "prepared for the Hawaiian Government" and presents a listing of "Native Manufactures and Implements," including *kapa* and *kapa*-making implements, stone implements, Ni'ihau shell *lei,* woven mats, braided hats, drums, baskets, *poi* beaters, nets, canoes, fish hooks, and "ancient" *lei* and *kapa.* Unlike the New Orleans exhibition strategy, which had collapsed Native Hawaiians into the single category of "natives," at the Paris exhibition the names of "exhibitors" appeared alongside individual items. Many of the personal items were listed as belonging to Her Royal Highness Princess Lili'uokalani, and a number of the ancient and historical items were listed as belonging to the Hawaiian government's collection, repositioning cultural authority and agency with the monarchy and emphasizing that it was invested in creating a credible image for the kingdom through international representation. Another notable difference in the Parisian presentation is that the "manufactures and implements" of Native Hawaiian artisans were represented as living traditions—a marked contrast to the New Orleans representation of Hawaiian objects as artifacts of a vanishing and primitive past. Old and new were presented side by side, metonymically evoking an adaptive Hawai'i possessed of history, not just a prehistorical preface to the civilizing forces of foreign colonizers. Instead, the Hawaiian elite were situated in an acculturated present (Hassinger 1889). By presenting Hawaiian cultural objects as historically embedded, vital, and meaningful, the monarchy used this exhibition to make a bid for international recognition and support at a time when its powers were becoming more and more constrained (Kaeppler 1992).[8]

By comparison to the monarchy's dignified self-representation in Paris, Hawai'i's 1893 appearance at the World's Columbian Exposition in Chicago reveals inverted power relations in which Native Hawaiians were racialized and symbolically demoted on the scale of social evolution. Rather than inanimate objects appearing as the emissaries of the Hawaiian Islands, in 1893, the year of the overthrow, actual Native Hawaiians were part of a world exhibition for the first time. However, the placement of the *hula* dancers—who had once danced for Kalākaua's affairs of state—on the carnivalesque and entertainment-centered Midway Plaisance devalued and objectified them as erotic exotica.[9] It is unclear under whose sponsorship they appeared at the Columbian Exhibition since those in the provisional government had been vocal in their disapproval of *hula;* however, Adria Imada argues that these dancers were not without agency and may very well have represented a level of covert resistance. The exposition provided them with opportunity for travel and economic gain, and many of them went on to become dancers in the vaudeville circuits. These dancers may also have used travel to the United States as an opportunity for protest during a tumultuous period when the United States was investigating allegations of illegality against the political usurpers, and the deposed queen was actively entreating Congress and the president to reinstate Hawai'i's rightful government (Imada 2002).

The overthrow and annexation shifted the locus of institutional power that defined and presented Hawaiian culture both in Hawai'i and to the outside world. Ideological changes in government led to attempts to reactivate restrictive policies toward Hawaiian traditions. Practices such as *hula,* which Kalākaua had reinstated as central to Hawaiian cultural and political identity, were seen by the *haole*-controlled provisional government as antithetical to Americanization and thus suppressed. The power of dance to embody political subversion was therefore quelled. Hawaiian language was evaluated as a political threat, since there were many Hawaiian-language newspapers, and an obstacle to Americanization. In 1896 the territorial government mandated compulsory education in English and in 1900 shut down Hawaiian public schools (Chapin 1996, 11), effectively interrupting and devaluing the Hawaiian language, the principal means for conveying oral traditions through intergenerational communications. New generations of young Native Hawaiians were subsequently schooled in English rather than Hawaiian, accelerating their assimilation away from Native Hawaiian traditions and enforcing a sense of cultural inferiority on Hawaiian-language speakers. This process was probably further exacerbated by the importation of more virulent forms of American racism, which applied primitivist racial stereotypes honed on blacks to Native Hawaiians—a by-product of the campaign to discredit the monarchy[10] and increase American military presence in Hawai'i. As a result, young Native Hawaiians were given little incentive to follow the cultural practices of the past.

The *ali'i* had utilized exhibition to present Hawai'i and Native Hawaiians as politically and culturally dominant in the islands. By participating in exhibitions, they had also demonstrated their assimilation into Western culture as an assertion that the kingdom of Hawai'i was an equal player in an international context. American exhibitions in 1893 and immediately after touted expansionism, social Darwinism, and progress as their principal themes (Rydell 1984). In 1901 *hula* dancers performed in the Hawaiian Village at the Pan American Exposition in Buffalo, New York. The village was part of a collective, adjacent to a display of wild animals, designed to show off the new Pacific and Caribbean prizes America had acquired in the Spanish-American War (Desmond 1999, 144–145). Performers may have felt in control of their individual destinies, but inasmuch as it could affect public opinion through visual spectacle, control of Hawai'i's cultural representation was in the hands of the American empire.

The new government in Hawai'i took a different approach to international exhibition in the 1909 Alaska-Yukon-Pacific Exposition in Seattle and the 1915 Panama-Pacific Exposition in San Francisco, producing a whitewashed version of Hawai'i for international consumption. In 1909 the Hawai'i Pineapple Growers Association capitalized on the beauty of *hapa-haole* (part white, part Native Hawaiian) girls to represent the industry by serving juice. In 1915 a commission sponsored by the government-backed Hawai'i Promotion Committee (HPC) spent $100,000 to construct an impressive Hawai'i Building (Desmond 1999, 66). In San Francisco as in Seattle, a major HPC goal was promotion of the pineapple industry, and in the horticultural portion of the 1915 exposition, a large pineapple exhibit was presented. Another motive was the solicitation of the "right" kind of immigrants in order to shift the population balance. A promotional brochure stipulates,

> While there is a general clamor for a larger American population, no American is advised to come here in search of employment unless he has some definite work in prospect, the means enough to maintain himself for some months and to launch into some enterprise. Clerical positions are well-filled; common labor is largely performed by Japanese and native Hawaiians, and the ranks of skilled labor are also well supplied.

Throughout the brochure, seemingly empty landscapes traversed by open roadways beckon the reader with money and initiative enough to qualify as a desirable Hawai'i resident to call Hawai'i home. To attract wealthy American immigrants, Hawai'i's non-*haole* population is neutralized to calm American xenophobia and American racism. The Chinese population is carefully not mentioned, and Japanese and Native Hawaiians are presented as an available force of unskilled labor. Native Hawaiians are redeemed as a "stalwart, healthy race." They are said to be "generous, pleasure-loving, natural musicians and orators, usually well-educated" people who "were never cannibals" and who speedily embraced early visitors, Christianity, and Americanization. To differentiate them from blacks and Indians, the publication claims that they were "barbarians but not savages at the time of the arrival of the white men." Native Hawaiians and part-Hawaiians are then characterized as ideal citizens who are "among the leaders of society" and whose "hospitality is famous" (Paradise of the Pacific Press 1914).

At the exposition, a domesticated version of Native Hawaiian culture—quaintly exotic and contained—was used to embellish a vision of Hawai'i as predominantly American. The commission constructed an elaborate and successful Hawai'i Building based on Western aesthetics. The Hawai'i Building, ideologically in tune but stylistically at variance with the Spanish Colonial theme of the overall exposition, was neo-classical Greek in design. Its interior walls held aquariums full of tropical fish, and latticed kiosks displayed landscape photos. Inscribed around the interior walls near the roofline was the simplified text of a Hawaiian legend. The names of the eight major islands appeared across the upper portion of the exterior façade (Hawai'i Exposition 1916). That official attitudes in Hawai'i had changed about the value of Hawaiian culture is evident, for at scheduled intervals each day, Native Hawaiian musicians and dancers entertained wildly enthusiastic crowds with *hula* and Hawaiian music accompanied by *'ukulele* (Morton 1921; Hawai'i Exposition 1916; Desmond 1999).

While it is certainly true, as Imada has argued, that expositions offered performers employment and travel opportunities and rewarded them with extremely appreciative audiences, in the larger scope, the question is one of relative benefits (2002). In the midst of an exposition dedicated to American territorial and trade expansion by way of the Panama Canal, the Hawai'i Building underscored the Hawaiian Islands as another U.S. project and possession. The representation of the islands in a classical-style building embellished with a translated Hawaiian legend relegated Hawaiian cultural traditions to a superficial, decorative role. Hawaiian music and dance were symbolically and actually contained, much like the tropical fish in the aquariums, as colorful specimens of island life.

The de-politicized representation of Hawaiian performance at the 1915 Panama-Pacific Exposition aestheticized Hawaiian music and dance, as well as Hawaiian bodies. Participation in the exhibitions had been intended to market Hawai'i as a business prospect, but the government's efforts to manage the image of Native Hawaiians and Hawaiian culture through scripted exhibition had unintended results in another direction. The Panama-Pacific Exposition kicked off a Hawaiiana craze that swept the United States and set off an era of mass appropriation and consumption of Hawaiian culture.

There were earlier productions that had paved the way: for example, when the musical *Bird of Paradise* opened in 1912, it quickly became the biggest Broadway hit of its time. The production featured Native Hawaiian musicians, but cast a *haole* woman in the "Hawaiian" lead role. The play went on tour and popularized Hawaiian music in elite circles throughout the United States, Europe, and Canada. After the exposition, Hawai'i culture was a popular phenomenon, and everyone wanted to "go native" and play *'ukulele,* sing *hapa-haole* songs (predominantly English lyrics with some Hawaiian words), and dance *hula.* The budding recording industry played a major part in disseminating Hawaiian music, and soon it was outselling all other kinds of music on the mainland. While the American fascination with Hawaiian music and dance created a lucrative market for Hawaiian performers, this popularity ultimately benefited larger Native Hawaiian interests only peripherally. Furthermore, it led to misrepresentation of Hawaiian cultural practices and exploitation of many performers as Hawaiian music and dance were extracted from their contexts and reinterpreted as Tin Pan Alley knock-offs (Kanahele 1979, 366–390). Soon the film industry followed suit. Starting in 1932 with the film version of *Bird of Paradise,* starring Dolores Del Rio—another non-Hawaiian in a Hawaiian female role—Hawai'i-themed films took off and soon matched the popularity of musical recordings. Although over twenty early films featured Hawaiian musicians, in most of the Hawaiiana films, non-Hawaiians played mutated versions of native people that perpetuated primitivist stereotypes.[11]

Tradition and Tourism

From the turn of the century, American's fascination with newly circulating images of Hawaiian culture—represented in postcards, stereopticon views, travel literature, exhibitions, recordings, and films—helped stoke the tourist industry in Hawai'i. Through the combined forces of mobile Hawaiian entertainers, American mass marketing, and Hawai'i's government-backed tourist industry, Hawai'i became America's new frontier of the imagination, to be possessed for as little as the price of a cellophane skirt and a *hula* lesson or as much as a Matson steamer ticket and a stay in a luxury hotel in the glamorous beach resort area called Waikīkī.

In Hawai'i, tourist desire for the exotic had eroded official disdain for *hula*. The result was a change from presenting native culture as ethnographic relics of the past in spaces like the Bishop Museum[12] to staging public performances for visitors. Seeing the commercial benefits of promoting island tourism, the state established the HPC in 1903. The HPC found creative ways to frame tradition in public spectacles. In its 1906 Midwinter Festival, it presented a historical reenactment of Kamehameha's landing. The "natives" in that spectacle wore long underwear under their historical attire for the sake of modesty, but by 1910 a less compromised version of *hula* was part of the early tourist industry's entertainment. In 1919 the HPC became the Hawaii Tourist Bureau (HTB), later renamed the Hawai'i Visitors Bureau (HVB), and by 1925 it was spending $125,000 a year on promoting Hawai'i as the "Paradise of the Pacific" and actively calling for Hawaiian performers to go on tour to promote Hawai'i as a tourist destination (Imada 2004, 118).[13]

As Waikīkī was developed in the early 1900s, the tourism industry emerged as an extension of the plantation system. This is not surprising given that much of the money to develop tourism came from a conglomerate of companies known as the Big Five (Castle and Cooke, C. Brewer, American Factors, Theo H. Davies, and Alexander and Baldwin). The principal source for the accumulated wealth of this *kama'āina haole* (Hawai'i-born *haole*) elite had been the sugar and pineapple industries. Through a complex web of intermarriage and cross-representation on governmental and commercial advisory boards, the Big Five held economic and political control in the islands. Landowners in the plantation system profited enormously from the underpaid labor of contract laborers from China, Japan, the Philippines, and other locations. With the construction of hotels, a similarly hierarchical system emerged in which low-paid labor was provided by non-*haole* and profits went to the elite. The industry depended on Native Hawaiians for its image, and Native Hawaiians entered into this stratified system as entertainers, marketing their performance skills.

The Hawai'i government's entrenchment with the tourist industry and the adoption of Hawaiian culture to signify Hawai'i to the world had several far-reaching effects on the imaging of Hawai'i. First, the endorsement of native bodies and traditional culture to signify Hawai'i effectively concealed other populations, making Hawai'i appear monocultural. Second, the adoption of the *hapa-haole hula*-girl image served to make Native Hawaiian men, immigrant populations, and the *haole* infrastructure that controlled the representation of Hawai'i invisible for its own economic benefit.[14] Third, the government suppression of Hawaiian language and disapproval of some types of performance, combined with its later approval and sponsorship of modified performance, resulted in the promotion of de-politicized, aestheticized, and hybridized versions of traditional culture that catered to tourist expectations. For example, the popularity of the *'ukulele* and *hula* in the United States after the Panama-Pacific Exposition gave them increased value as tourist attractions in Hawai'i, and by the 1920s Waikīkī tourism had become an important venue for acculturated versions of *hula,* or *hula auana* (modern, Western-influenced *hula*). As part of its promotional campaign, in 1928 the HTB funded the syndicated radio show *Hawai'i Calls,* which would continue for forty years and become popular worldwide as a venue for *hapa-haole* music.

HTB's projects inspired a host of private and corporate enterprises that capitalized on the images of *hapa-haole hula* girls. One of these was Mossman's Leilani Village in 1930s Waikīkī. Mossman's was a family-run native theme park replete with authentic grass shacks. It was unique in that it was the setting for films that perpetuated an image of primitive Hawai'i that existed only in such tourist productions while also encouraging cultural preservation by employing skilled traditional artists (Imada

2004, 119–123). Later, the famous Kodak Hula Show was created, a corporate-run mainstay in Waikīkī from 1937 until 2002. Together, the projects of tourism—state, private, and corporate—engraved an image of Hawai'i as an American playground graced with Hawaiian *aloha*. It is an image that has proved indelible, persisting through the military tourism of wars, the advent of mass tourism with the introduction of jet planes in the 1950s, into the recent revitalization of Waikīkī.

As Hawaiian culture was capitalized on as a marketable "natural resource," promotional imagery was transformed from turn-of-the-century depictions of Hawai'i as virgin territory with vanishing natives to fetishization of Hawaiian culture in images of native women draped in flower *lei* and holding *'ukulele*. The popularity of Hawaiian music and *hula* created a demand for performers. However, despite the seeming advance from government depictions of Hawaiian culture through ethnographic relics to incorporation of live performance, there was still little change in the overall message. In museums, film and stage representations, and tourist productions, Hawaiian traditions were romanticized, eroticized, primitivized, and consumed as safe and soft savagery.[15]

Ethnography and Cultural Preservation

At the same time that hybridized Hawaiian culture was being exploited for commercial gain, some citizens of Hawai'i raised concerns that traditional cultural forms were rapidly vanishing. There were many causes, such as loss of elderly cultural practitioners, disruption of language, rapid modernization and acculturation, government suppression, economic rewards for modified cultural forms, media saturation, urbanization, and cross-cultural marriages. Private, religious, and government groups responded to this sense of imminent loss of tradition in different ways and with different motivations.

Ever concerned with managing the image of Hawai'i, the same *kama'āina* elite faction that had previously disapproved of *hula* changed perspective in the 1920s and became its self-appointed protectors. Alarmed by trends toward what they perceived as crass commercialization of Hawaiian culture by Native Hawaiian performers, the media, and the tourist industry, they used publications like the magazine *Paradise of the Pacific* to decry the taint of tourism and mass marketing and urge a return to authenticity. This yearning for an earlier purity and authenticity, as Imada points out, smacked of "imperialist nostalgia," the phenomenon wherein colonizers long for the culture they have destroyed.[16]

Some private enterprises saw opportunity in perpetuating authentic traditional arts. For example, in his Leilani Village, Mossman hired a Native Hawaiian craftsman to build his grass houses according to the old style, and tourists could observe traditional cooking practices like *poi* pounding and *imu* building. Traditional *hula* and *oli* were performed there in addition to *hapa-haole* productions. Several respected Native Hawaiian *kumu* (teachers) stayed on the premises and passed on their stores of knowledge to Native Hawaiian students. Although Mossman, a part-Hawaiian married to a Native Hawaiian, was an entrepreneur who capitalized on tourist desire for the primitive, Leilani Village both engaged and resisted the tourism discourse in Waikīkī. It also contributed to the preservation of Hawaiian culture by providing a backdrop for its transmission (Imada 2004, 119).

The publication of Hawaiian storytelling in collections of myths and legends also contributed to both the preservation of aspects of oral culture and misrepresentation of Native Hawaiians. Cristina Bacchilega argues that the collection and publication of Hawaiian narrative traditions marks a boundary between appropriation and resistance. Prior to the overthrow and annexation, several collections of Hawaiian myths and legends had been compiled, and the Hawaiian-language papers often published traditional tales (2007). After annexation, and in response to American interest in things Hawaiian, the HPC translated and included some of these tales in promotional materials. It also sponsored the publication and circulation of illustrated collections that served to historicize Hawai'i while relegating Native Hawaiians to the past. This reframing of Hawaiian culture had the effect of creating what Bacchilega refers to as a "legendary Hawai'i" for American consumption (2007).

Anthropologists and folklorists played a pivotal role in cultural preservation efforts by selecting, collecting, and interpreting cultural materials. In some cases these collections formed a knowledge base, albeit a flawed one, for future cultural revivals. Martha Beckwith (1871–1951) is a case in point. Born and reared in Hawai'i, Beckwith occupied the first academic chair in folklore and thus was instrumental in establishing folklore as an academic discipline in the United States. As a student of well-known anthropologist Franz Boas, Beckwith became a staunch defender of cultural relativism and the necessity of understanding folklore in cultural contexts. She was instrumental in instigating serious academic study of Hawaiian culture as an integrated system of meanings and practices, but her study and life also point to anthropology's complicity with colonialism. Beckwith spoke fluent Hawaiian and spent many years collecting Hawaiian mythology and other forms of oral narrative. In 1905 she went to Columbia University, where she wrote a dissertation on a Hawaiian oral narrative epic—"The Romance of Laieikawai." She returned to Hawai'i to collect Hawai'i mythology and folklore from 1913 and 1915, and in 1916 she published an article on *hula* in the *Journal of American Folklore*. Later she would publish, among other things, an extensive study on Hawaiian riddling (1922), a comprehensive volume on Hawaiian mythology (1940), and a translation and study of the Hawaiian creation legend called "The Kumulipo" (1951).

Beckwith, who was given an honorary researcher position at the Bishop Museum in 1928, represents many of the contradictions inherent in who or what has been accepted as the ultimate authority on Native Hawaiian culture. She was a *kama'āina haole* who lived through the transition of Hawai'i from monarchial to territorial rule, and despite her insistence on the embeddedness of traditional cultural expressions in daily life, she separated Hawaiian culture from Hawai'i politics. She came from an elite family, and her position as distinguished chair at Vassar College was financed through the estate of a friend whose family was involved in the overthrow of the Hawaiian monarchy. Beckwith did much that is commendable and visionary by valuing Hawaiian lore, translating it, and attempting to represent it in terms of the unique culture from which it had emerged. Her work and teaching inspired a generation of women ethnographers, some of them Native Hawaiian, who would become instrumental in recording the rapidly changing traditions in Hawai'i. On the other hand, she was a product of her times, missionary schooling, and colonialist upbringing. Despite her appreciation for the cultural materials she collected, she continued to refer to Native Hawaiians in terms of Victorian assumptions—as backward and primitive (Bronner 1998, 237–265).

When the government decided to sponsor cultural preservation, as an outgrowth of the Hawaiian Rehabilitation Act passed by the legislature in 1920 and amended in 1921, one of Beckwith's students was hired for the project. The tourist industry presented Native Hawaiians as happy and carefree, but in reality there was an enormous gap between that image and the reality. The first decades of the twentieth century saw many Native Hawaiians landless and living in poverty and degradation.

Introduced by Jonah Kūhiō Kalanianaʻole, Hawaiʻi's first delegate to Congress, a prince descended from the monarchy, and author of the Rehabilitation Act, this bill was passed in 1920 to establish the basis for Hawaiian Homelands and numerous services for Native Hawaiians, who were deemed in dire need of not only social services and government protection, but also cultural protection. To address the cultural concerns expressed in Act 126 of the bill, the territorial governor appointed a Hawaiian Legends and Folklore Commission whose members were John R. Galt, Edna J. Hill, and Emma Havana Taylor, the latter a Native Hawaiian who was a chanter and composer. The committee was charged with collecting, printing, and publishing the ancient stories, songs, and music for posterity before they vanished.

After deliberation, the committee contracted two outsiders to Hawaiʻi to accomplish this task. For the collection of legends, they hired Patrick Cohm, an Irish poet who had produced a well-known volume of children's literature. To relegate Hawaiian narrative to the level of children's literature says a great deal about the relative level of importance at which these cultural artifacts were being perceived despite one member of the commission being a prominent native educator and *kumu hula*. It can safely be assumed from the speed of assembly and the replication of the stories used in other sources that Cohm collected only from previously published sources that had been translated into English. For the *mele* and *oli* project, they hired Helen Roberts, an anthropologist from Chicago who had studied with Boas and worked in Jamaica with Beckwith. The commission's choices at first might seem very strange. Neither "expert" spoke the Hawaiian language or knew Hawaiʻi. Although Roberts was at first hesitant, Herbert Gregory from the Bishop Museum argued persuasively on the basis of her transcription skills and familiarity with Edison's new recording device that there was no one else to do the job. Roberts employed a Native Hawaiian helper who transcribed Hawaiian lyrics from songbooks loaned to Roberts. Roberts herself was technologically proficient in the new recording equipment and became a student of Hawaiian language. She was given research space at the Bishop Museum and traveled through the islands of Oʻahu, Kauaʻi, Maui, and Hawaiʻi (also referred to as the Big Island) to record elderly Native Hawaiians.[17]

The Roberts collection of *mele* was later translated and interpreted by Native Hawaiian scholar Mary Kawena Pukui. Most of Roberts' recordings and field notes were housed at the Bishop Museum, where they became the basis of later research, especially during the *hula* revival of the 1970s. Although her findings can and are disputed on the basis of her lack of cultural background, her questionable grasp of the heavily metaphorical language of *mele* as a beginner in the language, and the limited scope of her travels in the islands, her recordings form at least a partial catalog of *mele* and *oli* that had survived into the 1920s.[18]

What entrepreneurs like Mossman and ethnographers like Beckwith and Roberts shared is the position of being early culture brokers, a role that would become increasingly more authoritative. The *kama'āina haole* elite and Mossman defined Hawaiian traditional culture within the frames of the tourist industry, and Beckwith defined oral narrative tradition within academe and to the elite Bishop Museum, which had previously been concerned only with Hawaiian antiquities. Roberts defined Hawaiian musical tradition by collaborating with both the territorial government and the Bishop Museum. Where Mossman's enterprise contributed to cultural transmission by traditional oral means, the Beckwith and Roberts collections recorded cultural productions for the future through the nontraditional means of publication and technology. Of course, Hawaiian-language newspapers and collectors had already published many stories and *mele,* so Beckwith and Roberts, and the ethnographers who followed them, built on extant materials in many cases. These collaborations between ethnographers and local government illustrate the complex positions culture brokers occupied in relation to "salvage ethnography."[19] By recording selected traditional Hawaiian cultural practices, these figures played a critical role in the future cultural revival and debates over the ownership and interpretation of culture. In their own time and academic disciplines, they established themselves as authorities on Hawai'i culture.

Institutional Intervention and Cultural Revival

While state- and museum-sponsored ethnographers had worked to collect remnants of vanishing traditions, within the next couple of decades other institutions would generate policies and activities that had direct impact on revivals of certain cultural traditions.

Although intervention from Protestant missionaries had negatively impacted *hula,* another religious institution was an agent in perpetuating it. The Church of Jesus Christ of Latter-Day Saints (LDS), or the Mormon Church, was instrumental in a *hula* revival in the 1930s. A presence in the Pacific since 1850, the LDS took a practical stance on the traditional practices of Polynesians that was very different from the views of the Calvinist missionaries who came to Hawai'i. Rather than suppressing the practices of its indigenous converts, the LDS tolerated traditional practices as long as they did not conflict with Mormon beliefs and values. As a result, some forms of *hula* and *oli* were perpetuated in slightly modified forms. The revival in the 1930s involved a few *kumu hula* who passed on their stores of knowledge of *hula pahu* to their students. Most of these *kumu* had been asked to conduct classes at the Mutual Improvement Association of the Mormon Church (Kaeppler 1993, 39–41). The public effect of these *hālau* was somewhat limited at the time; they performed mostly in elite settings like the Honolulu Academy of Arts. However, some of the most respected current *kumu* today trace their *hula* lineages to this critical time period and these *kumu*. It is unclear whether fund-raising was one of the motivations for encouraging *hula* transmission in the 1930s, but tourism did become an important fund-raising and recruitment activity for the LDS. When the LDS temple built in 1919 burned down in 1940 and could not be immediately rebuilt due to World War II restrictions, the LDS instituted a monthly *hukilau* (literally, "fishing lines") and *lū'au* (feast) gathering on the beach.[20] The famous "Hukilau" song by Jack Russell was inspired by the first Lā'ie *hukilau*. Visitors from Honolulu and elsewhere were welcomed and crafts items were sold at this event that successfully continued for twenty years.

The LDS also organized a Polynesian dance troupe, which traveled to Honolulu starting in 1959. In 1955 the LDS opened a Church College at Lā'ie for Pacific Islander students, and in 1963 it combined education and fund-raising with tourism when it opened the Polynesian Cultural Center (PCC), the most successful and longest-standing ethnographic theme park of its kind. More entertainment than ethnography, the student performances of Polynesian music and dance at the PCC accomplish a religious and educational mission for the LDS by showcasing their missionary activity and participating in tourism as a source of funding (Stanley 1998, 39–55). Like Waikīkī tourism, the LDS portrayal of Pacific culture is focused on indigenous culture, and as in early Hawai'i travel literature, the effect is a limited picture of Polynesian culture.

In the 1930s the city of Honolulu's Department of Parks and Recreation became an important site in which grassroots interests and government support collaborated in cultural preservation through classes, programs, and special events. According to *lei* maker and former department employee Marie McDonald, the Parks and Recreation arts projects came about because so many employees were Native Hawaiian. Some of these employees, like McDonald, who is a retired educator and has been recognized as a National Heritage Fellow for her flower *lei*-making skills, were talented tradition bearers themselves. For example, Alice Namakelua, slack-key guitarist and composer of over 180 songs, worked for the Parks and Recreation Department for twenty-three years. As playground director, Namakelua taught children's classes in *hula* and singing (Kanahele 1979, 263–265). The Parks and Recreation Department classes included a range of Hawaiian activities, such as *hula,* instrument making, and *lei* making. When interest in these programs flagged, it was reignited through publicity and special events. McDonald remembers at one point being charged with reviving the annual *lei* contest and having to involve all of her family members to ensure that it would be a success and not discontinued.[21] For musicians, the department provided an alternative venue when, in 1933, it sponsored a weekly local musical show that showcased local talent and stayed on the air until 1968 (Kanahele 1979, 321–325). It also provided opportunities for new talent by creating an annual singing contest in 1950 (Kanahele 1979, 360–361).

The Parks and Recreation Department classes were unique in that they went beyond exclusively covering Hawaiian traditional arts. Previously, the arts of immigrants had been fostered through neglect. A plantation system that had divided peoples by ethnic group to create enmity and thus suppress the possibility of labor strikes inadvertently fostered cultural preservation in its resultant ethnic enclaves. The exploitation of laborers eventually produced the solidarity it had tried to prevent, along with creolized cultural products like Hawaiian pidgin (creole English) and shared musical traditions.[22] While state economic interest continued to look to indigenous culture as tourist capital, the Parks and Recreation Department catered to working-class communities. Recreational workshops were given in immigrant crafts and performance since these, too, were endangered as people made the transition from plantation to urban life and in the face of increasing cultural homogenization.

Parks and Recreation Department dance and craft classes continue to the present as a public venue for the perpetuation of traditional crafts and performing arts. They are geared toward children and amateurs and do not necessarily produce students who aspire to emulate the skill level of their teachers, yet they have played an important historical role in cultural preservation. These classes provided public education about traditional arts—like playing *'ukulele* and making kites or *lei*—and public access to arts education. They also provided opportunities for local children to learn about their heritage and traditions devalued in the schools. Finally, they set the stage for further local government shifts in arts policy.

The Hawai'i State Foundation for Culture and the Arts

Missionization, capitalism, and political upheaval had effected a sea change in traditional arts and the imaging of Hawai'i during the first half of the twentieth century; a wave of populism in both Hawai'i and the mainland triggered another one in the second half. Economic and social changes in turn introduced changes in the political sphere, which thus affected arts policies. On the level of economics, this change began with the disruption of the plantation system. From 1910 on, Hawai'i was under the tightly woven control of the Big Five companies, whose major economic interests were tied to the plantation system. Plantation owners had imported large numbers of contract workers, and they controlled them through a surveillance system that regulated everything from their labor to their votes. Although plantation policies had implemented a racist "divide and conquer" policy of separating immigrant groups according to country of origin and paying them unequal wages, workers eventually were organized under the International Longshore and Warehouse's Union (ILWU) in 1946.

Unionization and shifts in the sugar trade weakened the profitability index for the industry in the early 1950s. There were sociopolitical changes afoot as well, as immigrant groups came of age. With American eyes turned to the Japanese during World War II, twenty-five hundred Japanese *nisei* (second generation of Japanese immigrants, born in Hawai'i) enlisted in the American military to prove their loyalty. They returned from the 442nd Regimental Combat Team with honor, G.I. Bill benefits that allowed them to acquire college educations and property, a strong sense of identity as Americans, and a stronger desire to oust the *haole* elite from government.

Out of this ferment, two *nisei* senators emerged: Daniel Inouye and "Spark" Matsunaga. Following in the footsteps of other political leaders since the 1940s who had discovered that with the advent of labor consciousness political power could be had only with the resounding support of non-*haole* residents of Hawai'i, Democrat John Burns, a former Hawai'i delegate to Congress, cultivated the support of local Japanese. In 1962 *nisei* Japanese and the ILWU were major factors in electing Burns, who ran on a populist platform, as governor of the state of Hawai'i.

Although Noel Kent argues that Burns was basically a conservative, his election marked a major shift in Hawai'i politics from a one-party system dominated by the *haole* elite to a two-party competition in which non-*haole* working-class voters had a say (1983).

Working among groups that had often harbored deep suspicion and resentment of each other—the *haole* elite, *nisei* professionals, Native Hawaiians and part-Hawaiians, and other ethnic groups—Burns signed into law major changes in some areas of the arts while enhancing the status quo in others. What distinguished these new policies as unique was that they institutionalized public education as the underlying principle for government sponsorship of the arts and made inroads toward democratizing both their access and their definition. These educational initiatives reached in a different direction from the economic initiatives involved in government sponsorship for the tourist industry. This is not to say, however, that there were no connections between these seemingly disparate agendas. Burns had high hopes of making Hawai'i the cultural capital of the Pacific (Kent 1983, 140–163).

Hawai'i became a state in 1959, and within the next decade a sweep of political and social change that would further affect Hawai'i arts programs took place at the federal level. In 1964 President Lyndon Johnson established a National Council on the Arts and on September 29, 1965, he signed Public Law #89-209, which founded the National Endowment for the Arts and Humanities as an umbrella for its two branches: the National Endowment for the Arts (NEA) and the National Endowment for the Humanities (NEH). The NEA quickly funded a states initiative that made grant money available to each of the states to establish public arts programs. To qualify for federal funding from the NEA under this initiative, Governor Burns established the Hawai'i State Foundation for Culture and the Arts (HSFCA) in 1965. According to its website, the official mission of the HSFCA was (and is) "To promote, perpetuate, preserve and encourage culture and the arts, history, and the humanities as central to the quality of life of the people of Hawai'i."

In 1966 Burns appointed architect and state planning coordinator Alfred Preis to the position of director and local Japanese businessman Masaru "Pundy" Yokouchi as chair of the Board of Commissioners.[23] In June of that year Preis attended the first national meeting with the Arts Councils of America, the American Symphony League, and members of the NEA. Together, Yokouchi and Preis attended the first national meeting of State Arts Agencies, held January 27–29, 1967, in Chicago.

Burns was a strategist whose choice of Preis, a European elite, and

Yokouchi, a local Japanese, illustrates how he straddled political factions. Preis could cultivate the support of wealthy *haole* who preferred Western fine arts, and Yokouchi would represent the local Japanese and other groups. Yokouchi may also have been correct in saying that he was chosen because he was a friend of Burns and an amateur art collector with strong views about equal access to the arts. Having grown up in his parents' bakery business, he felt he knew nothing about the arts except his own taste. To emphasize his sense of alienation in the national arena, he told a story about how at the meeting in Chicago he felt intimidated by the educated people from the other states and decided to align himself with someone else who was from a marginal area—South Dakota. To his chagrin, he soon discovered that the representative from South Dakota knew all the dignitaries and was a big city transplant.[24] From these meetings on the mainland, Preis and Yokouchi brought back new ideas about the government's relationship to the arts.

The odd partnering of Preis and Yokouchi illustrates a tension in state and national arts sponsorship that continues to this day. Classically trained and educated Preis was primarily interested in the collection and elevation of fine arts. He was also wise enough to realize that because he was a foreign-born *haole,* he would do well to allow Yokouchi to be the public face of the HSFCA. Influenced by his own underprivileged background, Yokouchi was a strong advocate for arts access in working-class communities, and through his exposure to NEA ideals and programs for under-served communities, he developed an appreciation for traditional or folk arts. Although he was brought up to look down on Native Hawaiians, he realized early on that HSFCA money was best spent on fostering the preservation of Hawaiian art forms perceived to be endangered. He said that the other groups could go to their home countries to learn their traditions, but for Native Hawaiians, there was nowhere else to go to find their roots.[25]

Reiterating the pattern begun in the 1920s with the hiring of Helen Roberts to survey Hawaiian music, but this time instigated by the NEA, mainland consultants arrived to assess the arts in Hawai'i. These consultants presented reports on their findings and made recommendations for programs that would use NEA resources to their best advantage. What they reported did not please Honolulu's social upper crust, who had hoped to expand the fine arts. Mainly interested in what was being taught in schools, the consultants said that they were very impressed with the quality of ethnic dance, but pronounced Hawai'i a "musical disaster area" after reviewing school music programs. The consultants emphasized the need for preservation, encouragement, and development of cultural dances, especially indigenous dance. This they felt should be done by "first reviving what is authentic." They recommended the creation of a statewide dance association to offer leadership and serve as a liaison between rural counties and the HSFCA. No doubt reflecting the attitudes of academically trained mainland folklorists, they repeatedly expressed concern for preservation of ethnic traditions in Hawai'i. In terms of music, they recommended less stress on standard European music and more music activities for enjoyment and group singing. They also recommended that *'ukulele,* guitar, and ensemble music be included. In visual arts they recommended a de-emphasis on competition and grading and more correlation with other arts.[26]

NEA-backed initiatives in Hawai'i were kicked off in style with a statewide conference in June 1966. At the conference, which included workshops and panels, NEA directors and affiliates laid out goals for NEA funding, and Robert P. Griffing, a curatorial assistant at the Honolulu Academy of Arts, spoke about Hawai'i as a hub of Eastern and Western cultures. The conference staged the first Hawai'i Arts Festival, an unprecedented event that featured a combination of traditional and non-traditional arts that weighed heavily on the side of elite preferences for Western fine arts. The festival featured a hybrid East/West, elite/folk theater production titled *Dragon of the Moon* at Kennedy Theatre. The Seventeenth Annual Artists of Hawai'i Exhibition was the visual arts facet of the festival and included the First Annual Arts and Crafts Design Exhibition, which displayed the drawings of children along with its presentation of arts and crafts. That it proudly featured the refined art of *ikebana* (Japanese floral arrangement) suggests that the exhibition organizers had previously not considered including immigrant crafts, since the only concession in this direction was to an elite foreign art form and the work of schoolchildren.

The musical highlight was an inter-island chorus that performed a commissioned piece with the Honolulu Symphony. This piece, "The Waters of Kane" by George Barati, was loosely based on a Hawaiian *mele.* It was followed by a concert of religious music whose selections were based on multi-ethnic religious expressions: Buddhist, Catholic, Jewish, and Protestant. Dance was represented by traditional Hawaiian and choreographed Asian performances. Because Hawai'i did not have a ballet company, the Harkness Ballet from New York performed. According to the HSFCA Annual Report, the most highly acclaimed segment of the Festival was the "Dances of Asia," performed by the Halla Huhm dance company, which received a subsequent invitation for a nationwide tour. Huhm's group of four performers "was rated by mainland experts as superlative," and the show was described as "exquisitely performed and staged."

Overall, the arts chosen for presentation appear to have been an uncomfortable fit between organizers' efforts to match NEA interest in seeing and sponsoring traditional art forms and their own prejudice in favor of elite art forms. The result was the creation of hybrids, with traditional arts selected out, enhanced, and "improved" through an infusion of Western fine art aesthetics. In contrast to the mostly fine arts presented to showcase Hawai'i culture to the NEA officials, so-called "authentic Hawaiian dances" were performed by Hoakalei Kamanu and Ku'uipo Enos to an overflow local audience at Washington Place even though they were temporarily upstaged by the arrival of actress Loretta Young.[27]

This split between support for folk and fine arts was present in the NEA from the outset and entered into some of the early codification of educational goals and objectives of the HSFCA set out in 1969:

- To preserve the culture of the Hawaiian people and to develop authentic knowledge of their arts and crafts.
- To preserve the arts, crafts, and traditions of the people who immigrated to Hawai'i, in order to deepen their pride in the culture of their forbears, and to expose them to the best traditional and contemporary performances, exhibitions, and demonstrations, including those from the countries of their origin.
- To devise programs and to establish the means whereby culture and the arts can be brought to those who would otherwise not have the opportunity to participate.[28]

These three goals teeter between elite surveillance and progressive cultural ideals. Native Hawaiians are selected out as most in need of cultural preservation efforts, although it is not clear from the first goal who will develop the "authentic knowledge" or how authenticity will be determined. Meanwhile, the specter of extant inauthenticity is raised. The traditions of immigrants are included in preservation efforts, but it is implied that they, too, are veering toward inauthenticity and either losing interest in their ancestral cultures or practicing them in an inferior fashion. Home country templates are offered as a corrective that will lead them back to what is "traditional," further suggesting that immigrant traditions need uplifting and implying that tradition is static in the country of origin. Overall, this view shows little understanding of the uniqueness of cultural development in Hawai'i or of traditional culture as dynamic and adaptive. The third goal seeks to democratize access to the arts, yet presumes that culture and the arts must be imported into communities.

In addition to the NEA arts funding, Hawai'i attracted other attention and funding from the federal level. In 1964 Honolulu was selected by the U.S. Department of Housing and Urban Development as one of seventy cities to participate in the Model Cities Program, part of President Johnson's War on Poverty. Nānākuli-Wai'anae (on the western side of O'ahu) and Kalihi-Pālama (a neighborhood of Honolulu) were targeted for funding when the program was officially authorized in 1966. Although the Model Cities Program was devised to involve communities in designing affordable housing, when the HSFCA was given responsibility for administering the program in Hawai'i, Preis added a cultural component to how it would be interpreted. The goal was "to prepare the organizational basis for the widest participation of the peoples of Hawai'i in expanding and improving cultural and artistic life." In 1965 the county governments of the islands of Hawai'i, Kaua'i, and Maui had each set aside ten thousand dollars in anticipation of matching federal funds. Between June and November 1966 community arts councils were established on the islands of Moloka'i, Maui, Lāna'i, Kaua'i, and Hawai'i (in the cities of Kona and Hilo), with NEA funding distributed directly through the HSFCA on O'ahu. New alliances were also formed; for example, a state conference on Hawaiian dance was collaboratively planned by the Bishop Museum, the Hawai'i State Dance Council, and the HSFCA.[29]

In the course of these changes, new models for tourism—plural, authentic, and community centered—were envisioned, and the Hawai'i Festival of Pacific Nations was planned for the Waikīkī Shell, an outdoor amphitheater in Honolulu, as a beginning. These efforts operated under the rationale of "improving" ethnic groups through the arts. For instance, in reference to planning the first State Conference of Hawaiian Dance, the HSFCA stated, "Residents interested in Hawaiian dance—there are very many—will be encouraged to join pre-conference dance workshops so they will be fully accomplished when the conference will commence and will be able to participate as proud equals with the best dancers of Hawai'i in seminar discussions and dance workshops."

Although later in the same report the HSFCA claimed that there were far too many dance companies in Hawai'i that produced only amateurs, organizers ignored all research on traditional Hawaiian *hula* transmission to simplistically assume that a pre-conference workshop would produce experts. The Hawai'i Festival of Pacific Nations, on the other hand, would bring in performers from the Asia Pacific region so that they could contribute to the educational uplifting of Hawai'i's immigrants: "Not only will our own Filipino, Japanese, Chinese dancers and musicians be exposed to classical and traditional arts, as they are currently interpreted, but they will have the opportunity to refine and perfect their own arts in workshops, seminars, and master classes given by the guest artists."

Hawaiian dance was to be the foundation for all other cultural development programs. The long-term plan was for the Hawaiian Civic Club to assume leadership and establish programs in all other facets of Hawaiian arts and crafts and stimulate other community groups, such as the Filipino Community Council and the Samoan associations, to emulate the Hawaiian program.

To this end, statewide dance performances were sponsored in which Asian and Hawaiian traditional dance was performed by the companies of Iolani Luahine, Halla Huhm, Koshiro Nishikawa, Alfred Durano, and other "ethnic dancers." Modern dance and ballet troupes also performed. The final dance performance of the Asian-Pacific Dance Workshop was performed at the Waikīkī Shell in two parts that illustrated the same ambivalence about traditional arts evident in the first festival. Part one showcased "ancient *hula*s" from pageantry to statehood. Part two was billed as the "Hawai'i of the Future" and presented "festival *hula*" as part of a commissioned Hawai'i opera choreographed by the University of Hawaii Theatre and Dance Department and co-sponsored by the Houston Symphony.[30] These programs superimposed institutionally determined aesthetics and standards of excellence on Hawai'i ethnic communities. In some cases this intervention altered the direction of traditional arts, and in other cases it may have also ensured their survival. It also provided important avenues for empowerment, identity, and increased visibility in economically depressed communities while expanding the official view of traditional culture to include the culture of immigrants. Where this attention to ethnic arts was met by community interest, it provided a financial impetus for grassroots cultural revivals.

In the ensuing years, the HSFCA continued to expand its sponsorship of ethnic culture—via a division called the Ethnic Development Program, subsequently the Cultural Development Program and Cultural

Heritage Program—through inter-island workshops that included a full range of Hawaiian traditional cultural practices: ancient dance, quilting, Hawaiian language, featherwork, weaving, instrument making, and music. These efforts often dovetailed with community efforts. For instance, *kumu hula* Iolani Luahine and Lokalia Montgomery oversaw two Model Cities state conferences on Hawaiian dance; civic clubs organized classes under master teachers selected from the community; and dance conferences continued to be organized by community groups after being set in motion by the HSFCA. As the HSFCA had hoped, the Hawaiian program set a precedent for other ethnic communities, and a Philippine Culture Development Program was initiated in 1970. This program started with two festivals in the Model Cities areas with accompanying classes in *rondalla* instrument making and Filipino dance. Despite this new development, the State Council on Hawaiian Heritage, comprising thirty-two organizations under one umbrella, continued to receive the largest portion of HSFCA funding for cultural development.[31]

The state's new recognition of traditional arts was also extended to individuals, based on an Asian model and reflecting Governor Burns' vision of Hawai'i in relation to the Asia/Pacific region. After the Japanese government's custom of recognizing exemplary traditional artists as National Treasures of Intangible Heritage, Burns presented Iolani Luahine with the first Hawaiian Order of Distinction for Cultural Leadership at the Second State Conference on Dance in 1970.[32] Four years later, the award was given to *kumu hula* and cultural researcher/writer Mary Kawena Pukui. This award was the first of its kind in Hawai'i and preceded by nearly a decade the National Heritage Fellowships later developed by the NEA.

That the efforts of the state were geared as much toward social rehabilitation through culture as they were toward the aesthetics of cultural preservation is illustrated by the following statement from the 1973–1974 HSFCA Annual Report: "The HSFCA aims not only to recover, restore, practice and perfect the authentic traditional arts, crafts, skills, customs and lore of the various ethnic groups in Hawai'i; but through the immersion in cultural pursuits, the people themselves will learn to look at their ancestors with pride."[33]

This kind of cultural uplift was attempted in different ways in different ethnic communities, with authenticity and excellence as the standards required by NEA backing. It also reflected the aesthetics of individual communities, since receiving grants beyond the original Model Cities initiatives required that proposals be generated by the communities themselves. The Hawaiian community employed master teachers to conduct classes and, following Burns' example, gave awards to recognize cultural expertise combined with meritorious service to the community and the state. In immigrant communities, also following the state model, a foreign "roots" model was generally introduced as the standard, implying not only the cultural inferiority of hybrid and evolved arts in relation to those of ancestral countries, but also emphasizing the transnational identities of immigrant communities. Under HSFCA initiatives, National Treasures and performance troupes were brought in from Japan, Okinawa, and Korea to perform and conduct workshops. This practice was not, however, limited to state standards. In May 1973 the community-generated Philippines Barrio Festival in Wailuku was modeled on village festivals in the Philippines. It was "constructed to create the traditional village atmosphere."[34] This attempt to re-create "old country" aesthetics collapsed Filipinos from both Hawai'i and the Philippines into a rural pan-ethnicity.

Another uplift strategy was to improve traditional arts. A Filipino *rondalla*/vocal ensemble was funded with the idea that it would be "of such high quality it will encourage pride." Tanghalan Repertory Theatre was funded to present plays on Filipino immigrants. These projects were co-authored by communities, and the HSFCA/NEA Asian programs in Hawai'i sought cultural validation transnationally rather than internally. The traditions being cultivated were often court music, theater, and dance rather than actual folk arts practiced by common people. Likewise, the Samoan Chiefs and Orators Society, which became a regular HSFCA recipient beginning in 1976, focused on high culture through chiefly arts. What the NEA had defined as efforts to democratize the arts through representation of the traditions of "minority constituencies" consequently became suffused—through both HSFCA and community directives—with hierarchical thinking within those communities.

In a decade, what had begun as the Ethnic Development Program and become the Cultural Development Program underwent many changes. It evolved from an intervention effort that supported the focus on the preservation of authentic Hawaiian dance in economically depressed areas of O'ahu into inter-island sponsorship of a full range of ethnic cultural practices. It fostered the creation of civic organizations and cultural development programs in other ethnic groups, some of which were also economically depressed, but others of which were simply feeling the cultural losses of rapid assimilation. In 1976 the Model Cities areas were "liberated" to continue under their own direction. They could continue to receive federal funding, but without direct HSFCA control. An important goal of culture brokering at the federal level—sponsorship that leads to independent community action—had been accomplished.

As new ethnic communities came into range, ethical issues in culture brokering were raised. In the late 1970s the HSFCA received applications from Laotian, Vietnamese, and other Indo-Chinese groups. Interaction with these groups spurred a certain amount of self-reflection about cultural intervention projects having "certain impacts on people whose consciousness of heritage is expected to benefit." A key question with regards to intervention was raised: should methods and goals be adapted to community needs and values in efforts to solidify community solidarity/identity? For example, the 1978–1979 HSFCA Annual Report states that Tongan and Samoan immigrants found the transition to "taboo-free, authoritarian-free society" strange and difficult, with the result that young and old tended to break with the past in order to adapt to the new environment. The HSFCA was discovering that the arts were neither neutral nor apolitical within the ethnic groups it sponsored. Rather, traditions have different social functions over time, particularly in periods of transition. Introducing programs emphasizing traditional arts can reassert traditional values that may not be equally desirable to all members of a community in a particular time and place. In relation to this issue, the HSFCA assessment was that "the programs thereby established are divisive within a society and temporarily lead to a sort of cultural chaos. HSFCA must adapt to these conditions."[35] The implication was that community elite and the HSFCA had been complicit in proposing or introducing programs toward which some community members felt ambivalent or even hostile.

HSFCA programs also sparked incentive for cultural differentiation and cultural revival in very acculturated communities. Under the NEA directive to reach out to new constituencies, an extensive program was started for cultural development among the Portuguese in Hawai'i, the only former plantation labor immigrants who had not been funded thus far. The Annual Report notes that "for a long time there has been little incentive for the Portuguese to distinguish themselves from other Caucasian people" and emphasizes that the Portuguese in Hawai'i all originated in the Azores and were of rural, island roots rather than being from Portugal proper. Although the Portuguese were categorized as Caucasian in this report, usually referred to as *haole*, they were distinguished as non-*haole* because of their plantation labor history.[36] The value of a separate category was a funding advantage. An occasional small grant was given for "European folk arts"; for example, a Ukrainian dance group received five hundred dollars in 1979, and in the early 1980s a Scandinavian Centennial was funded, but the majority of HSFCA funding was earmarked for non-*haole* groups.

The authority of the HSFCA to define ethnic arts and ethnicity in Hawai'i grew exponentially with its federal funding. As the number and variety of applications expanded, funding was shaped into three categories: Polynesian, Asian, and Other. This categorization has persisted into the present with only minor changes. In 1980 the "Other" category was a blurry catchall that included the Polynesian Voyaging Society, the Bishop Museum, Puerto Ricans, Scandinavians, Portuguese, and so on. Clearly it was used to lump together proposals from mixed groups and those that did not fit the first two categories.

By 1980–1981 the HSFCA was administering a budget of nearly $3 million, with $447,819 going to the Cultural Heritage Development Program. The lion's share of the HSFCA program money was still designated for fine arts, and much of the Cultural Heritage Program's budget was earmarked for established organizations like the University of Hawai'i Oral History Program ($90,000), the Bishop Museum ($150,000), the Polynesian Voyaging Society ($12,000), the two Filipino programs ($323,000), and Korean studies at the University of Hawai'i ($6,000). Many of the grantees had been previously funded. *Hula* was now funded through the Hula Master Teachers Program, which gave four grants of $5,000 each to individual teachers like Kau'i Zuttermeister. Among Asian groups, Halla Huhm's dance company received the largest grant ($6,000).[37]

In 1979 Alfred Preis finally retired as director of the HSFCA, and Sarah Richards was hired. Because public arts funding was and is tied to politics, in 1980 the HSFCA's NEA-funded bottom fell out. Due to a general economic recession, Congress requested that funding from the federal Department of Management and Budget to the NEA be cut by 50 percent. Anticipation of these cuts caused a great deal of consternation at the HSFCA. While Democratic senators Daniel Inouye, Daniel Akaka, and Spark Matsunaga gave strong support for funding local communities, the new director at the HSFCA stressed the importance of funding major institutions, such as the symphony, in the case of downsizing. Ethnic arts could not be deleted, however, since the NEA gave its monies to the state with certain stipulations. When the money crunch did come, it created a change in the way that the HSFCA would address ethnic arts from then on. "Ethnic Heritage" became a category that administered funding to local organizations representing individual ethnic groups.

Despite the organization's reduced funding, through a new NEA initiative the Folk Arts Program was created as an HSFCA entity that would deal directly with traditional arts through special projects and apprenticeship grants. Repeating the sequence that had set the HSFCA in motion in the 1960s, starting in 1980–1981 the NEA provided seed money to get the new division under way—in this case money was designated for a folk arts coordinator and field services.[38] Lynn Martin, a recent University of Hawai'i master's graduate in Pacific studies, was hired and an advisory committee formed. The members of the committee, some of whom were academically trained culture experts, were all representatives of influential institutions on which the HSFCA depended for support: Ricardo Trimillos (University of Hawai'i, Department of Music, Ethnomusicology), Roger Rose (Bishop Museum), Deborah Waite (University of Hawai'i, Department of Art), Richard Via (East-West Center), and Linda Moriarty (East-West Center). Martin, mentored by Bess Lomax Hawes, director of the Folk Arts division of the NEA and founder of the National Heritage Fellowship, established the HSFCA Master and Apprentice Program in 1987, a program that provided small grants to individual tradition bearers as an incentive to transmit their knowledge to skilled students.

Throughout this period, the NEA served as a resource and legitimizing force for traditional arts in Hawai'i, often an unsung one. In the 1980s the NEA made grants directly available to nonprofit cultural organizations working with traditional artists. These grants required that the organizations abide by NEA standards, and funded organizations were evaluated by a representative of the NEA. Early site visits were made by Robert Garfius of the University of Washington and later by local cultural authorities from the University of Hawai'i or the HSFCA. Trimillos and Martin both served as evaluators for community projects.

The goal of public arts support is to empower communities, so it logically follows that it is critical that supported communities, however dependent they may be on public financial aid for survival of their traditions, not be made to feel or look dependent on the granting agency. To do this successfully, granting agencies must cultivate invisibility. In many cases they grant seed money as an initiative to get community agencies started and then phase out their support as the agency becomes independent. Whereas the imperial exhibitions of the past highlighted the national frame to emphasize the dependency of colonized subjects, effective contemporary arts agencies deliberately hide the frame in order to forefront the activity of community artists and arts. Idealistically speaking, for the role of the NEA and HSFCA in cultural revivals to be overlooked might be the ultimate sign of their success at empowering communities. At the same time, their invisibility masks the extent to which they define and survey the traditional arts of communities and, by doing so, define authenticity, tradition, and even ethnicity. In looking at the disappeared frames for cultural rehabilitation and representation, it is worth noting that many of the same cultural authorities have appeared on virtually every arts advisory board dealing with "ethnic arts" in Hawai'i since the advent of the HSFCA cultural programs. This core group of advisors and culture brokers was invested, by the HSFCA, with the responsibility of being the guardians of cultural integrity in Hawai'i and would be enlisted in shaping Hawai'i's representation at the Smithsonian in 1989.

On the other hand, HSFCA and NEA attention could not have had the impact they did if they had not been met by community efforts emerging at a time of political ferment and growing unrest among the groups they served. The majority of the early funding went to Hawaiian communities to support the Model Cities Programs, the Hawaiian Civic Clubs, the State Council on Hawaiian Heritage, and the State Conference on Dance. These projects either developed community leadership or were generated in the communities they represented. Other organizations, such as the Polynesian Voyaging Society and the Queen Lili'uokalani Children's Center, applied and received funding for specific projects. Timing was critical, and it is safe to say that federal and state funding for the perpetuation and preservation of traditional arts contributed indirectly to the sociopolitical changes that emerged among Native Hawaiians in 1970s Hawai'i. A generation that had learned organizing and leadership skills in the Model Cities Programs was coming of age.

Re-politicized Culture in the Hawaiian Renaissance

Hawai'i is a Pacific crossroads, and national and international issues affected the direction of social upheaval in Hawai'i in the 1970s. Through travelers and transplants, returning residents, and the media, Hawai'i was influenced by the American civil rights movement and Native American movements, the Vietnam War, decolonization in the Pacific, and, in particular, the success of the Maori political and cultural revival in New Zealand from the 1960s onward. That this climate of change most deeply affected Native Hawaiians among Hawai'i residents testifies to the uniqueness of Hawai'i's colonial history and neo-colonial conditions.

The 1960s had ushered in an era of growing resentment over the established economic and political control of *haole* (*kama'āina* and newcomers), the economic advancement of local Chinese and Japanese, rampant development for tourism, and the non-distribution of promised Hawaiian homelands to Native Hawaiians. These issues first came to a head in 1970 in Kalama Valley when farmers were evicted so that trust lands, administered by the Bishop Estate, which had been set up to benefit Native Hawaiians, could be commercially developed. The resistance that this provoked was the first such action in the twentieth century, and because of its identification with Hawaiian lands, it came to be identified as a Hawaiian resistance against the state, although it actually involved many other groups.

The Kalama protest set a precedent for similar disputes, identified land as central to Hawaiian political issues, and cemented the groundwork for an ideological connection of land and culture. Additional protests ensued over evictions in Wailuku, non-distribution of Hawaiian homelands, development issues on Moloka'i, and an unpopular appointment to the Bishop Estate Board of Trustees. These protests brought many Native Hawaiians together and infused them with a sense of purpose that spurred them to create organizations like The Hawaiians, the Council of Hawaiian Organizations (COHO), Hui Ala Loa, and Aloha as a way of combating what they perceived as the state's flagrant disregard for the rights and well-being of Native Hawaiians. Political mobilization also divided indigenous Hawaiians between those who identified as American-Hawaiian and those who preferred to see themselves as Hawaiian only, those who wanted Hawaiian-only organizing and those who chose to include sympathizers of other ethnicities. Disputes over identity heated up when demands for reparations were made by Aloha in 1973. The result was the creation of the now official label "Native Hawaiian."

The allocation of federal money to be paid to Hawaiians in 1974, through the efforts of a group called Alu Like and Senator Inouye, further complicated Hawaiian identity issues since it required potential recipients to be able to trace their genealogy to before 1778. Melanie Chait asserts, "It was only from 1976 with the Protect Kaho'olawe 'Ohana movement that culture, land, and political power were to be united in one struggle, which resulted in a stronger sense of pride, entitlement and nation" (1999, 98). Hawaiians rallied around the campaign to stop the use of the island of Kaho'olawe for military testing and reclaim it as a Hawaiian sacred site, and Kaho'olawe, like Kalama, became an important icon for Native Hawaiians advocating political change.

In response to the momentum of a grassroots organization called Haole Kanawei, the state of Hawai'i established the Office of Hawaiian Affairs (OHA) in 1978 and designated it as the agency to hold title to all real or personal property set aside or conveyed to or entrusted for Native Hawaiians. To some activists, the creation of OHA was a government co-optation of a grassroots movement and a betrayal. Meanwhile, the issues that had crystallized around Kaho'olawe led to the beginnings of a vital sovereignty movement with groups like Ka Lahui Hawai'i. When John Waihee, the first elected governor of Hawaiian ancestry, took office as Hawai'i's fourth governor in 1986, the future appeared more promising for many Hawaiians. The renaissance seemed to have come of age when 1987 was declared "The Year of the Hawaiian."

The Hawaiian renaissance had multiple impetuses and manifestations, including its growth out of the earlier programs and collaborations I have discussed, but it was primarily political and it politicized culture as a part of its unfolding. There are multiple narratives in circulation about the events and ideas that sparked the renaissance—some exclusively political and others exclusively cultural. Together they represent a discourse on Hawaiian identity that entered into the narrative constructed by the Smithsonian in 1989.

Historian Lawrence H. Fuchs dates the renaissance to 1959. He relates that at a faculty meeting of Kamehameha School for Boys "it was agreed that 'a psychological rebirth of the Hawaiian people'" was in process despite the fact that the majority of their students were of diluted Hawaiian ancestry. Fuchs claims that the renaissance was led and is best symbolized by Abraham Akaka, reverend of Kawaiahao Church and president of the Council of Hawaiian Congregational Churches. In 1959 and under Akaka's leadership, the council inspired the Hawaiian Civic Clubs to agree "that festival, *lū'au,* and fashion shows were not enough" and that political and educational goals should be foregrounded (Fuchs 1961, 446–449). While this narrative nods to community agency and the important role of certain institutions, Fuchs' choice of Akaka as a symbol of the renaissance grants catalyst power to a symbol of colonial power—the church founded by missionary Hiram Bingham—effectively containing political dissidence by co-opting and neutralizing it. Fuchs' version adopts Akaka's beliefs in the positive contributions of intermarriage and his stress on *aloha* as the unique mission and message of Hawai'i to the rest of the world. Although he cites much evidence to the contrary, Fuchs' underlying message resonates with that of Akaka: that cross-cultural marriage and exchange in Hawai'i, despite the inter-ethnic and class tensions, constitute an ideal of *aloha* that the mainland would do well to learn from. This ideological stance asserts benign multiculturalism and effectively negates Native Hawaiian claims to a separate identity and the political nature of the Hawaiian movement that followed. It is a popular version due to its inclusivity and avoidance of conflict.

In the same year that Protect Kaho'olawe 'Ohana was organized, the Hawaiian movement adopted the *Hōkūle'a,* a replica of a traditional Polynesian voyaging canoe, as another symbol, spawning the basis of one of several exclusively cultural origin narratives for the renaissance. The Polynesian Voyaging Society was conceived by Ben Finney in 1966 and made its first voyage in 1970. The society's goal was to collect data on early voyaging, using the mostly forgotten arts of celestial navigation, and to prove the validity of the early migration accounts preserved in indigenous oral histories. According to the society website, by its third and much publicized voyage in 1976, the *Hōkūle'a* had become another icon for Hawaiian identity: "Navigated without instruments by Micronesian navigator, Mau Piailug, the canoe arrived 33 days later in Papeete, Tahiti, to a crowd of more than 17,000—over half of the island had turned out to greet the canoe. What had begun as a scientific experiment to prove a theory about the settlement of Polynesia had touched a deep root of cultural pride in Polynesian people" (2004).

The voyages did not, however, happen alone, nor was the *Hōkūle'a* as grassroots as some claimed. It was generously funded both by private donors and the HSFCA. This funding allowed its highlights to be filmed and distributed for maximum media coverage. The *Hōkūle'a* itself was made almost entirely of fiberglass, the crew was a cross-section of ethnicities, and the original navigator was from Micronesia because there was no one in Hawai'i who knew how to navigate in the ancient way. One Native Hawaiian who traveled to New Zealand related that among themselves, the Maoris derogatorily referred to the project as the "Plastic Fantastic" because of all the hype and glitz surrounding it.[39] The *Hōkūle'a* origin narrative, however, is attractive as a colorful beginning for the Hawaiian Renaissance because it is replete with heroic pageantry and public acclaim. It is also a predominantly masculinist tale that holds up an image of warrior virility against the eroticized and feminized native tropes of tourism. That Kalama and Kaho'olawe are often eliminated from this narrative bespeaks an avoidance of politicization. Like *hula*, which also emerged as a powerful symbol of identity, the *Hōkūle'a* is easily co-opted when severed from political resistance.

Three other cultural narratives bear mentioning. One focuses on *hula* as the ultimate symbol of the renaissance and the Merrie Monarch Festival as the instigator. In 1969 Dottie Thompson took over the failing Merrie Monarch Festival in Hilo. In the ensuing years it became the most important *hula* festival of its kind and a much-disputed arbiter of *hula* standards. The festival invigorated *hula* competition and altered its public face by staging public competitions in *hula kahiko* (ancient *hula*) and *hula auana*. The problem with this narrative is that the festival, although deigned a venue for *hula* for Native Hawaiians rather than tourism, was always a tourist event (Whitney 2001). It set new standards and heights for *hula* performance, but tourism and institutionalization are also important factors in its development and survival as a *hula* venue.

George Kanahele, in his book on Hawaiian music, also omits the political side of the renaissance when he locates its beginnings exclusively with musicians and traces it to the release of Sunday Mānoa's third album, *Guava Jam*, in 1971 (1979, 332–333). Although there was a resurgence of interest in Hawaiian music at this time, this cultural narrative is problematic as a local genesis story in that it locates the origins of even that with wealthy investors and a recording industry that happened to be in the right place at the right time. The talent, it appears, had been there all along and was merely waiting for the funding. The political actions over land and identity are missing in this explanation as well, along with the body of protest songs that were written to embody the renaissance and the important role of music in Hawaiian resistance at the end of the monarchy and in the 1970s and 1980s.

A third narrative, the reinstitution of the Hawaiian language, blurs the boundaries between culture and politics. At the 1978 Constitutional Convention, after decades of suppression and neglect, provisions were passed granting Hawaiian language the same official status as English and mandating that the study of Hawaiian language be given special promotion by the state. A group of Hawaiian-language teachers on Kaua'i organized in 1983 to form an organization called Aha Punana Leo, Inc., to promote Hawaiian-language education. In 1987 the first elementary-school-level indigenous language immersion classes in the United States opened: one at Keaukaha Elementary School in Hilo and the other at Waiau Elementary School in Pearl City, O'ahu. One year later the Hawai'i State Board of Education proclaimed the public schools' language immersion program a success and granted the program permission to continue. The suppression of Hawaiian language in 1896 had been a political move with drastic consequences for Hawaiian politics, culture, and identity, and the establishment of immersion schools was equally as political. Like *hula* and voyaging, it became a symbol of resistance, but without Kalama and Kaho'olawe, this, too, was only part of the story.

Obviously, narratives of the history of the Hawaiian Renaissance are divided between political and cultural explanations. In another direction, cultural practitioners and culture workers who participated in the projects of the early Department of Parks and Recreation and HSFCA workshops find grassroots revival narratives flawed because they omit important activities in which they participated and out of which they feel the renaissance emerged. This omission is understandable, however, if recognition of institutional support as key in the revival and perpetuation of Hawaiian traditional arts is seen as downplaying and even compromising community agency in the political and cultural changes that transpired. To see the renaissance as entirely the end result of internal combustion gives it a subversive spin. To suggest that its momentum was in any way due to institutional initiatives is to imply that survival of Hawaiian culture was dependent on the agencies of the state apparatuses that had once threatened it with extinction and cultivated its appropriation and commodification.

The history of the Hawaiian Renaissance, like all pasts, is contested ground, and the selection of a limited narrative of its genesis can serve to select out certain aspects of its trajectories while masking others. Chait argues that what the array of narratives about the assertion of Hawaiian identity from the 1970s on and the resurgence of interest in Hawaiian culture does attest to is the fluidity of Native Hawaiian identity and the importance of historical narrative in the construction of identity (1999, 221). Who narrates the past and determines how it is articulated also controls representation and identity in the present.

Hawai'i Re-imagined for the Festival of American Folklife

As Richard Kurin remembers, it was 1987 and Waihee was in Washington for a governor's meeting when they first met face-to-face to seriously discuss the possibility of Hawai'i being represented at the Festival of American Folklife (FAF) on the National Mall. A few months earlier Mark Talisman, a longtime supporter of the Festival, had traveled to Hawai'i on other business and had introduced the idea of a Hawai'i program to the governor. He had called Kurin to say that Waihee was very interested, and Kurin then sent Waihee some preliminary specifications. Kurin says he "really didn't know what was going on in Hawai'i at the time," but it was clear that the idea "resonated with something he [Waihee] had on his agenda." Waihee visited the Office of Folklife Programs (OFP), talked with Kurin and the staff, and made a quick decision. As Kurin recalls their meeting,

> Basically we talked about the Festival. We showed him our video fundraiser. . . . We talked about what it would take to have Hawai'i on the Mall and why it might be good, and I think his big thing was that it might be good for Hawai'i to do some promotion on the East Coast—that it was a nice way of doing that in a kind of dignified and respectful way. And he was very much taken by the fact that it could be multi-ethnic, that it could be really Hawaiian. And this was a neat thing to try to do. So I remember he went out, I was walking him out into the hallway, to the elevator—he had a quick conversation with his assistant, and he basically said, and I overheard him, "Give the man his money!"[40]

According to Lynn Martin, a Hawai'i program at the Smithsonian had twice been suggested to Governor George Ariyoshi, Waihee's predecessor, but it was not until Waihee took office that the idea met with a receptive audience.[41] Kurin said that before talking with Waihee, he had talked with Sara Richards at the HSFCA to assess the HSFCA infrastructure that would be available, and she made it clear that she was not interested.

Although the timing for the occasion of the thirtieth anniversary of statehood appears to have had great symbolic value, it was, according to Kurin, "an afterthought, but not a central thing."[42] Festival organizers point out that the scheduling of their festival programs is not always a predictable factor and that a program emerges when they have what staff refer to as the "three-legged stool": a convergence of "our kind of people," adequate funding, and local institutional support.[43] Seen in a larger time frame, however, the program's form and content were very much inflected by the convergence of Smithsonian and Hawai'i histories, ideologies, and agendas that coalesced when the festival planning process began. Kurin felt that both he and Waihee saw the Hawai'i program with a sense of its possible social impact, rather than as a national gesture: "This was an opportunity where people threw out 'we have interesting cultural things happening in Hawai'i.' We saw that, and this was a very useful thing to do at the time. I think in part it was because it was able to take something that was happening in Hawai'i and cast it on a bigger screen that was also off island and allow a lot of things to play out."[44]

At the top level, the Hawai'i program was to be a practical and conceptual partnership between the Smithsonian—the National Museum—and the state of Hawai'i; within that frame, it was conceived of a collaboration between the divisions of each of those agencies—the OFP and the Folk Arts Division of the HSCFA—that dealt with unofficial, nonelite culture. With the decision to do Hawai'i, these agencies took on a major logistical challenge, as well as a conceptual one. In Hawai'i that meant treading carefully between the officials, scholars, culture workers, and community experts who would be convened to craft a Hawai'i narrative that could be inserted into a ten-day tourist event representing national culture. It was a challenging task and a process that crystallized much of Hawai'i's history of cultural intervention and resistance as well as its uneasy relationship with authorities at the national level.

Upon returning to Hawai'i Waihee connected Kurin and Festival director Diana Parker to his fund-raisers, Pat Brandt and Norma Wong. Based on Kurin's insistence on the critical role of folklorists in a successful festival and despite Richards' reluctance to do the program, Waihee appointed the HSFCA to be fiscal agent for the project and provide the services of Martin, who was enthusiastic about the project. Kurin called Martin on March 1, 1988, to give her the go-ahead—letting her know that he had committed to the festival and would clear $100,000 immediately so that research could begin. He asked Martin to begin thinking about staff and advisors.[45] At the Smithsonian, a model contract was drawn up that outlined the rights and responsibilities of the OFP and the HSFCA. The attachments included "Guidelines for the Research and Development of a Hawaii State Program for the 1989 Festival of American Folklife" and a detailed budget setting the program cost at $795,000. The deal was signed by Joseph Shealy, contracting officer for the Smithsonian, and Richards, executive director of the HSFCA, on May 27, 1988.[46]

Martin's first task was to work with the HSFCA and the governor's office to amass a community think tank in order to solicit input from community leaders and scholars. This kind of brainstorming was crucial to the success of the program for a couple of reasons. OFP methods required that the conception of a program and the selection of its participants be achieved in as egalitarian a fashion as possible. In Hawai'i, hashing out differences of opinion between various groups from the outset would ensure a stronger and less contested production later on. At a practical level, the logistics and costs of exhibiting Hawai'i also mandated soliciting community financial support. Two lists were drawn up: one of community scholars with expertise in Hawai'i folklife and representatives of local cultural institutions and agencies, and one of "VIPs" who were possible financial backers.[47] Because the goals were different with regard to these two groups, separate letters of invitation were sent from Parker's office to the individuals on the "community scholars" and VIP lists.

Planning meetings are a critical first step in creating a festival. Kurin has found them useful for getting a sense of social relation, even if there is conflict involved: "I find those meetings very good because they give you a quick thumbnail sketch of the lay of the land—who's into what, who you're going to be stepping on, who we'll be perceived as stepping on, where are the possible partnerships."

Clearly the OFP was concerned with creating good relationships with and understanding the communities with which they would be working. The planning meetings also provided a venue for the directors to set the tone by showing Festival promotional material and explaining the Festival mission and style based on previous programs. Kurin and Parker flew to Honolulu on July 25, 1988, to participate in the Hawai'i planning meetings. To elicit their ideal of partnership and consensus, it was also important that they learn what they could before the meetings. Kurin and Parker stayed at a quaint, older hotel called the Waikikian and spent their first evening talking over dinner with Martin so that they could be briefed on what to expect from the groups they would meet. The next morning they met with Richards and Martin, then with the Native Hawaiian Culture and Arts Program Board of Directors at the Bishop Museum. Armed with books from the Bishop Museum gift shop, articles on Hawaiian issues, and a Hawaiian dictionary, they retired to the Waikikian to educate themselves for two days of intensive meetings.[48]

Two "working" or "planning" meetings, also referred to as "community scholar meetings" were held from 1:00 P.M. to 4:00 P.M. in the Senate conference room of the State Capitol on July 27 and 28, 1988.[49] It is unclear whether the lengthy lists of suggested meeting participants were whittled down from the original suggestions made by HSFCA director Sarah Richards to the governor's office or the attendees represented only those who were interested in the project. Fourteen invited people and two guests, in addition to HSFCA and OFP staff, attended the first meeting. Fifteen persons attended the second meeting. Each group comprised a who's who of local organizations that had advised or otherwise been involved in arts programs since the onset of federal arts funding in Hawai'i: scholars from the University of Hawai'i and local museums and organizers from community centers and projects. Only a few attendees were also traditional arts practitioners. According to the minutes, each of these meetings followed the same "open" format: a welcome and thanks by the Smithsonian staff, introductions around the table, agenda and ground rules, history of the OFP and videotapes of the FAF, a general discussion covering the various genres and formats of Festival presentation, a timetable for Festival production, and concluding remarks.[50]

The VIP meetings took an altogether different tone since the VIPs were being wooed for donations while community scholars worked on program planning. This meeting, referred to as the "resource meeting" and "political meeting" in HSFCA notes, took place in more elegant surroundings and with decidedly better trappings. It was held from 5:00 P.M. to 7:00 P.M. at the Honolulu Academy of Arts on July 28 and was followed by a catered reception in the academy's elegant sculpture garden. The community scholar meetings had been conducted to brainstorm ideas for the Festival concept and identify potential research areas and resources. The stated purpose of the VIP meeting was "to brief community leaders on the plans for Hawai'i's presentation as a featured state at the Smithsonian's annual Festival of American Folklife,"[51] and its underlying intent was to present the project to individuals and businesses that might potentially serve as financial sponsors.

The next morning Martin, Richards, and Norma Wong joined Kurin and Parker in a courtesy visit to Governor Waihee, and then Richards, Martin, Kurin, and Parker gathered at the HSFCA for a final debriefing over all three meetings before the OFP directors departed for Hilo early that afternoon. The Smithsonian directors would spend another four days sightseeing on the Big Island, and then Parker would go to Kaua'i for an additional two days of vacation.

Given a historical basis for local suspicion about the ability and motives of a *haole*-run federal agency proposing to represent Hawai'i, some initial resistance was inevitable. Kurin, however, was undaunted by the hostility that occasionally surfaced in the meetings. In fact, he said he found it instructive: "Some people really put it to us—You're the dumb Smithsonian and what do you guys know about this?—we have this going on."[52] Local authority was questioned as well. One of the planning meetings included scholars from the Bishop Museum, but at the other meeting where the museum was not included, there was consensus among the local scholars that the Smithsonian should definitely not go to the Bishop Museum for its information on Hawaiian culture. Mediation was at least partially established through scholars who straddled the divide, mostly university professors who had worked with Hawai'i communities and established a degree of trust.

The opportunity to present Hawai'i to the nation and to present a Hawai'i that was different from that constructed by the tourist industry was eventually accepted as desirable by everyone present. A bigger challenge was crafting a unifying strategy that would allow many cultural groups and their overlapping histories to be presented cohesively. In a region where a manufactured version of culture has been packaged and repackaged for tourism, it should come as no surprise that someone asked if they would be representing the "myth" or the "reality" of Hawai'i. Some Native Hawaiians saw the Festival as an opportunity to correct a whitewashed history. This raised questions about whether they were going to represent the past or the present and the degree to which history could be introduced in a production that was centered on living traditions. Parker and Kurin explained that despite the focus on the present and the avoidance of historical re-creation, history could be employed to inform the present, to show how the present had evolved. No one asked about the limitations imposed on history by an exclusively cultural representation or a focus on only traditional culture.

The many questions raised in the planning meetings followed the lines of identity issues in 1980s Hawai'i and illustrated tensions between groups. The debate over how Hawai'i would be represented in general turned to the central issue of who would be represented—everyone in Hawai'i according to demographics, only those unique to Hawai'i, those who had emigrated prior to a certain date, or those who had made unique contributions to the social fabric of Hawai'i? Would the program focus be on indigenous culture or would it include introduced elements? A particularly critical issue given the recent political visibility of Native Hawaiians was how the balance between indigenous and immigrant groups would be determined. Barbara Smith, ethnomusicologist and professor emeritus at the University of Hawai'i, added another layer of complexity by observing that immigrant groups had arrived in waves, so it could not be assumed that members within an ethnic group had the same history. Linda Moriarty, a Native Hawaiian cultural consultant from Kaua'i, volunteered that she would like to see at least half of the representation be Native Hawaiian. Trimillos added that "the host culture requires a different rationale." This recognition of Native Hawaiians as the host culture and the separation of Hawai'i peoples into two camps—indigenous and immigrant—expressed strong post-colonial, post–Hawaiian Renaissance sentiments.

The issue of ethnicity also generated heated discussion. The Festival promotional video made it clear that Festival programs tended to fall into one of three categories: theme, region, or ethnicity. Waihee had proposed a multi-ethnic festival, and multi-ethnicity was one way to present a counter-narrative to the mono-cultural flattening of Hawai'i in touristic imaging. Ethnicity, however, is experienced and defined differently in Hawai'i than it is on the mainland. As evidenced by the HSFCA reports, ideas about ethnicity had shifted even in official evaluations. In both planning meetings, the problem of categorizing Hawai'i culture by ethnicity was underlined when examples were given of people who identified with multiple ethnic categories through intermingling of blood, proximity, and/or cultural practice. Dolly Strazar, a historian for the HSFCA, encapsulated the general argument presented by *haole* at the meetings when she claimed that everyone who comes to Hawai'i is affected by Hawaiian culture and eventually becomes "local." Although the term "local" was a topic at both meetings, this optimistic view of the category as inclusive was apparently advanced only by those whom it usually excludes.

Given only a day to come up with themes, each group did its best to arrive at a workable solution. When they floundered, Parker and Martin nudged them toward inclusive rather than exclusive themes. Martin offered symbols that would cut across difference, such as *'ohana* (family), celebration, and the calabash (often used to imply family-type relations). A Native Hawaiian artist suggested flowers as a possibility, pointing out that the *lei* has been universally adopted and that flowers are used in *hula*. A Native Hawaiian scholar protested that outsiders would be drawn to introduced varieties and superficial symbolism. Martin and Parker assured the group that the Festival audience was highly sensitive and should not be underestimated, so the discussion moved on. *'Ohana* was toyed with as a possible theme, but fell apart when it was juxtaposed with ethnicity. Celebration got equally as messy when people began to note the many crossovers between ethnic communities in terms of celebrations. The theme that the groups finally were able to agree on was "A Sense of Place," one that indirectly brought the discussion back to a unified representation of the state of Hawai'i and was in accord with the intent of all three of the sponsoring agencies—the Smithsonian, the HSFCA, and state government. Ironically, it also centered the festival theme on the very issue that has been most contentious in Hawai'i's history and especially the Hawaiian Renaissance: the land. Whose place and whose privilege is it to be there?

In the meetings, as if on cue, questions turned to concrete issues of how to represent an island in the Pacific in an enclosed space that bears little resemblance to the tropics. Kurin asked how Hawai'i could be re-created in Washington and prompted community scholars to think about architecture. A *yagura* (Japanese *bon* dance tower), gardens, taro patches, *paniolo* stone corrals, mom-and-pop stores, plantation houses, and a canoe shed were among the suggestions. A last stab at the cross-cultural was made when someone suggested Hawai'i comedians and ethnic humor as a cross-cultural link, but it was quickly voted down as a practice that everyone agreed would be misinterpreted by outsiders. Kurin returned the questions to visual depictions by asking, "How do you represent the ocean?" This was a challenge to which the groups responded with an uncertain but pragmatic question: "Photos?"

The Smithsonian delegation was viewed by some with suspicion, as just another example of know-it-all, mainland *haole* showing up with their ideas about what was good for Hawai'i. Yet at the end of two days, the colonial, resistance, and revival histories had been collaboratively leveled into a unified and congenial image of Hawai'i multiculturalism. With so much extant conflict and an acknowledged distrust of outsiders, what had transpired to contain the meetings? That both groups came to the same conclusions speaks to the subtle guidance and prompting they received. The theme "A Sense of Place" established a safe, unifying frame for the program. Martin gave the groups a limited choice between two "realities" by asking if they wanted to represent the "best of Hawai'i" or "everyday reality."

Self-censorship also played a part in the discussions. It was made clear in the meetings that indigenous and plantation histories were not the same, and topics and agendas sifted out along ethnic lines. Native Hawaiians wanted to make it clear that the neighbor islands are different and that historical "skeletons" should not be hidden. The cost of *poi* (a staple food made from pounded taro root) production and the exploitations of tourism were expressed as Native Hawaiian concerns alongside a stronger desire to move away from negative depictions of Native Hawaiians in the present. Many Asians, on the other hand, wanted to move away from negative representations of the past. Those whose ancestors had come as contract laborers preferred to stress how the plantation system had preserved culture rather than how it had exploited laborers. As the discussions progressed, the grid of the Festival concept and form was gently but effectively imposed. Festival emphasis on visuality and performance formed a template that limited the messiness of Hawai'i's past and present and ultimately refocused the discussion away from Hawai'i's colonial legacy and cultural hybridity toward how to "put Hawai'i's best foot forward" instead.

Culture workers explain that there is a custom of reticence in the islands that takes precedence with outsiders, dictating that local people act as welcoming hosts without divulging personal information, and perhaps it is this custom of reticence that made the meetings mostly polite. However, there were other dynamics at work as well. The scholars who were invited to the planning meetings were the guests in this case and were not in the position of acting as hosts. It was the officials from the state—in this case the HSFCA—who played host for this enterprise, parties with much at stake in sponsoring the proposed event. Clearly these persons had good reasons for being cordial and putting their best foot forward, a phrase that Martin repeatedly urged they adopt as the Festival modus operandi. In trying to understand the dynamics of the meetings, it is worth noting that the HSFCA was represented by three *haole* women who offset the multi-ethnic composition of the invitees.

Although the community scholar meetings were conducted according to Smithsonian ideals of democratic collaboration, they were also carefully orchestrated and monitored. Before each discussion, the Smithsonian directors set the stage by showing videos of previous festivals and lauding the value of the Festival. They then deferred to local experts with whom they had previously met. An ethnomusicologist from the University of Hawai'i music department had been invited to each of the meetings, and in each meeting was asked to give the preliminary comments. This protocol served at least a couple of purposes. Their selection by the Smithsonian established their cultural authority, and it established the primacy of musical performance for the cultural representation at the Festival. Whenever the conversation veered "off course," as it frequently did, it was steered back to more concrete issues of Festival planning by one of the Smithsonian directors with focused questions such as, "What is it that you want to say about Hawai'i?" and "How would you show that on the Mall?"[53] The community scholars who were invited to the planning meetings hailed from University of Hawai'i ethnomusicology, dance, and language programs, various ethnic civic groups, and local ethnographic museums. Intentionally not invited were Native Hawaiian political activists. Some of the university and community people had worked with the Smithsonian already, and most of the other groups had received federal and state funding.

In the planning meetings, Hawai'i's histories emerged in issues of who and what would represent Hawai'i to the nation, but the potential for these questions to stir controversy was contained by the Festival concept. After all, a festival is presumed to be a conflict-free and joyous occasion. Second, a folklife festival generally represents elders and stresses cultural continuity. Although the history of cultural revival in Hawai'i indicates quite the opposite, folklife tends to be understood by the public in conservative terms—as traditionality posed against radical change and modernity. And while Smithsonian folklorists are well aware that folklife is inherently political, it is a secret they hold close to the vest when staging it in the midst of the National Mall.

The difficulties of eluding the tropes of tourism are apparent in the rhetoric of the meetings. In attempting to find ways to represent cultural fusion, multi-ethnicity, and creolization, people were at a loss. In trying to symbolize the local, they offered only trite symbols employed by the media, tourism, and popular culture such as the mixed plate, plate lunch, and rainbow multiculturalism. As with the various accounts of the Hawaiian cultural renaissance, essential parts of the narrative are eclipsed when the political is avoided.

* * *

The Festival model presented both opportunity and dilemma. After the turn of the century, institutional interest in Hawai'i's traditional culture slowly changed from a concentration on salvage ethnography to a focus on cultural conservation and community collaboration, but ethnographic authority was still construed from center (East Coast academia and its offshoots) to periphery (Hawai'i), and determinations of what was traditional, authentic, and worthy of revitalization were determined by academically trained outsiders. Ironically, the intervention of mainland experts and federal cultural monies in Hawai'i has had, for the most part, the effect of counteracting the local elite's colonialist preferences for elite art forms and devaluation of folklife. The various cultural revitalizations of the 1970s and 1980s in Hawai'i emerged out of local and national politics, and their accompanying reclamation of traditional arts for ethnic identification was often, despite claims to the contrary, in part a collaboration with granting agencies.

In looking back, Kurin remembers that the OFP assessed Hawai'i as a "hot spot, a cultural hot spot" in the 1980s.[54] By bridging the gap between cultural conservation and cultural tourism, the Smithsonian proffered an opportunity to represent a differently calibrated vision of Hawai'i, one that repudiated the primitivizing of indigenous culture and the erasure of immigrants. Timing was critical. The Festival planning drew on identity issues of the moment while building on federally and state-funded cultural programs of the past. As in Kalākaua's Jubilee and the Panama-Pacific Exposition, the Festival would demonstrate the unity and strength of the government through the arts of its subjects. Its potential for educational value was valorized by mainland authorities working for national agencies, just as educational cultural projects had been in the 1920s, 1970s, and 1980s. As a national spectacle, the Festival offered the state a venue in which it could be promoted as "more than beautiful beaches." The Festival's populist roots and democratic ideals assured ethnic groups of the chance to self-represent and be heard.

The Hawaiian Renaissance had established the *'āina* (land) as the central symbol of Hawaiian identity. The planning committee appropriated that symbol and made it both abstract and inclusive in selecting "A Sense of Place" as its multicultural theme. The following chapters examine how this and other tensions unfolded within the various phases of the Hawai'i program.

Chapter 2

Finding and Defining Traditional Hawai‘i

Cultures are not like clocks and motors that can be taken apart into neat and separate pieces. Thus in any listing of cultural categories there will be some overlapping areas, and many cultural objects and practices will not fit exactly into one category or another. This fluidity is what makes cultures and communities the dynamic force that they are and presents people who hope to study and document them with exciting challenges.

—Lynn Martin, *A Guide for Surveying Pacific Island Folk Arts*

Caucasians are strange people / Caucasians are strange, strange people / Caucasians are not like you and me / They put sugar on their poi and butter on their rice / They're always giving you advice. . . . / We don't want no Caucasians 'round here!

—Frank Delima, *The Best of Delima too*

The 1989 Hawai‘i program in Washington, D.C., lasted for only ten days, but it was over a year and a half in the making. Fundamental to the festival-making process was the six-month-long "fieldwork phase"—the research-based process determining which tradition bearers and what traditions would be selected to represent Hawai‘i in the national arena of the Smithsonian's Festival of American Folklife. Widely constructed as an exotic American playground, Hawai‘i was an ideal candidate for a Smithsonian makeover and a guaranteed draw. Furthermore, the state's complex pluralism—the only state purported to be without a majority population—made it an ideal choice for the Festival mission of celebrating American cultural diversity. A successful program would require careful re-imaging to strip away the tourism and media myths and reveal an alternative view of island culture(s). Local scholars and culture workers at the planning meetings had made it clear that the representation of Hawai‘i should circumvent primitivist images of island culture as *hula* girls and surfers and instead present the traditional culture of the state's many ethnic groups as it is practiced unself-consciously and within local communities. The Smithsonian staff assured them that Hawai'i's tradition bearers would have a hand and a voice through multiple modalities: performance, dialogue with audiences, craft and food demonstrations, and on narrative stages.

Fieldwork was central to the vision of a collaborative, polyvocal outcome. The fieldwork phase had three concrete goals: to create an archive of traditional arts practitioners for the state of Hawai'i from which culture workers and others could draw for future in-state projects; to contribute to the national store of information on cultural heritage in the United States and form a resource for future Smithsonian projects and researchers; and to establish a basis for the Hawai'i program. Ideally, documenting ethnic communities, tradition bearers, and traditions would provide the pool of people and materials for Festival selection, and the selections would, in turn, influence the conceptualization of the program, from narrativization to site design. Given the complex and calendrically driven process of festival making, the fact that fieldwork is seen as a necessary step is already surprising. Good fieldwork takes time and patience. Folklore fieldwork is generally a delicate and fluid process in which relationships of trust are established and time and collected materials are not under the control of the fieldworker. In fact, in his classic nuts-and-bolts guide to fieldwork methodology, folklorist Bruce Jackson warns against predetermining goals for fieldwork: "I would probably say that if you finished the fieldwork project and got exactly what you'd expected and did with it exactly what you'd planned, that you'd planned a simple minded project to start with and your fieldwork was superficial and so was your thinking about what you'd seen" (1987, 18). In Festival planning, however, time schedules, budgets, personalities, and politics greatly restrict the fluidity of the fieldwork process and make the depth of findings questionable.

Alongside the process of gathering fieldwork data on which to construct the Hawai'i program was the process of sorting this data into a system of meaning that would, in turn, form a coherent conceptual narrative. Advisors at the planning meetings had arrived at "A Sense of Place" as a theme for the program and made preliminary suggestions about how that might be accomplished, but fieldwork findings would determine who would go to Washington, D.C., what they would perform, and how folk and folklife would be framed. In other words, in order to make sense of the fieldwork, culture workers needed to subject it to museum methodologies. The Folklife Festival bills itself as a disruption of the sobriety of the national museum, as the museum taken outdoors and brought to life (Kurin 1998, 30–40). What examination of the fieldwork phase reveals that is not readily apparent in the Festival itself is that it is constructed on museum classification and narrativization strategies. According to Eilean Hooper-Greenhill, the role of museum narratives is to impose order through various strategies.

> The master narratives that museums construct depend on a number of techniques of inclusion and exclusion. These include hierarchies of value (which relate to the intentions of the museum), authenticity (the object is both there to be observed and is presented as the "real thing"), and verifiable knowledge (the provenance of an object demonstrated through documentation). These combinations produce apparently reliable and trustworthy material evidence. (2000, 24–25)

Techniques of inclusion and exclusion were present in each step of the fieldwork phase of the Hawai'i program, and the final selection that emerged both shaped and was shaped by the master narrative constructed for the program.

This chapter looks at the role of the fieldwork process in shaping the version of Hawai'i that was performed on the National Mall in 1989 and its implications for the representation of Hawai'i as a multicultural paradigm on a larger scale. I argue that a close look at the fieldwork phase reveals gaps between local and national definitions and uses of multiculturalism and that while the final selections were intended to challenge simplistic notions of Hawai'i, they unwittingly reinforced some of the very tropes they sought to undercut.

Insiders and Outsiders in the Islands

Given the complexity of 1980s identity politics in Hawai'i, it might seem a recipe for disaster for mainland *haole* culture brokers to take responsibility for creating the 1989 Hawai'i program. Once the initial planning phase was completed, the key players in the creation of the program were Richard Kennedy (OFP) and Lynn Martin (HSFCA). Kennedy had been hired by Kurin and Parker, and on August 20, 1988, he agreed to take a year off from his job at the National Council for the Traditional Arts (NCTA) and curate the Hawai'i program. He arrived in Hawai'i on October 6 to begin the fieldwork phase. According to Kennedy, his first official encounter with the politics of representing traditional culture in Hawai'i occurred at a Hawai'i Museum Association Conference held in Hilo October 7–8, 1988. In a report written to Parker two months later, he recounted,

> During the three days of conference talks I had a chance to meet many of the program officers of the more than 60 some small museums across Hawai'i and to be introduced to some of the issues facing preservationists in the state. I also had the opportunity, first day "on the job," to justify and defend the Smithsonian's presence in Hawai'i as well as its plans for a 1989 festival. Trial by fire!
>
> The keynote speaker and discussant of the sessions was [the] Director of the Museum of British Columbia. On this first day [he] decided not to comment on a very controversial talk about the role of hotels in the preservation of Hawaiian culture and stated, after my introduction to the group, that if someone from Ottawa came to British Columbia to do a festival about the Province he would tell him to go home. The room went silent; the audience clearly was not accustomed to controversy. In response, I feel I presented our case well and answered the many questions that arose. Eventually someone commented that he was tired of the issue and suggested that we move on.[1] (1993)

For Kennedy, this incident sounded a cautionary note about his position as a cultural authority in Hawai'i. The interchange hinted at a much larger issue, one that has become particularly virulent in the "post-colonial" Pacific: a debate over who owns and defines culture. Cultural practitioners, local governments, anthropologists and culture brokers, and national and international agencies like the Smithsonian Institution and UNESCO are all part of this debate (Smith 1999, 177–178).[2]

In his retelling of this story, Kennedy takes seriously the concerns raised by his heckler. He may also have been accurate in interpreting the silence in the room as discomfort with conflict. In his midterm report to Parker, Kennedy acknowledges the state's "highly politicized culture" and says that he is aware that "many people in Hawai'i are extremely self-conscious and proud of their traditions and are critical of the role played over the past 150 years by Caucasians from the mainland, especially the federal government." He also astutely notes that "in many cases it is only the 'Aloha Spirit' that softens some of the criticisms." Yet he ends his report by saying that he has not received "even an inkling" of resentment from anyone he has met.[3] That no conflict was expressed might be attributable to the customary reticence of "local culture." Kirkpatrick argues that the defensive identities shaped by the colonial and plantation experiences have shaped an acute sensitivity to conflict. Jonathan Okamura further argues that confrontational behavior has been associated with *haole* behavior and is often referred to as such; consequently, it is avoided to elude being stigmatized. It makes sense, then, that *haole* who work with non-*haole* cultural groups are careful to avoid confrontational behavior in their desire to adapt to local culture and in order not to be alienated.[4] Kennedy's naturally quiet demeanor and cultural sensitivity no doubt played an important role in his acceptance within various Hawai'i ethnic communities. Kurin confessed that he could never have succeeded in Hawai'i, that he was "too New York" for the subtle social codes of the islands.[5]

As the planning phase had revealed, the cultural environment in which the fieldwork process was expected to operate was complicated by multiple histories and agendas, intermarriage, and the degree of cultural sharing that permeates many groups. Communities living in close proximity to each other had dropped, borrowed, adapted, and reinvented traditions, combining their own practices with elements adopted from other groups as well as what they had assimilated from the dominant culture. In Hawai'i, the catchall term applied to the resulting sensibilities and practices—from language to foods—is "local." In the 1980s terms like "mixed plate" and "chop suey" were also common. These terms had all been appropriated by the tourist industry and advertising, along with pidgin expressions like "howzit" (a greeting) and "da kine" (a context-specific general referent) to connote an inherent geniality and inclusiveness in Hawai'i culture. Over time and on the street, however, the term "local" had been more ambiguously employed. In the territorial period, it was a pejorative used by elite *kama'āina haole* (local-born *haole*) to enforce a racialized class differential. This was particularly true after the infamous Massie case of the 1930s, which had resulted in a national media slur depicting nonwhite men in Hawai'i as bestial and subhuman (Rosa 2002). David Stannard argues that the outrage among nonwhites in Hawai'i at the unjust outcome of that case, in which a murderer and her accomplices served a one-hour sentence, prompted the beginnings of inter-ethnic solidarity and laid the foundation for a "local" identity in opposition to *haole* rule and privilege (2005). With the Hawaiian Renaissance, "local" acquired additional currency as non-

haole.[6] In addition to simply designating someone as born in Hawai‘i, the term “local” might be used to racialize or de-racialize, to exclude *haole*, to collapse non-*haole* groups into a conglomerate, or to claim a sense of belonging (when used by *haole*).[7]

In Hawai‘i a long-standing tradition of everyday banter and comedic performance that openly, and usually playfully, stereotypes people by ethnicity often causes uncomfortable outsiders to remark that people in Hawai‘i are obsessed with race and ethnicity. Meanwhile, the popularity and uses of ethnic humor indicate that many longtime residents see this kind of labeling as good-natured and benign play that functions to stress inter-relationships between groups rather than to separate them. However, as Okamura points out, this good-natured playing with difference does not necessarily obviate underlying social tensions. In fact, he argues that it may actually conceal them (1998). In Festival preparation, it fell to Hawai‘i culture workers to translate “local” in a way that could be understood on the mainland with its very different notions of multiculturalism and identity politics. By choosing “A Sense of Place” as a unifying theme and “putting our best foot forward” as a rubric, the program planners had already begun to pick their way through the ethnic complexity in Hawai‘i and construct a narrative that would shape the fieldwork process and order the resultant information.

Cultural Authorities

A festival program is framed by the particular vision of the people who craft it, and the Hawai‘i program is no exception. Personalities, educational backgrounds, and institutional affiliations were key factors in the direction of the two-day planning meetings and wielded even more influence in the six-month-long fieldwork process. Each of the coordinators of the fieldwork process in 1988 represented a major institution, and they enhanced each other’s expertise. Neither Kennedy nor Martin had been academically trained as folklorists, but they both had acquired ample experience related to traditional culture. Kennedy received his Ph.D. from the University of California at Berkeley in South and Southeast Asian studies and was working for the NCTA, where he had helped produce six National Folk Festivals, folk art/music tours, and performances for the Library of Congress and the NEA. Although he had not previously traveled to Hawai‘i, he had worked with National Heritage Award winners from Hawai‘i and had helped organize a *hula* tour to Italy.[8] Martin, the HSFCA Folk Arts coordinator, had lived in

Hawai'i and the Pacific for many years. In an interview she referred to herself as a "de facto folklorist," one who has been trained on the job. Part of that training had come from the national level when Bess Lomax Hawes helped her to set up the Master and Apprentice Program at the HSFCA.[9] Martin also had ample Asia/Pacific exposure; she had lived in Japan and studied in Guam and Hawai'i. She received a master's degree in Pacific studies from the University of Hawai'i at Mānoa and was a proficient weaver and *lei* maker before being hired by the HSFCA as state folklorist. The Hawai'i program was her third and largest project for the HSFCA. When Martin discovered early in the festival-making process that she was pregnant and would not be able to play as active a role in the festival as she had originally planned, a co-curator was sought on the Hawai'i end. However, Martin continued to play a central role in the creation of the Hawai'i program.

Choosing a coordinator who was part-Hawaiian was a definite asset and put a local face on the project. Kennedy's trip in 1988 was his first visit to Hawai'i, and after arriving he watched numerous documentary videos to familiarize himself with the people, culture, and politics. In one of those videos he saw Linda Moriarty, a part-Hawaiian from Kaua'i who worked for the East-West Center and was on the HSFCA Folk Arts Advisory Board. Kennedy says that he was so impressed with her that he decided then and there that she was the co-curator he wanted. He found out that she had traveled extensively in Asia and the Pacific, had her own Pacific import company, and had published a book on shell *lei*. He convinced her to sign on to the project, and they have been close friends ever since. Another non-*haole* who played an important behind-the-scenes advisory role was Dr. Ricardo Trimillos, a professor of ethnomusicology at the University of Hawai'i. Trimillos, a Filipino from California, had served as an advisor to the HSFCA since its inception, had been on the Folk Arts Advisory Board since 1985, and had done previous consulting work with another office of the Smithsonian. The most valuable aspect of Kennedy's new team was their combined access to local communities. Martin had HSFCA files from earlier state projects as well as from her own projects as state folklorist. Moriarty had lived on three islands, where she had met many craftspeople through her business and research ventures. Trimillos was a musician and an expert on world music with access to several communities, especially the Filipino, local Japanese, and Okinawan communities. Most important, Martin, the only *haole* other than Kennedy, had the weight of a state funding agency to complement her familiarity with Pacific culture and Hawaiian language. She also had her weaving and *lei*-making skills as a point of access. The results of the fieldwork process would reflect the combined styles, dedication, and expertise of these four culture workers.

The Bible of Hawai'i Folklife

When Kennedy agreed to take on the curatorship of the Hawai'i program, Martin wrote an ecstatic letter to Festival director Diana Parker congratulating them on their choice. Kennedy was a newcomer to Hawai'i, a *malihini*, but he arrived armed with a twenty-two page document titled "Overview of Folklife in Hawai'i and Possible Field Research Topics/Themes" that he still says was his "bible."[10] Martin had begun preparing this document immediately after the initial planning meetings in Honolulu, at the request of Parker and Kurin, and it would become Kennedy's lens for viewing Hawai'i culture, making it feasible to pull together the elements needed for the program in the time allotted.[11] It summarizes the suggestions made at the planning meetings, provides HSFCA information on the main ethnic groups and suggestions for areas of further research, suggests themes and workshop topics, and details "special concerns." This document demonstrates the degree to which Martin and her advisors had already shaped the program concept in the interim. Their project had been to distill the community debates of the planning meeting discussions into the working concept of folklife used by the OFP. This concept was based on the definition contained within the Folklife Preservation Act of 1976 that resulted in the establishment of the American Folklife Center at the Library of Congress:

> the traditional, expressive, shared culture of various groups in the United States: familial, ethnic, occupational, religious, and regional. Expressive culture includes a wide range of creative and symbolic forms, such as custom, belief, technical skill, language, drama, ritual, architecture, music, play, dance, drama, ritual, pageantry, and handicraft. Generally these expressions are learned orally, by imitation, or in performance, and are maintained or perpetuated without formal instruction or institutional direction. (Hufford 2002, 244)

This definition—focused on orally transmitted, unofficial, expressive culture—provided the operating principle for fieldwork selections, and the document that Martin sent Kennedy represented its application to Hawai'i ethnic communities, although the official definition of folklife does not mention ethnicity. Instead, it presents a number of ways in which cultural groups might be formed, such as by family or occupation, and a range of folklife genres. This catalog of genres, while broad enough to include cultural expressions not usually valued as folklore, is also limiting in ways that would come to light in the fieldwork process. Applying this definition within ethnic categories at times and outside of them at others, Martin's document generally adheres to the planning meeting proposition that a different logic should be applied to the "host culture" in Hawai'i. As a result, different organizational strategies were employed for Hawaiians and "others."

From the opening, Martin's overview vacillates between thematic and ethnic category approaches. Setting an overall tone, the notion of Hawaiians as the host culture is expanded to present Hawaiian culture as pervasive and the base for immigrant culture. Under the heading "Hawaiian Folklife and Arts," a paragraph on kinship and *'ohana,* the Hawaiian word for family, explains that *'ohana* is an inclusive extended-family concept utilized by many ethnic groups in Hawai'i and that terms like "calabash cousin," "auntie," and "uncle" are commonly applied outside of blood relations. Martin notes that the idea of *'ohana* as a festival theme was brought up at the planning meetings; however, she does not mention that the suggestion was promoted as a way to move the divided group toward inclusivity or that "sense of placc" had been the consensual choice. Nor does she note, as she later does with *aloha,* that *'ohana* is also a term much appropriated by tourism.[12]

Although the HSFCA had for years organized its projects into the broad ethnic categories of Polynesian, Asian, and Other, Martin's report changes tactics to express the focus on folklife. It is divided into four major parts: Hawaiian Folklife, Local Traditions, Culture and Ethnic Groups Represented through Themes of Celebration, and Special Considerations. The first two categories served to separate out Native Hawaiians from immigrants, and the third category acted to subdivide the immigrant category within the constraints of an inclusive theme, like *'ohana,* that had been introduced at the planning meetings by Martin. These categories, the HSFCA response to the Festival parameters, would regulate every aspect of the fieldwork process, determining who and what would be selected.

In line with Moriarty's planning meeting assertion that the Festival programming should be 50 percent Hawaiian, over half of the overview is devoted to genres of Hawaiian folklife. The disproportionate focus on Native Hawaiians was due to several factors, one of them being HSFCA familiarity and extant data. Since its inception under NEA directives, the HSFCA had targeted Native Hawaiians for "cultural development." Native Hawaiians had been given top priority because the HSFCA, which administered the NEA funds, saw indigenous culture as endangered and because Native Hawaiians were considered to be on the lowest economic and educational rung in the islands. Over the years prior to the creation of the Folk Arts Division, the HSFCA had amassed a large body of data on Hawaiian performance arts. Through its collaborations with Hawaiian organizations, the HSFCA also had an extensive database on Hawaiian arts practitioners who had been funded by the HSFCA and the NEA. Furthermore, Martin had majored in Pacific studies and was familiar with many of the crafts. Her initial HSFCA assignment had been to assist with Hawai'i's participation in the Festival of Pacific Arts, a project that had introduced her to a number of the *hālau hula* and immersed her in *hula* protocol and Pacific identity issues. Finally, the Native Hawaiian cultural revival had intensified since the 1970s, so Native Hawaiian arts had high visibility along with political volatility. As well as being an ethical imperative, it was politically prudent for the HSFCA to devote the majority of its attention to Native Hawaiians. For the same reasons, the categorizations required to do this were complex.

According to the Smithsonian philosophy of the time, the Festival was interested in folklife that showed evidence of continuity, and arts that had fallen into extinction and been reinvented were to be excluded. Martin's overview divided Native Hawaiian folklife into three main categories and several smaller ones that demonstrate the difficulties of trying to impose the Smithsonian template based on continuity onto actual cultural practices that had been altered by a variety of historical and political factors.

The three main genres in Martin's breakdown are Hawaiian Folklife and Arts (*hula,* chant, music, and costuming), Hawaiian Crafts, and Hawaiian Architecture. The category of Hawaiian Crafts is further subdivided according to assessments of traditionality: Crafts of Continuance (feather work and stonework), Crafts of Revival (voyaging and crafts such as *kapa* making, which had allegedly died out but had been recently revived), and Crafts of Acculturation (quilting and various forms of weaving that incorporate elements introduced from elsewhere). Discrepancies abound. For example, *hula* and *oli,* Hawaiian music, and instrument making could easily fit into all three of the subcategories of continuity, revival, and acculturation. Certain "crafts of continuance," such as featherwork, had been perpetuated, but only by a very few people and through acculturation. Some crafts of revival, such as voyaging and canoe building, were well on their way to being iconic of Hawaiian tradition despite their reinvention, while at least one of the crafts of acculturation, *lauhala* weaving (mat and hat weaving with pandanus leaves), owed its rescue from extinction to sponsorship by the HSFCA Master and Apprentice Program rather than traditional modes of transmission. The remaining categories for Hawaiian folklife are uneven. Native Hawaiian architecture had virtually disappeared, except for ruins and canoe sheds, from everywhere except reconstructed historical sites. While there were still a few elderly *kahuna* (healers) who were knowledgeable in *lā'au lapa'au* (traditional healing arts), the HSFCA had no information on children's games or sports (other than surfing).[13] On the other hand, the Hawaiian language was undergoing a comeback due to the University of Hawai'i language program and the establishment of experimental immersion schools for Native Hawaiian children beginning in 1970.[14] What Martin's list emphasizes is the cultural richness of the Hawaiian renaissance, the history of collaboration and adaptation in Hawai'i, and the interplay of loss and revival. It invokes the complex relationship between colonial structures and indigenous culture and illustrates the necessity to rethink accepted definitions of folklife in application to an indigenous Pacific context.

"Local" traditions required yet another kind of thinking—one that defied ethnic categories. Some people at the planning meetings, particularly the *haole* organizers, had insisted that shared, or "local," traditions predominated over those of individual ethnic communities. Following the emphasis of the planning meetings, Martin lists "Local Traditions" before she lists the remaining ethnic groups in Hawai'i, giving greater weight to shared culture than she does to particular traditions that ethnic groups might use to distinguish themselves from each other. This "local" segue between indigenous and immigrant traditions is sorted into standard folklife genres. These are interpreted for the most part as indigenous-derived practices that had spread to other groups and some practices introduced by foreigners: Occupational, Local Language, Local Vernacular Architecture, and Local Foodways. Due to its orientation around "traditional" occupations that fit into folklife categories, this is a very limited list. Under taro farming, Martin notes that although taro has spiritual significance for Hawaiians, its actual cultivation is much reduced from earlier times and is mostly done by a few Japanese farmers. Plantation agricultural crops such as coffee, pineapple, and sugar are categorized as horticulture, and the traditional Japanese arts of *ikebana* and *bonsai* are designated as ethnobotany. Fishing and boat building are acknowledged as practices with multiple influences, mostly Hawaiian and Japanese. *Paniolo,* a group on which Martin had done extensive work for a traveling exhibit in 1987, are offered as an ethnic crossover occupation.

The "local" overview also details ways in which shared traditions are found in multiple sites where cultural groups have coincided, such as local pidgin, "mom and pop" stores, painted churches, the "plate lunch," and "shave ice." Again, Martin emphasizes a line of cultural descent from Hawaiians to immigrants and superimposes "local" over the particularities of ethnic traditions while merging tradition and identity: "Food is a very important element of local culture and life in Hawai'i. The sharing of food is an important bonding experience in Hawaiian culture and this feeling is shared by most of the immigrant groups in Hawai'i. There is a tremendous sense of 'local identity' that surrounds the food of all groups."[15]

Illustrating the tension between an inclusive "local" and distinct ethnic traditions, the plate lunch—a popular combination meal that features foods from several ethnicities—is first used as an inclusive symbol of "localness" and is then sorted into ethnic categories food by food, according to the Festival logic of differentiated ethnic presentations. The effect is the same as that given by the symbolic gesture of listing local traditions before individual ethnicities—the parts are subjugated to the whole.

With Hawaiians selected out through logics of both history and place, Martin frames the remaining ethnic groups with a theme suggested in the meetings: "Cultural and Ethnic Groups Presented through Celebration." In doing so, she subordinates non-Hawaiian groups to an inclusive frame that will bind them into a harmonious unit in the interests of performability. The goal that had emerged in the planning meeting was to select a theme that would show Hawai'i's diversity with its "best foot forward," that would simultaneously highlight shared culture and demonstrate difference. A theme of celebration would accomplish two things: show everyone at his or her holiday best, and demonstrate the dynamics of sharing and of difference, not just highlight difference. Through such a theme, the Hawai'i program could portray pluralism transported into the ideal, and possibly idealized, dimension of interactive multiculturalism.

Incorporating immigrant traditions under the umbrella of Hawaiianness to evoke a hosts/guests dyad, Martin begins this section with the Hawaiian term for celebration, *ho‘olaule‘a,* and *ho‘ike* (to exhibit), and a lengthy section on multicultural celebrations highlighting parades with *pā‘ū* (literally, "a divided skirt") riders and first-year *lū‘au* for babies. Although she correctly presents these as multicultural celebrations derived from Native Hawaiian practices, their shift to multicultural celebrations has occurred in different ways. The parades have been appropriated and commercialized, and first-year celebrations have been adapted in a variety of forms by other ethnic groups. As a frame for the information on ethnic traditions that follows, Martin then offers a qualifying statement that stresses the amount of slippage between practices and particular groups.

> In Hawai‘i there is a certain amount of blurring of ethnic barriers and yet some very distinctive characteristics in some of the cultural practices. Many people are made up of people from different ethnic groups. It is not unusual to meet some one who is Hawaiian/Portuguese/Chinese/Filipino, or Chinese/Japanese/Hawaiian/Puerto Rican, or Scottish/Portuguese/English. There is a local expression for something or someone that has a mixed cultural/ethnic make-up—"chop suey."

It is clear from her previous emphasis on multicultural traditions and this statement about mixed ethnic identities that Martin was uncomfortable with rigid ethnic categories as a grid for Hawai‘i folklife, but she struggled with them as a way to fit Hawai‘i to her conception of Smithsonian expectations.

After the section on shared local celebrations, twelve ethnic groups are listed, each with a (very) brief evaluation of its relevant folklife and what the HSFCA had in its files about cultural practices and practitioners. The brevity of information on some of these ethnic groups (nine lines for the Chinese, eleven for the Koreans, three each for the Samoans, Greeks, Scottish, Black Gospel, and Southeast Asian, and two for Tongans) may be due to several factors, such as the limitations imposed by the theme, a group's degree of assimilation, and lack of available information at the time the document was compiled. The latter is the least likely explanation since some of these groups (and others, such as a Swedish group) had been funded by the HSFCA in the years prior to the program planning, albeit not always for traditional arts endeavors.

At the planning meeting, University of Hawai‘i professor of ethnomusicology Barbara Smith had pointed out that immigrants had come to Hawai‘i in waves, making it presumptuous to assume that groups were internally homogenous in terms of culture. Following this logic to some extent, Martin divided immigrant groups into earlier and later groups. The earlier groups she linked through the idea of plantation history, although their plantation experiences were not necessarily concurrent. More problematically, members of each ethnic group had arrived in more than one time period, so groups now include members who share neither ancestral nor actual connections to the plantation experience. For example, Koreans in Hawai'i immigrated in two distinct waves—the first during 1903–1910 and the second from 1969 on (Nordyke 1989, 84–91). These two groups of Koreans in Hawai'i have different historical memories and cultural proclivities. The temporal division between early and later immigration was a line that would be both employed and crossed in the selection and conceptualization processes of festival making.

The groups listed as the major ethnic groups in Hawai'i are the Chinese, Japanese, Koreans, Filipinos, Portuguese, and Puerto Ricans. This list is tagged with inside information geared toward access and performability. For example, Martin notes that there "are many good music groups playing in Chinatown" but that the "Chinese community is difficult to penetrate" and would require a "Chinese person to do primary field research." Limited by the theme of celebration, the acculturated early immigrant groups are summarized according to their folklife calling cards. Martin says that the Japanese are known for *bon* dances and once developed a kind of work song called *hole hole bushi.* She states that the first wave of Korean immigrants brought little traditional culture with them but that the second wave is identified with a particular school of dance. Filipinos, she says, are very well integrated but have some *rondalla* groups that have been supported by the HSFCA. Portuguese, once the *luna*s (overseers) on the plantations, are revealed as the butt of local jokes but celebrated for their contribution of the *branguiha,* adopted as the Hawaiian *'ukulele.*[16] She speculates that the Puerto Ricans may have some *barinque* and *salsa* bands. Later groups are listed as Samoans, Tongans, Greeks, Scottish, Black Gospel, and Southeast Asian, and each is relegated to a mere two or three lines in the overview. Of course, there are many ethnic groups in Hawai'i that are missing from this top-twelve list. When this list was stripped down to the fieldwork model, only nine groups would remain to be woven into a narrative of shared history.

Following these sections on who and what to represent are suggestions for workshop subjects and issues, based partly on planning meeting discussions. Narrative stages are a standard feature of the Festival, and the directors had explained at the planning meetings that they offer a space where cultural issues can be foregrounded and in which intangible aspects of culture can be presented. This is where Martin placed politically charged issues such as language revival, tourism, and land access.

A separate page of Martin's report is devoted to the special considerations of dealing with Hawai'i cultural groups—attesting to Martin's sensitivity to the highly politicized nature of Hawaiian issues at the time. Set as an attachment to her revised version of the overview, these "concerns" make a full circle back to her *'ohana* opening. They fall into two categories that reiterate the same point—a successful Festival program will require that the person in charge be an expert in mediating and avoiding conflict between the various groups of participants, and the group must be molded according to a unifying template.

> Though there are many disagreements within the native Hawaiian population and some strained relations among ethnic groups, there are some ideals which most people in Hawai'i strive for: *aloha*—which though overused in the commercial sense still is a powerful concept meaning love, affection, mercy, sympathy, kindness, sweetheart, and a greeting; and *ho'olokahi*—which means harmony or unity. Therefore it is critical that when selecting the participants for the festival, we should look for not only the best representative of each tradition, but the best "mix" of representatives and how their individual spirits, skills, and personalities will harmonize with one another. We have numerous examples here of delegations to international and mainland events that were successful and unsuccessful in this regard and the repercussions thereof.[17]

The first batch of "concerns" focuses on logistical strategies for creating a sense of *'ohana* by notifying people of selection decisions early, by providing people with ample opportunity to "bond" both before and at the Festival, and by choosing people whose personalities will blend harmoniously. Martin warns that she is aware of other cultural delegations where these strategies were not undertaken and the results were unsuccessful.

Martin's other stated concerns apply specifically to Native Hawaiians and touch on some of the political issues raised by Hawaiian activists prior to and in 1988, such as bomb testing on Kaho'olawe and self-determination. However, these issues are undercut by Martin saying that most of the activists are university-based intellectuals who are not cultural practitioners and that many of the cultural practitioners feel uncomfortable about such radical views. This separation of politics from culture may suggest a generational difference, but it overlooks many of the comments made at the planning meetings. It is also possible that some cultural practitioners did not air their differences to representatives of the HSFCA. As Merry points out, resistance can take subtle forms, and adaptation may be yet another strategy for resistance for those who choose to work within institutional frameworks (2000, 15). The stress laid on the necessity to create a sense of *'ohana* and instill a feeling of *aloha* in the participants, along with the mention of unsuccessful endeavors in the past, strongly points to the existence of ethnic conflict that needed to be managed in order to pull off a vision of the state's "rainbow multiculturalism" in a form that would manifest the harmonious ideal. This process of containing potential conflict resonates with Okamura's argument that the image of *aloha* is utilized by government agencies and the tourist industry to tamp down protest and impose harmony on cacophony (1998).

Fieldworker Selection

Martin's report may have been Kennedy's Hawai'i folklife and identity politics "bible," but he also set out to self-educate. After the museum studies conference in Hilo, he arrived in Honolulu and moved into the East-West Center's official guesthouse, Lincoln Hall, which is conveniently located on the edge of the University of Hawai'i Mānoa campus—a short walk to Hamilton Library's Hawai'i-Pacific Collection and Sinclair Library's Wong Audiovisual Center. Trimillos had helped to secure Kennedy an office at the East-West Center itself, just a few buildings away. Kennedy lived in Lincoln Hall for the next six months, long enough to oversee the fieldwork phase of the Festival pre-preparation. During his stay, Kennedy traveled to the neighbor islands, familiarized himself with Hawai'i history and culture through books and videos, and consulted with community culture workers from various ethnic groups who took him for visits with cultural practitioners in the communities they represented.[18]

Selecting the right tradition bearers depended on selecting the right cultural authorities to find them, and Kennedy's first major task was to find and train the next tier of cultural authorities—local fieldworkers.

Martin, calling on her HSFCA, University of Hawai'i, and East-West Center connections, had already put out feelers in many directions. She had sent a form letter to a list of prospective fieldworkers and to community organizations that she hoped could produce other prospects.[19] Although anthropologists and folklorists generally agree that good fieldwork is not done in a hurry, the Festival works on a tight time schedule, and the fieldwork reports had to be in by the end of December if the program was going to be ready in June of the following year, necessitating that what was being called fieldwork was really more of a preliminary survey with supporting documentation. This meant that the fieldworkers needed to have more than the standard characteristics of research and listening skills; they needed to have community familiarity and immediate access. Kennedy needed fieldworkers who could show up with a list of contacts or potential participants already in hand. Some communities required minimal work and others required much more. For example, the insular Chinese community (actually many communities) would require considerably more effort than Native Hawaiian groups because the HSFCA had been actively involved in sponsoring Native Hawaiian groups since the 1960s and because of the public nature of the Hawaiian cultural revival. Consequently, the overview stated that only secondary research was needed to compile a survey of *hula* and *oli* practitioners. Martin had recently researched *paniolo* arts herself, so there was a store of already prepared research and a solid list of contacts for that occupational group. Groups that had received little or no institutional attention would require investigation via community contacts. Based on the HSFCA directory, Martin sent a form letter to academic departments, civic organizations and leaders, museum scholars, and community arts organizations. Attached to the letter was a four-page list of "Possible Fieldwork Topics," and interested applicants were to specify their areas of interest or suggest additional ones. The letter presented the fieldwork time frame as being from October through early January when, in fact, résumés were due in by October 24, with fieldworker selection still to follow.[20]

Selected fieldworkers received information packets dated November 24 and a letter urging them to get film to Kennedy by December 22, with a final deadline for reports on January 10, 1989—leaving only a little over one month in which to accomplish the actual survey.[21] Kennedy did meet with individuals and give go-aheads in the interim, so the information packet may have been more follow-up than directive. Still, it was a severely truncated period in which to do the actual fieldwork on which the participant selection would be based.

Choosing to use all Hawai'i-based fieldworkers partially shifted the locus of cultural authority for the program in ways that would not necessarily be visible in the final production. It was an inspired move for a Smithsonian program since the usual procedure to date had been to bring in academically trained culture workers from outside to do preliminary surveys. In addition to the problems of dealing with a limited time frame, Kennedy had realized early on that outsiders would not have the kind of access or cultural sensitivity required for the Hawai'i program. He personally interviewed fieldworker applicants, aware that in politically sensitive communities the wrong choice can stymie the fieldwork process. *Hula* was a particularly sensitive selection. Teri Skillman, a *haole* who was chosen to research *hālau hula,* feels she was chosen partly because she was an outsider. She was a *hula* practitioner, but she had been out of the country for some time prior to the fieldwork project and the *hālau* with which she had been affiliated was defunct, so she would not be seen as a threat among the fiercely competitive *hālau* that had emerged since the Hawaiian renaissance.[22] The final fieldworker team comprised local scholars, community leaders, artists, museum personnel, and consultants, each of whom had some specialized knowledge in one or more aspects of traditional life in Hawai'i.[23]

Prepping Fieldworkers/Defining Tradition

The job of the fieldworkers was threefold: to survey the folklife of designated ethnic communities (communities designated as ethnic), to identify tradition bearers whom the communities held in high regard as exemplars of their traditions, and to recommend which tradition bearers should be considered as Festival participants. Even at this preliminary stage in the festival-making process, Festival parameters altered the fluidity and open-endedness deemed desirable in a less product-oriented fieldwork environment. Looking at the politics of festivals, Barbara Kirshenblatt-Gimblett assesses the problem as one inherent in tensions between community and academic definitions of authenticity: "The curatorial problem in folk festivals is the delicate one of determining not only what meets certain standards of excellence but, first and foremost, what qualifies as authentic folk performance. As a result, performances at folk festivals are often artifacts of the discipline of folklore, whatever else they may be" (1998, 76).

This issue was both surmounted and complicated by the hiring of untrained local fieldworkers to do research for the Hawai'i program. Local culture workers had knowledge of and access to communities to which outsiders would find it difficult to obtain entry, at least in the limited amount of time. However, they needed to be trained in how and where to look for folklife. In the initial solicitation letter, fieldworkers received a statement about the purpose of the Festival, but most of them still had to be familiarized with folklore research concepts and terminology.[24] To be sure that they were all operating from the same mind-set, the packets that they received included several pages about Festival philosophy, program development procedures, and two articles by Richard Kurin—"Why We Do the Festival" and "The Festival of American Folklife: Building on Tradition"—in addition to forms, sample reports, and guidelines on how to submit their collected materials.[25]

Contrary to standard conceptualizations of folklore as static, the Smithsonian guidelines stress that traditionality incorporates change: "The Smithsonian does not regard traditions as unchanging nor gauge authenticity solely by conformity with some past (possibly the oldest) practice." Acknowledging that traditions are "culture conserving," this view also assumes a dynamic view of traditional cultural practices—that they are continually negotiated; that they can be forced underground in the face of intrusive policies, change, or socioeconomic change as well as re-emerge after periods of dormancy; and that they can be synthesized and creolized when juxtaposed with other cultural practices. Repeatedly stated to fieldworkers was the edict that the traditionality of a cultural practice was to be determined by its being community based, and tradition bearers were "those individuals engaged in an exemplary practice of particular traditions, as indicated by their status and recognition within a community." Fieldworkers were given a definition of tradition/traditionality outlined by the American Folklife Center at the Library of Congress.

> Community-based cultural traditions can be generally defined as forms of knowledge, skill, and expression learned through informal relationships and exhibiting intergenerational continuity. Typical genres include oral tradition (i.e., narrative, epic, poetry, proverbs, riddles, speech), social custom (i.e., festivals, celebrations, games, rituals, vernacular religion, customary behavioral codes and their practice), material culture and its supportive knowledge (i.e., crafts, architecture, costuming, foodways, agriculture, fishing, medicine), and the arts (i.e., music, dance,

> drama, puppetry). Forms of culture are traditional to the extent that they maintain standards or values which have continuity with, and are informed by, past practice. They are living traditions to the extent that they are practiced, are socially integrated within community life, and can speak to its cognitive, normative, affective and aesthetic concerns.

The combined effect of the documents in the fieldwork packet was to reinforce Festival ideology by establishing a set of common definitions designed to break down assumptions that folklife was static or peripheral to everyday life and that the value of cultural expressions should or could be determined by outside experts.

For Festival selection, however, the guidelines added that it was not enough for a cultural practitioner to be exemplary. One also had to have potential for performance since the Festival required that the chosen participants be able to "convey rich information about themselves and their traditions in an interactive situation," preferably through demonstration and narration.[26] The Festival is a public stage that requires a certain amount of stage presence, implying that the unself-conscious cultural practices, deemed desirable by culture workers, would have to be transmitted through practitioners with enough meta-consciousness to perform, articulate, demonstrate, and otherwise mediate between folklife practices and a large audience.

Fieldwork Interviews and Reports

According to Kennedy, among state programs produced by the Smithsonian, the Hawai'i program stands out for having involved an exceptional amount of fieldwork. Sixty-two interviews and twenty-eight fieldwork reports were produced in the fall of 1988. As might be expected, they vary in quality and depth, but they still form the only comprehensive body of material on Hawai'i folklife that is publicly available.[27] The reports comprise both primary and secondary materials—interviews, newspaper and journal articles, overviews, and commentary. Some fieldworkers were meticulous about following the fieldworker guidelines, while others skipped critical steps, such as making recommendations. Fieldworkers were instructed to be careful not to let participants think that being interviewed was an invitation to be in the Festival, but news travels fast in a small state with wide-sweeping community networks, through what is often referred to as the "coconut wireless." A few fieldwork reports openly state that certain individuals were eager to participate in the Festival. Although the planning meetings had stressed unself-conscious and continuous traditions, groups that had undergone cultural revivals, often with the help of HSFCA and NEA funding, were the most eager to participate in the fieldwork project because they saw it as an opportunity to express their recovered or reinvented identities. In fact, it is clear from the fieldnotes that many of the informants were already aware of the possibility of being able to participate in the Festival. Whether the coconut wireless or fieldworker indiscretion was responsible for this slip is unclear.

Community conflicts of several kinds are revealed in these reports. For instance, the fieldworker who surveyed woodcarvers used his report to note his discomfort with the way that traditionality was being defined. He wrote that artists like Rocky Jensen were using traditional methods and materials in innovative ways, but were often criticized within the Hawaiian community for blurring the boundaries between traditional and "fine arts." The same fieldworker, a Hawaiian, indirectly endorsed himself as the best choice over the several woodcarvers that he had interviewed, albeit in the third person and by stating that he was aware that, if known, his recommendation would provoke resentment in the politically charged environment. Some of the conflicts were inter-cultural and illustrated the prevalence of ethnic stereotypes. For example, one Hawaiian weaver wanted to know if the fieldworker interviewing her was Japanese and said that she would like to have a student interviewer, but not a Japanese one because her father had always told her that Japanese would steal her ideas and make money off of them.

Due to time constraints and the use of people who had done previous fieldwork, some of the material submitted was "canned" in that it had already been analyzed within another context and was being recirculated. Scholars who had done previous research in particular genres of Hawai'i traditions tended to cite or include their own published work. Many of the reports reflect enthusiasm for the program but frustration with the lack of time for the project; they function more as suggestions for future fieldwork than as the in-depth archival contributions they were supposed to be upon completion. For instance, Skillman, who was experienced in the fieldwork process, recommended that interviews be undertaken with all of the *kumu hula* and stated that all she had time to do was one in-depth interview, the assembling of materials from *hula* competitions, and a survey of archival materials. Martin's extensive work for the *paniolo* exhibit she had produced in 1987 came complete with a celebrity, in the form of Clyde "Kindy" Sproat, and catalog material that could be infused into signage. Martin had successfully nominated Sproat as a National Heritage Fellow for his singing, so he was already known in Washington. That this material had been pre-packaged made it likely that it would appear in the Festival program and that her research would be definitive. Likewise, Judy Van Zile of the University of Hawai'i Department of Theatre and Dance had written several articles on Japanese *bon* dance in Hawai'i, which were submitted as her report along with three interviews with previous informants. The use of previously compiled work expedited the process, but it also blurred the boundaries between Festival ideals and Festival logistics.

Perhaps the most poignant reminder of the effect of imposing Festival parameters on fieldwork is the breadth of the sixty-two taped interviews in comparison to traditions selected for performance. Copies of fieldwork and Festival recordings are routinely sent back to the originating state by the OFP after a Festival program is completed. The Hawai'i recordings were sent to the Hawai'i State Archives, where they were rejected and passed on to the University of Hawai'i. Twelve years later, in 2001, they had still never been accessed. Languishing in this collection of recordings is an invaluable body of life stories, memories, and folklife—much of which fell outside of the Festival grid. They exist as a reminder that not all folklife is showy, and not all tradition bearers are showmen and women, nor is the excellent and exemplary necessarily what is most meaningful outside of the limelight.

Fieldwork Review Meeting

The fieldwork process culminated in a fieldworker review meeting—actually a series of meetings—held at the East-West Center during January 25–27, 1989. According to firsthand accounts, it was grueling. From the Smithsonian OFP, program coordinator Barbara Lau and technical coordinator Fred Nahwooksy flew in to be part of the process. It would be their task to translate the selection decisions into a conceptual and spatial design on the Mall. In this meeting, as at the planning meetings in January, Festival philosophy and logistics met the conflicting narratives and realities of Hawai'i culture and identity politics.[28] Hawai'i culture simply did not fit into academically defined, presentation-friendly categories. At the planning meetings, discussion about how to represent Hawai'i was hypothetical, and dissent had been transcended with grounding questions like "How can you represent the ocean?" that focused discussion back on the concrete issues of actual representation. At the fieldwork meeting, however, organizers, advisors, and fieldworkers had much more at stake since they knew they were influencing final decisions. A few of those present at the planning meetings had gone on to be part of the fieldwork process—Martin, Trimillos, "Benjie" Bennington, Nathan Napoka, Dolly Strazar—but much of the cast had changed, with the result being that many of the same thorny issues were resurrected.

The first day of discussion covered the critical topic of demographics. It formed the nucleus of a debate that would persist throughout the three days. The second day was devoted to crafts, and the third allotted to conceptual and spatial design. In each of these lengthy discussions it was clear that even after conducting fieldwork into ethnic traditions, a number of the people at the meeting were uncomfortable with the use of ethnic categories to delineate Hawai'i populations in the present. While Kennedy retained ethnic categories as an underlying organizing principle for the program, disputes by the Hawai'i culture workers led to some novel solutions that blurred ethnic boundaries and refocused much of the Festival concept on cultural creolization.

One challenge was to pare down the long list of communities, traditions, and culture bearers produced by the fieldwork reports to what was actually feasible and budgetable. At the planning meetings, when Moriarty had expressed a desire to see at least half of the program represent Native Hawaiians, there was no dissent. This choice, however, stirred debates over who was really Hawaiian and to what extent authentic Hawaiianness was reflected in the traditional arts. According to HSFCA statistics, in 1988 pure Native Hawaiians made up only 1 percent of the population, and 33 percent of the population claimed to be part-Hawaiian. On the other hand, many participants in Hawaiian traditions, especially *hula,* were not Native Hawaiian since Hawaiianness was not a prerequisite for membership in a *hālau.* Crafts were less of a problem since most of the practitioners in Native Hawaiian crafts tended to identify as Native Hawaiian.

Clearly, demographics promised to be a sticking point as people debated the pros and cons of using compensatory or actual demographics as the basis of selection for a multicultural production. Trying to explain Hawai'i inter-group dynamics to the Smithsonian crew, someone at the meeting cited a well-known local saying that points to perceptions about asymmetries in economics and power: "In Hawai'i, the Chinese own it, the Japanese run it, the Hawaiians remember it, and the *haoles* enjoy it." According to meeting notes, the group was working with the following demographic figures.

25 percent	*haole*
25 percent	Japanese
5 percent	Chinese
14 percent	Filipino
5 percent	Puerto Rican
5 percent	Portuguese
1 percent	Hawaiian
33 percent	part-Hawaiian

These odd numbers leave no catchall for other populations in Hawai'i. Although no source is cited, it is also noted that 50–60 percent of marriages in Hawai'i are mixed. A look at statistics in Eleanor Nordyke's *The Peopling of Hawai'i* (1989) shows the figures used at the meetings to be in the range of the 1980 census, with some notable exceptions that illustrate how U.S. official racial categories were being broken down into ethnic categories in Hawai'i. According to Nordyke, the U.S. Census Bureau survey had no separate categories for Portuguese and Puerto Ricans; however, both tend to identify by ethnicity in Hawai'i and be assigned to non-*haole* status by virtue of plantation history. In the U.S. census, these groups were subsumed into a generic "white" racial classification. National figures also did not distinguish between Hawaiian and part-Hawaiian. Like the category "black," a person was all or nothing. The Hawai'i Health Surveillance Program also did not present Portuguese as a separate category; on the other hand, it broke out categories of Pacific Islanders and thus offered statistics based on some specific regions of origin: Samoan, Guamanian, and others (Nordyke 1989, 183). What these statistics demonstrate is that in Hawai'i even official ethnic designations tend to accord with ancestral country of origin rather than employ the racial designations used on the mainland.

To narrow the final selection to a manageable number of groups and people, Kennedy established some selection parameters. Based on the theme of "A Sense of Place," he determined that they would accept only tradition bearers born in Hawai'i. This rule streamlined the selection process by eliminating some tradition bearers and including others. For example, it included Okinawan master *sanshin* (three-stringed plucked lute) player and folksong singer Harry Seisho Nakasone, who had been born in Hawai'i but raised in Okinawa, but it excluded recent immigrants. The second condition was that tradition bearers who were selected as Festival participants needed to be linked by a shared narrative, and for this plantation history was chosen. Chinese, Japanese, Portuguese, Koreans, Puerto Ricans, Filipinos, and Okinawans could all be tied to plantation culture. The plantation past was a useful linking device in that it provided a way to select out only the groups who had arrived as contract laborers and would provide a locus for presenting cultural creolization and sharing. The problems associated with this—that immigrants had arrived in waves rather than all at once—revisited points raised in the planning meeting. The drawbacks to the plantation as a frame were that transcending the issue of non-parallel histories required the plantation history to be essentialized into the plantation "experience." Of course, fitting immigrant groups to this narrative also falsely implied that all members of the selected ethnic groups or their ancestors had shared this experience.

For the immigrant groups who could not be fitted to a plantation history and were not born in Hawai'i, other thematic links had to be forged to merit selection—numbers were not enough. Nordyke's figures show blacks numbering more than Samoans, and they were mentioned in Martin's preliminary report as having "gospel culture," but they were discounted as mostly military and therefore transient. Samoans were the only group of later immigrants chosen to go to the Festival. The majority of Samoans had immigrated in the 1950s, meaning they were not born in Hawai'i, but they could be thematically linked to Hawaiian/Polynesian culture. They fit the compensatory logic of the selection process because they had been ranked by the HSFCA as on the "lowest socio-economic rung" along with Native Hawaiians, and they had a history of involvement with the HSFCA through cultural development grants awarded to the Samoan Chiefs and Orators Society. The fact that Samoa had a strong political and diasporic presence in Washington was duly noted.

The third condition used to narrow the groups selected was more ambiguous: these groups should have made a major contribution to the cultural life of Hawai'i through their folklife.[29] This determination, although never directly stated, allowed *haole* to be eliminated from representation at the Festival. While European and American influence permeates almost every aspect of cultural life in Hawai'i, using a folklife model that posed traditionality against dominant and official culture made it seem natural to omit this conglomerate group from a view of Hawai'i valorizing under-represented and unheard voices. The problem of what to do about *kama'āina haole* was sidestepped through the focus on traditional culture—it was presumed, based on perceptions of high economic status, that they had either acculturated into some form of "local" culture or were invested solely in elite culture. Although Scandinavian groups had been funded by the HSFCA and Scottish and Greek groups were listed among the later immigrant groups on the overview Martin sent to Kennedy, they had been edited out of the fieldworker recruitment letters. Martin also mentioned in the meeting that no HSFCA fieldwork had been done on *haole* or blacks. The decision to erase *haole* may have been the result of an organizational blind spot or of *haole* culture workers allying themselves with other groups due to awareness of "local" resentment toward *haole* as socioeconomically dominant and politically exploitative. Conveniently, the erasure could be justified through the use of a plantation frame that omitted plantation owners.

Remembering the review meetings, Hawai'i former fieldworkers insist that the central debate was over Hawai'i versus mainland ideas of multiculturalism and the slippage between racial and ethnic usages of the same terms in Hawai'i. In the meeting, local fieldworkers stressed that in Hawai'i everyday-use ethnic terms rely on fluidity and double entendre. What went unremarked was the irony of omitting *haole* from representation in contrast to the powerful administrative role they were playing in the festival-making process. The Festival goal was to represent culture occluded by the mainstream. In the service of that vision, the Hawai'i program was inverting power bases to portray an ethnoscape otherwise invisible by erasing the obvious. For outside appearances, however, an apparent inclusion of *haole* was accomplished through the selection of Portuguese music, foods, and crafts.

Erasure of *haole* was not just accomplished by narrowing the number of ethnic groups. They were also purged from within categories. Of the three rock-wall builders recommended, a Native Hawaiian was chosen over two non-Hawaiians despite the fieldwork report attesting to the skill of the others. One of the most heated moments in the demographics discussions occurred over the selection of Korean dancers. A debate erupted over whether to allow dance school founder Halla Huhm's leading pupil and teacher, Mary Jo Freshley, to perform. Freshley was Huhm's foremost assistant, but she was *haole*. Kennedy had established a rule that all Festival participants be Hawai'i born. She was not, and this was the stated basis on which she was eliminated; however, it is clear from all accounts that Smithsonian representatives, at the time, felt her appearance onstage would be inappropriate because she was not

Korean. After a proposal that she wear a black wig and despite her professional endorsement by Huhm and Professor Van Zile, Freshley was relegated to the role of stage presenter/manager for her own students.[30]

The other group perceived to have disproportionate demographic, economic, and political power was the local Japanese, but their power in contemporary Hawai'i would be downplayed through being limited to folklife representation. A five-person *bon* dance group from Kaua'i, a paper-doll maker, and a bulrush sandal maker were chosen as the Japanese contingent. This representation, numerically small and mostly rural, stands in marked demographic contrast to population figures for Japanese in Hawai'i and to commonly held perceptions of Japanese as upwardly mobile and saturating local government, state agencies, and schools in Honolulu (Okamura 1994). When asked about the small number of Japanese chosen, Kennedy mentioned the Okinawan group as part of the Japanese representation.[31] However, in Hawai'i Okinawans generally do not identify themselves first as Japanese despite the Japanese annexation of Okinawa.[32] Ironically, representing Japan through the Okinawans might be seen as in accord with the Festival's compensatory philosophy.

A different type of power perception was at issue in the selection of Hawaiian tradition bearers. Because of the volatility of Hawaiian issues and the politicization of *hula* and *oli,* decisions about *hālau hula*s had to be carefully handled. In fact, meeting notes flag the *hula* decisions as "sensitive." Skillman feels that one reason the fieldwork on *hula* was limited to secondary research was to avoid community politics.[33] The problem was resolved by choosing, according to her recommendations, that island variations, generations, and lineage be the selection guidelines. Accordingly, Kau'i Zuttermeister and her daughter and granddaughter, participants in an earlier FAF, were chosen to represent inter-generational transmission and the island of Oahu. *Hālau hula* from the Big Island and Lāna'i were balanced with Hawaiian musicians from Maui, Kaua'i, and Ni'ihau. A wood carver from Moloka'i was selected to round out the geographical distribution in an egalitarian fashion. Native Hawaiian craftspeople were also selected from throughout the islands. It was assumed by organizers that the four National Heritage Fellows from Hawai'i (Ray Kane, Meali'i Kalama, Kindy Sproat, and Kau'i Zuttermeister) would be selected along with other artists who had participated in Smithsonian-sponsored activities. These tradition bearers had already been recognized as exemplary. However, their selection meant it was a foregone conclusion that Native Hawaiians would be in large part represented through institutionally created celebrities rather than through the community validation purported to be the goal of the fieldwork discovery process. Fortunately, there was no debate voiced over the merits of these tradition bearers.

Ultimately, history and ethnicity drove the final selections. Grounded in the Festival concept of a "past informed by the present," ethnic groups were selected on the basis of a shared history, at least partially imagined. The concept of a shared history made for a clean and eminently presentable version of a dirty plantation history repackaged as "embraceable imagery."[34] It allowed for a unified strategy of representation for groups who had actually arrived at different times and who had in many cases been pitted against each other through unequal wages and segregated work camps. That Native Hawaiians had also worked on the plantations, although in smaller numbers, went unremarked since that would have confused the imposed division between indigenous and immigrant populations. *Haole* was a category that, by virtue of not being ethnicized, became invisible. In some cases, such as the Chinese and Filipinos, ethnicity was conceived in broad strokes that collapsed disparate regional/cultural parts into a manageable ethnic whole that was actually pan-ethnic. The emerging ethnoscape of the Festival program was a utopian place where the colonizers were invisible, the immigrants were equal, and the natives were both untainted and enriched by the cultural contributions of others.

Defining Tradition

The objective of a folklife festival is to present living culture, not relics of the past. Smithsonian literature made it clear that traditional culture was to be understood as unofficially transmitted, meaningful within communities, and having continuity, but to apply all of these conditions and reach community consensus was challenging in Hawai'i. Urban and rural areas, for example, had very different ideas of what was traditional and authentic. For example, Moriarty, who lived on Kaua'i, successfully persuaded the committee to select a *bon odori* group from Kaua'i because her perception was that the Honolulu groups were all very stiff and unfriendly. She preferred the Kaua'i group—a group considered "out there" and "maverick" by the more dignified Honolulu groups—because they were interactive rather than performative and thus fit better with the Festival's ethos.[35] Authenticity was a sticky issue as well. Hawai'i culture workers made it clear that they wanted to present a version of Hawai'i that was untainted by tourism, but many performance arts had been influenced by or grown out of touristic performance, such as *hapa-haole* music and *hula auana*. At the planning meeting Trimillos had proposed that what they really should be looking for was "backyard" culture, what people did at home rather than for money, but many performers participated in tourism as a way to make a living and incorporated tourism performance genres into their backyard culture. Furthermore, because island culture had absorbed large numbers of immigrants, determining authenticity and traditionality within particular communities was complicated by the intermingling of traditions, so trying to determine what was traditional and authentic within a particular ethnic group was not so simple.

At least one local tradition was eliminated because it would not translate well to Washington, D.C.: Hawai'i ethnic humor. Although Moriarty had suggested that humor be included, it was quickly dispensed with as too political, especially the ethnic humor of the islands. Kennedy thought the ethnic humor was a wonderful illustration of inclusivity and negotiation of multiculturalism, but insiders were afraid that what was considered funny and acceptable in Hawai'i would be misunderstood as racist in Washington. Based on the difficulties encountered in translating Hawai'i ethnicity into the frame of mainland multiculturalism, no doubt they were right.

Where fieldworkers were outsiders, sometimes definitions of traditionality were too rigidly applied. For example, the fieldworker for Chinese traditions recommended June Tong, a noteworthy Chinese cook and author of a cookbook titled *Popo's Kitchen*, but in the report the fieldworker expressed concern that Mrs. Tong did not know how to make noodles. Consequently, the fieldworker interviewed a man who owned a local noodle factory as another possibility. The noodle maker was too busy to consider the Festival (obviously the fieldworker leaked the purpose of the interviews), but he expressed willingness to teach Mrs. Tong how to make *lok fun* noodles. On hearing this story, a local Chinese man who is an avid cook scoffed at the fieldworker's ignorance, saying that everyone knows all Chinese cooks buy noodles readymade. Apparently the fieldworker was familiar enough with Chinese food to know that noodles were a staple, but not enough to know Chinese cooking habits. In the process, he imposed his own ideas of what was traditional.

Although Kurin notes that traditions can go underground and re-emerge (Kurin 1998), fieldworkers were told to look for practices that had been continuous. Traditional *hula,* which by 1988 had rebounded and was being performed in public venues like the Merrie Monarch Festival, is an example of this process of suppressed tradition revived after a period of near-dormancy and neglect. It had not, however, completely disappeared at any point, so while it had been resuscitated through institutional support, it could still be transmitted through unofficial transmission, albeit in changed surroundings.

Other native traditions had not fared as well and were dealt with selectively. *Kapa* making has now been revived, but in 1988 it was not selected for two reasons. First and most obviously, it had died out completely and was being reinvented. Second, the organizers feared invoking images of primitivity and felt that *kapa* might present an image of Native Hawaiians stuck in the past.[36] A similar argument was used to exclude certain kinds of wood carving, such as carved gods, often called *tiki*s, and fishhooks, while including others, such as bowls. This avoidance of primitivizing was further complicated by the resurgence of Native Hawaiian iconicization of ancient practices. For example, the well-publicized voyages of the *Hōkūle'a* beginning in 1976 were a case of a scientific experiment employing aspects of tradition being adopted as tradition. The committee chose as a compromise the maritime tradition in canoe building that would imply the ocean and voyaging without directly using the *Hōkūle'a.*

The continuity requirement was construed differently in communities the Festival organizers were anxious to represent but which had more discontinuous folklife. Kenichi Tasaka, a *nisei* living in Kaua'i, had begun experimenting with making bulrush sandals, a craft he reinvented based on a remembered traditional product rather than on a process he had been taught by traditional means. He produced something that had nostalgic community value but that did not have wide appeal since the majority of Japanese in Hawai'i are urban. In his case, even the inter-generational aspect came after the fact, as it was his children who helped him to obtain the materials he needed to make his sandals. In the Samoan community, a similar circumstance occurred. Faced with a dearth of crafts, the fieldworker had finally asked a group of Samoan elders if they could remember crafts they had practiced in the past. Some of them replied that they could do fine mat weaving but that they could not obtain the necessary materials in Hawai'i. The fieldworker made it a project to help the elders locate funding and materials to revive their weaving, and Kennedy noted that perhaps they would be ready for the next Festival. These examples demonstrate that having adequate multicultural representation was the committee's foremost objective.

In selection discussions about synthesized traditions, ethnicity and traditionality questions converged. Some cultural items and practices were so widely diffused that they resisted ethnic classifications—thus the need for "local" as a category for traditions like "shave ice," the Hawai'i version of the snow cone and a popular treat. Others had been absorbed by particular groups and then further appropriated by others. For instance, *paniolo* practices literally hailed from elsewhere. Mexican *vaqueros* had been brought in to solve the problem of wild cattle running rampant on the island of Hawai'i. The *vaqueros* adapted cattle ranching techniques to the new terrain and trained a generation of local *paniolo* in skills such as riding, skinning, and leatherwork. The Hawai'i-born *paniolo,* from various ethnic groups, infused ranching with their own cultural sensibilities, which included storytelling, music making, and *lei* making. In the 1980s some of the best *paniolo* music was sung by Kindy Sproat, a former mule skinner who had never been a *paniolo.* According to the fieldworker for Puerto Rican music, *paniolo* music was also a popular part of the repertoire for at least one Puerto Rican group in Hawai'i. This kind of exchange worked in other directions as well. In an interview, Moriarty pointed out that Puerto Rican *katchi katchi* music was regularly played at Hawaiian *lū'au* when she was growing up, thus it was a type of music with which everyone was familiar. Likewise, the Hawaiian *lū'au* had been widely adopted. The effect of Festival categorization was to reposition these traditions within ethnic communities of origin and grant these communities ownership based on origin rather than practice.

In the intimacy of the islands, traditions easily jump cultural fences and become dislodged from their original tradition bearers, and the curators found themselves trying to distinguish between what had been traditional prior to inter-group contact. Slippery linkages between ethnicity and traditionality are especially evident in the genres of Hawaiian music selected; for example, *hīmeni* is a tradition in which colonization and Hawaiianization converged to form a unique style of unaccompanied hymn singing (Kanahele 1979).[38] *Hīmeni* is an institutionally instigated, syncretized cultural practice that can be seen as either a religious musical tradition crafted with and for Hawaiians or as a hegemonic tool adopted as community tradition. Likewise, what is generally referred to as "Hawaiian music" incorporates other European musical elements, such as introduced instruments like the *'ukulele* and guitar and vocal styles like falsetto and harmony. The origins of falsetto singing are attributed to various sources such as male/female dialogues in *mele,* church choir training, and the introduction of falsetto and yodeling by *paniolo* (Kanahele 1979, 86–92). Whatever the origins, Hawaiian music is sung to Euro-American melody. Clearly, there is no getting around creative fusion as foundational in Hawaiian music.

In the process of choosing to represent these traditions, the organizers also had to consider how to narrativize them since they were subject to multiple interpretations, and one of the responsibilities of the programming would be to provide historical context through signage. Rather than representing Hawaiian cultural expressions as the result of colonization by European culture, they decided to present these practices in terms of cultural agency and creative appropriation, as having been claimed and synthesized by Native Hawaiians—Hawaiianized. This choice of narrative fit with both the agency of the renaissance and the "putting our best foot forward" idea that would undergird the program.

A mismatch between the search for ethnic authenticity and acculturated realities arose in certain contexts. Martin stated in her overview that the Koreans brought little traditional culture with them when they immigrated to Hawai'i just after the turn of the century. This view made it difficult to find a way to represent the Korean community. What was overlooked, however, was that at least a third of this community identified itself as Christian (Adamski 2003). In this community, as in the Hawaiian Christian community, hymn singing is central. Whereas Hawaiian hymn singing was qualified as "vernacular religion" due to its unique style, Korean hymn singing was apparently seen as derivative and overly acculturated. Instead, what was chosen to represent Koreans in Hawai'i was the Halla Huhm dance company. Halla Huhm was recommended by Judy Van Zile. As the proprietor of the sole Korean (and also Okinawan) dance company, Huhm had been repeatedly funded by the HSFCA and commended for her dedication to Korean traditional dance on more than one occasion. However, Van Zile admitted in her field report that Huhm received little attention from the Korean community. A Korean professor of ethnomusicology went further when he called Huhm's Korean dance "fake." According to him, Huhm grew up in Japan, where she learned Japanese court dance, which she passed off as Korean traditional dance in Hawai'i. Whether or not this is true, the lack of community identification with her cultural practices indicates that they were no longer meaningful for the community and that this selection was a case of academic and individual definitions of tradition being foisted on a community that had chosen to define itself in other terms.

A related but different situation arose with the so-called Chinese community, an ethnic group referred to as "hostile," "ethnocentric," "closed," and "uncooperative" in various planning and meeting notes. Unlike groups who had sought HSFCA support for cultural revivals, such as the Hawaiians, the Filipinos, and the Portuguese, the Chinese had been less than eager to participate in HSFCA projects. There are several possible reasons for the lack of relationship between the HSFCA and the Chinese. Economically disadvantaged groups—Native Hawaiians, Samoans, and Filipinos—had been sought out to be the initial recipients of NEA/HSFCA funding. The Portuguese had undergone a reassertion of Portugueseness after an era of identity submersion when they were informed that they were eligible to become grant recipients. What these groups had in common was institutional intervention and feared loss of identity in the face of rapid acculturation. This did not seem to be a factor for the Chinese, who had either been absorbed, in the case of early immigrants, or remained insular, in the case of later ones.

There is a wealth of Chinese tradition practiced in Hawai'i—such as music, herbal medicine, martial arts, and cooking. Much of it is practiced by later immigrants who have maintained more distinct Chinese identities, so little of it is practiced at the level of cultural revival. Early laborers came mostly from Guangdong Province. Later immigrants have come from Taiwan, Hong Kong, and, more recently, mainland China. As a result, Hawai'i actually has several Chinese communities, some very assimilated and others less so, with at least four first languages spoken in addition to English.[39] Descendents of early Chinese in Hawai'i are mostly of mixed ethnic heritage and often identify with their other ethnic groups. Very few young descendents of the early immigrants speak any Chinese language. What the combined forces of the NEA and HSFCA had done best was to forestall cultural bankruptcy, and the Chinese in Hawai'i were deemed, as a whole, neither economically nor culturally needy enough to be targeted for conservation efforts. There is little need for such conservation efforts to preserve traditions still actively part of daily life, and this may have accounted for the perceived lack of enthusiasm on the part of the community to HSFCA investigations. The Chinese traditional practices ultimately selected for Festival presentation were herbal medicine, lion dance, a Taoist priest, and calligraphy. Ironically, all of these represent practices that can be or are institutionally transmitted rather than folk practices that are orally and informally learned. Temple-based Chinese schools teach martial arts, lion dance, and calligraphy. The Taoist priest had attended a seminary, and there are colleges of herbal medicine—one in Honolulu. Again the desire to represent the seven major groups who had come as contract laborers had trumped the actual social complexity of the group's makeup as well as cornered the committee into blurring its own rules for determining what was and was not community folklife.

In sorting the fieldwork results by ethnic categories, most shared traditions were attributed to the ethnic groups from which they had originated, rather than evaluated according to their current social practice. *Imu* building, *lei* making, rock-wall building, and *lauhala* hat weaving, for example, were assigned as Hawaiian traditions by the selection of Hawaiian practitioners, although they had also been mastered by craftspeople from other ethnic groups.[40] Hybrid practices, such as quilting, were also presented as Hawaiian.

Some groups no longer practiced the traditions of their ancestors. Charlene Smurnap, fieldworker for Filipino culture, wrote in her report that "the young show no interest in learning to carry on the culture." She added that all the musicians were elderly, there was limited transmission of crafts, and food was the only cultural practice still intact. To emphasize this lack of continuity, Smurnap quoted from a book on Filipinos in Hawai'i by Robert Anderson: "Just as older immigrants cherish a life and culture that no longer exists in the Philippines, Filipinos born in Hawai'i will look back to life and culture plantation towns that are no longer there." Working with an ethnic group that had such a high level of acculturation and loss of tradition made it difficult to come up with enough material to make this group's folklife representation on par with the others. Smurnap did manage to turn up a six-person string band, or *rondalla,* and a weaver who had been in the HSFCA Master and Apprentice Program. Ironically, the focus on difference imposed homogeneity on certain communities. For example, most of the Filipino population in Hawai'i is Ilocano, but the only musical group that the fieldworker could locate was Visayan. Fortunately, this was not an issue since the Camarillo family repertoire included Ilocano songs and since there was no other *rondalla* group.

Community evaluations of what traditions were most valued were not necessarily the basis of final choices in other cases as well, sometimes due to logistics. In the Portuguese community interviewed on Maui,

Catholicism was foremost in terms of community identification, and the Holy Ghost Festival the most important annual event. To illustrate the importance of the festival, one informant told a story about how his particular community had used a handcrafted gold crown in its annual procession. The rest of the year the crown was kept in a prominent side chapel of the local church. When the parish priest, under directives from the pope to break down barriers between parishioners and the clergy, began to make changes in the church structure, the crown was removed to an area behind the sacristy. Parishioners protested, and some even went so far as to leave the church. Meanwhile, the crown disappeared and the informant expressed his belief that it was "borrowed" by a parishioner until the church could be restored to its former form and concept. Despite Martin's original recommendation to present non-Hawaiian ethnic communities through celebration and despite this Portuguese community's assessment of its traditions, the Holy Ghost Festival was not selected to represent the Portuguese in Hawai'i. Instead, the *forno* (beehive oven) was chosen—a tradition that the fieldworker had identified as extinct but that a cultural association had recently re-created as a historic exhibit in a park. While a fieldworker was able to come up with a family that still used a *forno,* this was obviously not a practice that was integrated into community life except as a memory for some elders who had lived on the plantation. Instead, a private family tradition was reconstrued, by way of a historical narrative, as a community symbol for the present. It was a symbol readily accepted since it connoted Portuguese baked goods, which are very popular in the islands.

Presenting private traditions has its own inherent problems. The Festival seeks to present private traditions in an extroverted environment that makes the private public. The goal of presenting unself-conscious culture was offset by the need to select tradition bearers who also had the potential to be good performers. They needed to be hearty enough to travel, extroverted, knowledgeable, and articulate enough to perform on a national stage.[41] If they were able to perform multiple functions, such as cooking and singing, this was a decided bonus—one that could ultimately save OFP money. Many of the musicians, dancers, and storytellers were veteran performers, but the craftspeople and cooks were not. It is one thing to prepare a meal, stitch handsome quilts, or cultivate taro in private and quite another to explain what you do to a curious crowd of onlookers. This is not to say that the people selected to travel to Washington did not have all of these qualities or the potential for them. In fact, many of them did, and that was exactly why they were chosen over other tradition bearers. Performers who had already been honored in Washington were natural choices both for their "star" status and for their familiarity with the Smithsonian cultural scene. Some tradition bearers had developed the ability to narrate their cultural practices through participation in former HSFCA programs that required public presentation as an educational element. And a few of them would develop that ability in Washington, D.C.

* * *

Blind spots are inevitable in the Festival selection process. The focus on tradition resulted in the domestication of powerful groups like the Japanese and the Chinese, erasing class and economic markers to create the illusion of egalitarianism, and elsewhere erasing the frames of socioeconomic power by eliminating *haole* altogether. The need to represent the selected groups equally, despite their level of traditional culture, also led to selecting nostalgic practices resurrected by revival groups alongside relics of the past and folklife that has been continuously practiced.

The Festival mission is to recognize how traditional culture changes and adapts to new circumstances. In practice this goal is often truncated by the need to select "embraceable imagery" and to categorize it in ways that are easily digestible by a moving target with a short attention span—Festival visitors. The limitations of the venue are built into the fieldwork process where fieldworkers are primed to look for cultural practices and artifacts that will fit within the program requirements. What falls outside may or may not be collected in the process of surveying and will not be used on the Mall. Martin, Kennedy, and various local advisors consulted about the Hawai'i program selection process were primarily concerned with articulating difference within a harmonious frame—diversity domesticated by unity.

The Festival fieldwork process illustrates that the Festival operates as a museum behind the scenes, and museums rely on master narratives, which are, according to Hooper-Greenhill,

> created by presenting a large-scale picture, by eliminating complicating and contradictory detail, by disguising difference, by hiding elements that don't quite fit, and by emphasizing those that do. Unity rather than difference is emphasized; gaps that emerge when the story doesn't quite work are filled somehow, and those things that would have shown a different interpretation of events are excluded. The whole is naturalized through links to other supporting discourses. A homog-

> enous mapping is produced, the constructed character of which is not often readily apparent, partly because of the confidence with which it is usually projected, and partly because of the network of other supporting material. These master narratives are therefore naturalized as universal, true, and inevitable. (2000, 24)

The danger in designing the grid on which the Hawai'i program would operate was that in using institutional paradigms to create a narrative counter to the erasures and distortions of the Hawai'i imaging in national, media, and tourism agendas, a new master narrative would be created. The challenge was to walk the treacherous path between regulating the program and regulating the image of the very people to whom it is designed to give visibility and voice.

Chapter 3

Interpreting an Authentic "Sense of Place"

Like sex, tourism is based on experience, juxtaposition, and contrast. Beauty rather than truth is the key word, and the eye of the beholder is the unpredictable key. Truth would instill too many doubts.

—Lucy Lippard, *On the Beaten Track*

Each year just prior to the annual Smithsonian Folklife Festival (SFF), the National Mall is a fenced-in flurry of activity as construction crews barrel about in trucks and carts, scurrying to get tents hoisted, stages and backdrops built, signs mounted. Electrical generators must be set up to run stage equipment and lights, food vendors and portable toilets must be set up, and most of the CFCH staff physically moves into portable trailers on site that become temporary offices. Elsewhere, the annual book of the Festival must be completed, and supplies must be obtained and delivered for everyone from cooks to volunteers. The production process leading up to this frenzy of activity happens primarily behind the scenes, but it manifests in the highly visible end products of site design, signage, and the Festival book that create the visual and textual support for performance. From design work to dirty work, from tracking down funding to searching for supplies, the Festival production phase is caught up in the construction of authenticity.

The Hawai'i program, like any museum exhibit, was skillfully crafted over a rhetorical and spatial armature. Once the fieldwork phase of the festival-making process, in which the performance content and performers were selected, was completed in Hawai'i, the torch was passed to the skilled Festival staff, and the production phase was set in motion in Washington, D.C., where an experienced design team began the complex process of transforming the program concept into a multi-sensory educational event. Skillful rhetoric about the reciprocal value of tradition and the ability of the Smithsonian to frame it authentically had garnered the donations of money and goods necessary to produce "the real Hawai'i" in the nation's capital while strategic mapping of authenticity ideology onto the space of the Mall manifested that "reality" as the stage on which "the real Hawai'i" would be enacted.

Seeking to produce authenticity is particularly problematic in a festival-making process that attempts to negotiate between community self-definitions and institutional definitions and applications. Regina Bendix's study of the how the history of folklore studies has developed in relation to changing ideas about authenticity claims that the issue is rooted in dichotomous thinking: "The notion of authenticity implies the existence of its opposite, the fake, and this dichotomous construct is at the heart of what makes authenticity problematic" (1997, 9). This avoidance of the "fake" was a central concern to the Hawai'i program staff as they worked to manifest an alternative to glitzy, market-produced images of Hawai'i. What had become clear in the early meetings in Hawai'i was that the Hawai'i and Smithsonian people had different interpretations of authenticity as it applied to Hawai'i culture and that these views were critical to envisioning the site and its accompanying textual support. For both groups, however, the "fake" was associated with tourist productions and the "authentic" with an ideal of non-commercialized cultural practices.

Although the objective was to present the real Hawai'i, Hawai'i reality did not necessarily sort out along these lines. For example, many Native Hawaiian living traditions had evolved in the spaces between communities and the cultural marketplace; however, limitations imposed to avoid the fake meant that traditions appropriated by tourism could be used only if they were pared down to roots traditions, symbolically returning them to their ethnic sources and eliminating culturally viable practices like *hapa-haole* music. The issue of root traditions as the measure of authenticity posed a different problem in relation to immigrant groups. Hawai'i fieldworkers had insisted that hybridity was authentic Hawai'i, and what was "traditional" was cultural sharing. Adhering to the multicultural model used by the Festival in the 1980s, with traditions clearly attributed to particular ethnic groups, made it difficult to place the many hybrid forms of culture that had evolved in Hawai'i's overlapping communities. How these debates were resolved in the production process solidified and transmitted the program narrative for public consumption. This chapter tracks the production phase of the Hawai'i program as the festival-making process was translated from Hawai'i to Washington, D.C. In examining the various components of the production phase, it explores how the Hawai'i program was fitted within and yet contested Festival paradigms.

"A Sense of Place" Out of Place: Envisioning Cultural Geographies

Although visitors to the 1989 Hawai'i program do tend to wax nostalgic over program memories, the construction of its "sense of place" was far from magical. If we focus only on the performance aspects of the program, we overlook the degree to which the production determined what happened within and around its performance zones. Pulling off a program of this magnitude is predicated on the deliberate erasure of its institutional frames, and a critical key to invoking festival magic is to design a performance zone that functions as what Dean MacCannell refers to as a "staged back region" (1976, 99). In tourism productions, this region consists of constructed illusion that caters to tourist desire for authenticity. For the Festival, such staging is integral to a festival ideology steeped in ideals of cultural democracy; it tutors visitors to look beyond surface display and define authenticity in local terms. In the process of rendering Hawai'i on the Mall, space was manipulated to disrupt tourist tropes of Hawai'i and to contextualize and narrate Hawai'i multiculturalism. Unveiling the festival-making process suggests the degree to which spatial design contains and constrains performance.

Robert Fairbanks, in discussing the work of Lefebvre, asserts that space is never neutral, never simply a stage on which human affairs are enacted: "Space shapes social life" and is "always constructed culturally through social interactions." Analyzing space as a factor in culture can shed light on "the way in which power operates through spatial structures" (Fairbanks 2003, 131). The Mall is the symbolic epicenter of American public space. A rectangular swath of green between the Capitol Building and the Washington Monument bounded by the imposing galleries of the National Museum, it has been the site of major protests and celebrations. For the Smithsonian to display a community, region, country, or even occupation there is to grant it a symbolic national center stage and, depending on who and what is being showcased in any given year, to temporarily invert power relationships between margin and periphery. Strategic mapping of space is central to this inversion. For visitors, a festival is primarily visual and aural, and a critical problem for program coordinators is designing the program's space so that its conceptual messages will be communicated visually and experientially as well as textually. Through effective staging, represented culture will not only be experienced as authentic and believable, but will also be seen as lived rather than museumized. The challenge in producing the Hawai'i program was to move beyond museumization using tools that are central to museum exhibition strategies: spatial design and textual interpretation. The final site plan was the result of painstaking negotiations between national and local perceptions that would shape Festival performance and reception.

The reconstituted real is at the core of Festival presentation style, in what Robert Cantwell refers to as "ethnomimesis" (1993). While the Festival staff does not aspire to mimic an actual context, they do use spatial designs to signify cultural contexts. On the Mall, authenticity is incurred through carefully chosen objects and environments that point to the real. For the Hawai'i program, this meant trying to signify Hawai'i without using commercialized images. As OFP director Richard Kurin summed it up in an internal memo to Ralph Rinzler: "the design of the Hawai'i program site must convey to the 1.5 million Festival visitors a sense of the physical and cultural landscape of the state. . . . Creating a Hawaiian site on the national Mall presents quite a challenge."[1]

The process of crystallizing the Hawai'i program site design began with preliminary discussions at the end of the fieldwork phase, and it is the fieldwork review meetings—where Hawai'i fieldworkers, Kennedy, Martin, and Moriarty were joined by Barbara Lau, Linda Moriarty's program coordinator counterpart in D.C., and Fred Nahwoosky, Festival technical coordinator—that we must revisit in order to understand the ensuing dilemmas surrounding the program site design.

Discussion of the Festival as a construction in space had been initiated at the planning meetings in early 1988. Richard Kurin and Festival director Diana Parker had posed questions about how the poetry of place could be invoked in space. According to notes from the meetings, Kurin had repeatedly nudged local scholars and culture workers away from vague notions and toward visualization with queries about how the ocean and abstract ideas could be concretely interpreted on the Mall.[2]

In the fieldwork process that followed, questions of what could be displayed and how drove much of the research. Fieldworkers, given limited time in which to survey ethnic communities, had been steered toward investigating and collecting information on traditions that would fit neatly into preexisting Festival genres: material culture, occupational culture, foodways, and performance. Shyer traditions, such as narrative traditions, were also surveyed, but always with stage presentation in mind. In the fieldwork review meeting, questions about presentability heavily influenced the selection of tradition bearers and traditions.[3] Fieldworkers and organizers asked: How would a person or group or activity appear to an audience outside Hawai'i? How well could a tradition bearer articulate a tradition? Could he or she handle a large, inquisitive audience? How would a tradition be perceived visually and aurally? The last day of fieldwork review meetings was devoted to translating the program concept into structural strategies and spatial possibilities for the environment in which tradition bearers and traditions would perform.

Reproducing "A Sense of Place" out of place was the obvious challenge. To evoke the ocean in a landlocked location was an additional obstacle. Featuring surfing and fishing were ventured, and although surfing had been ruled out as a featured tradition, those present at the meeting decided that it would be important to supply ample photographs of sand and sea. Greenery was less of a problem. It was quickly agreed that flowers and trees would need to be abundant in order to visually underscore a link between culture and nature and to instill tropical ambiance. A discussion ensued about whether to restrict the staging to native plants or to include plants that had been introduced from elsewhere—an attempt to reify the pure botanical past rather than reinstate the hybrid botanical present with its showy colors and shapes made familiar by the tourist industry. This point was considered, and meeting notes underline the need for the designers to obtain books on Hawai'i plants so that Smithsonian planners could accurately reproduce the flora and fauna. It was proposed that a learning center could portray the vegetation through photo text panels. Demonstrations were also suggested; *lei* making would add sensory integrity through the scents and colors of flowers.

Including natural structures was another solution to the problem of creating an atmosphere reminiscent enough of Hawai'i to feel authentic. Lava rock walls were suggested as a landscape feature, a reference to rural areas of the islands where they can still be seen. A taro field and family gardens were suggested as practical, multifunctional sites serving to incorporate nature with the occupational lore of *poi* making and of herbal healing while illustrating shared ethnic traditions. This brainstorming at the fieldwork review meeting was productive in solving the problem of how nature could be used to simulate familiar environments. In the process, however, participants called on many of the same signification strategies used by the tourist industry. Clearly, it was not going to be easy to represent Hawai'i without employing overused tropes.

In the fieldwork process, fieldworkers and Smithsonian staff had agreed that a different spatial logic needed to be applied to indigenous and immigrant groups. The proposal was to distinguish Native Hawaiians from other groups through structures that could be designated as exclusive to Native Hawaiians; however, Native Hawaiian architecture had been supplanted by foreign elements, and the Festival rule was to avoid historical reconstruction. Grass shacks were out, so a *hula* mound (a traditional earthwork construction) was suggested as an indigenous "structure" that could convey the connection between culture and landscape, but this solution was also problematic since site design relies on architectural elements rather than natural ones.

A related problem was crossovers with other groups. The next tier of suggested indigenous structures were a *lo'i* and an *imu*—both earthworks that would point to connection with the land. The problem was that both structures had also been suggested to represent acculturation with other groups. The only extant type of "indigenous structure" that the fieldworker who researched vernacular architecture had identified was canoe sheds, although the modern canoe shed is typically a structure used to house outrigger canoes for elite canoe clubs that charge high fees for membership. Likewise, other physical features suggested were Native Hawaiian by association with the past, not the present. Mortarless walls made of black lava still dot various parts of the landscape in the islands, in pastures, remains of fishponds, gardens, and in areas where *heiau* (ancient temples) still stand. Simulations are popular for tourist industry construction. At the time of the Festival, the few rock-wall builders skilled in mortarless wall construction were, however, from various ethnic groups. Clearly, Hawai'i ethnic traditions were far too layered and intermingled for any easy division by ethnicity, and translating indigenous Hawaiian traditions into physical space outside of Hawai'i was problematic.

Finally, the committee decided that the only structure that could be designated a Native Hawaiian space would be a generic one that would be Hawaiianized through performance: a *hula* stage. Meeting notes specified that it should be large and have an unsanded surface. The idea was to surround the stage with native plants to emphasize the relationship between *hula* and island ecology, redrawing the culture to *ʻāina* connection that is the mainstay of the tourist industry as well as a traditional principle in Native Hawaiian culture.

The different logic applied to immigrants had already been a topic of heated discussion in the fieldwork meetings by the time designers arrived at questions of physical structures. The OFP was employing a multicultural paradigm developed over the twenty years of the Festival's existence, one they had assumed was shared until it was disputed in the fieldwork review meetings. Meeting notes and memories from the Hawaiʻi end of the process emphasize how uncomfortable the fieldworkers from Hawaiʻi were with establishing firm divisions between ethnic groups—they chafed at classifications they considered artificial boundaries that belied local realities.[4] Rather than attributing cultural practices in the present exclusively to individual groups, they preferred to stress shared traditions such as *lei* making and exchange, foodways, and *hula auana*. This insistence on blended culture as authentic demonstrated that local interpretations of authenticity leaned toward cultural hybridity.

In this discussion, the focus on hybridity was segued into preliminary suggestions for Festival architecture that could represent the mixing of cultures in Hawaiʻi. Several suggestions were based on fieldwork research done on vernacular architecture. Throughout the Hawaiian Islands there are tiny painted churches, and one suggestion was to use a church front for the Hawaiian narrative stage in recognition of missionary history, the prevalence of Christianity among Hawaiians, and of the hybrid traditions that had resulted from missionary contact, such as Hawaiian quilting. Another idea was a "mom and pop" store modeled after the small stores that had sprung up as former workers left the plantations and went into business. The store, fieldworkers said, could stock rubber slippers and crack seed and sell shave ice as symbols of the "local."[5] The architecture fieldworker had contributed a stack of photographs of these ubiquitous one-room stores. Both the church and the store ideas could serve the purposes of the narrative stages at the Festival. Musicians and storytellers could assemble on the storefront porch. Quilters could work near the church door. The idea was that these spaces, through carefully researched detailing, would lend an air of authenticity to performance by their association with actual gathering places; of course, it was an idea more symbolic than realistic since the church steps are an unlikely place to actually find quilters, and the corner store is an unlikely place for a jam session.

Certain occupations made it easier to represent hybridity because they were tied to particular kinds of sites in which various peoples have traditionally congregated and learned from each other, combining skills and interests. One such hybrid occupation is *paniolo* culture. Martin had previously researched and exhibited the material culture of *paniolo* from the Big Island and Maui, so she was familiar with the landscape in which it had flourished and was still practiced, albeit on a smaller scale. Her request to the Festival staff was to consider erecting a tack shed/ work area for saddle making and rawhide braiding. Horses and cattle were added to her *paniolo* wish list.[6] Maritime culture was another cultural hub brought up at the fieldwork review meeting since Hawai'i has a long, multicultural maritime history that includes voyaging, merchant shipping, whaling, fishing, and canoe racing. The suggestion was to create a boatbuilding shed that would allow maritime history to be visualized and narrativized. Overall, the objective was to create structures that would balance cultural hybridity against the Smithsonian's emphasis on ethnic divisions.

A compromise to the standoff between the Hawai'i and Smithsonian views was to construct a spatial strategy to represent ethnic groups in physical proximity to each other. In figuring the demographics of the Festival program, as opposed to the actual demographics of the islands, a decision had been made to accord Native Hawaiians half of the Festival representation as the "host culture" and to divide the remaining representation equally among the eight other ethnic groups selected to participate. Of those eight groups, Samoans would be loosely linked to Hawaiians through shared geography and Polynesian cultural roots. The remaining seven—Chinese, Korean, Japanese, Okinawan, Portuguese, Puerto Rican, and Filipino—would be linked to each other through a theme of shared plantation history, despite that history not being necessarily contemporaneous. The insistence on connections rather than divisions between immigrant groups led to the proposal of a circular layout for demonstration booths that would allow ethnic groups to be exhibited separately while being symbolically linked within a spoked-wheel layout conceptually reinforcing the notion of shared culture and interdependency. Low stone walls or *ti* plants could provide minimal separation between the groups without obstructing the view. Improving on that notion, the committee envisioned a radial pattern traversed by adjoining paths rather than barriers and suggested that family gardens could be a way of identifying different ethnic groups through their food and medicinal plants while presenting a shared activity. In these solutions, juxtaposition became a compromise solution that would insinuate hybridity while maintaining ethnic distinctions.

Interactivity was a roundabout way to emphasize cultural sharing, and it was one that fit well with the mission of the Festival. Because the Smithsonian Festival is a museum extension, its success is measured by how well it communicates, and its methodology is geared toward interactive education. Structures were needed to provide a multi-sensory experience for festivalgoers that would form an intimate antidote to the hushed reverence and "don't touch" imperative of the surrounding museums and facilitate audience/participant interaction. Interactive spaces, such as a children's activity area, demonstration kitchens, and narrative stages, are standard components of the annual Festival. These standard features needed to be incorporated into the site design but could be adapted for the Hawai'i program's conceptual theme and visual image. To this end, the Hawai'i fieldwork review meeting notes are appended with recipes and a list of recommended cooks for the kitchens, plans for a learning center with photos and text on topics like tropical vegetation and *hula auana,* a children's area for games, and an open space for net throwing. Some proposed structures lent themselves to interactivity by their very nature, and these were favored by both the Hawai'i and the Smithsonian people.

Presenting Japanese *bon* dance required a *yagura*. In Hawai'i, *bon* dances are usually open to the public and outsiders are encouraged to join in (van Zile and Kirchhofer 1981, 118–23, 52–59). For the purposes of the Festival, the *yagura* was envisioned as a unifying strategy as well as an ethnically marked structure because it would be the center of interactive activities in which the public could participate. For logistical reasons as well, outsiders would be needed since there were far too few Japanese participants selected for the program to form more than just the nucleus of a proper *bon* dance. The *yagura,* with its strings of lanterns, would conveniently form the same radial design as the proposed immigrant exhibit, furthering a symbolic portrayal of cultural interconnectedness through the use of circular structures. It was these recommendations that the Hawai'i staff passed on to the OFP for its actual constructions.

Mapping Multiculturalism: From Concept to Festival Frame

Through careful suggestion of actual places being represented, a Festival program site functions as both a liminal zone and a living map once it is inhabited by participants and visitors. Speaking of the map as a metaphor for the museum, Hooper-Greenhill says, "Through the apparently neutral and technical processes of mapping, specific world pictures are constructed and that constructed picture is understood as 'reality'" (2000, 17). On the Mall, the same attention is paid to constructing an illusion of the real. Near the completion of the fieldwork phase, Lau and Nahwoosky, from the Smithsonian, left the program review meeting in Honolulu and set off on a fact- and atmosphere-gathering trip to the island of Hawai'i, locally referred to as the Big Island. There they videotaped and took extensive photographs of the lush vegetation that would inform the site design. In their quest for authenticity, they collected images of the Big Island from which they would construct a collective backdrop for urban, suburban, and rural residents of all seven Hawaiian Islands. Back in Washington, Lau located and hired Gordon Velasco, a landscape architect who had lived in Hawai'i and who had moved to the D.C. area. The final design would be a negotiation between the combined skills of Lau, Nahwoosky, Velasco, and Kennedy. The concern for faithful representation was reflected in an internal memo at the OFP that stated, "The space created for *lei*-makers, weavers, and boat-builders will be evocative of a Hawai'i that exists in reality and not in the imagination."[7]

Back at the Smithsonian, the design team had the task of physically manifesting Hawai'i on site where new factors came into play, such as the geography and dimensions of the actual site, the three other 1989 programs alongside which Hawai'i would be positioned (Caribbean, French Traditions in America, and Plains Indians), and the regulations of the National Park Service. Although more recent programs have all been located in the treeless center of the Mall due to the National Park Service's concerns over the health of the trees, the Hawai'i program area was under the trees that line the Mall where a certain amount of greenery was guaranteed. The Mall itself is divided into a number of rectangular areas separated by one-lane dirt walkways and service roads. The location designated for the Hawai'i program occupied two adjoining rectangular plots on the side of the Mall closest to Jefferson Drive and directly across from the Museum of American History. These two plots are bisected by a walkway and surrounded by fences. The site design for the Hawai'i program underwent several changes before it was finalized, and viewed in sequence, the site designs map the program's spatial conceptualization and concretization.

An early idea that was later rejected juxtaposed two plots side by side rather than end to end. The plan for the two plots accorded with the bifurcated fieldwork review strategy of dividing Hawai'i peoples into "First Immigrants" and "Later Immigrants," with 50 percent of the representation on indigenous culture. This proposed design recalled the linked strategy mentioned in the fieldwork phase, when some members of the committee suggested separating Hawai'i cultures into two groups according to their different relationships to land and history. Indigenous and immigrant groups had been suggested as representing, respectively, a split between "a sense of place" and "a sense of displace." Ironically, this early sketch gave "displace" a physical space while separating Hawai'i culture into two migrations, with Hawaiians labeled as the "First Immigrants."

In the layout of the First Immigrants plot, certain crafts and occupations—quilting, instrument making, lei making, rock-wall building, maritime activities—were relegated to Native Hawaiians despite the insistence of many of the Hawai'i fieldworkers and local cultural advisors that these were shared traditions. The spatial plan for the First Immigrants area was further subdivided by materials and/or activities. Two corners were defined by nature-related activities. Rock-wall building occupied one corner, and the opposite held foodways and *lā'au lapa'au* (plant-based medicinal lore), an *imu,* a *lo'i,* and an herbal garden. Next to a *hula*/music stage was a booth for *lei* makers and one for quilters and weavers. Across from the *hula* stage was a learning center, and next to that was a booth for the crafts of woodworkers: musical instruments, carving, and furniture. The last booth in this area was a maritime booth featuring fishing, canoeing, and surfing.

The second plot in this early layout, labeled "Later Immigrants," was organized by a different logic. A dance and music stage occupied one corner, and in the opposite corner on the same side were the food concessions and foodways. There are only two other exhibition/performance spaces—one was a semi-circular area for Okinawan, Japanese, and Filipino crafts, and the other was another half-round with a store in the center and a garden and Portuguese *forno* on the side. A few "concessions" were sprinkled across the area across from the foodways structure. This part of the plan obviously drew on the aforementioned circular concept. Less obviously, it constructed Hawai'i culture into three categories—Native Hawaiian, Asian, and Other (Portuguese)—that simplify the complexity of the fieldwork reports and subsequent recommendations.

That authenticity issues had resurfaced in this stage of production is evident in the variation between the first design and an intermediate design for the program. The interim layout retained the distinction between indigenous and immigrant groups and the desire to grant half of the Festival representation to Native Hawaiians, but drastically reinterpreted other features, especially the first site design's inclusive treatment of cultural hybridity. In one long plot, indigenous culture was placed at one end and a *paniolo* rodeo demonstration area was at the other. Halfway between the two was a maritime area reached through a gate called the "shell entry." On the Hawaiian end of the layout were a *lo'i,* a *heiau,* a *hula* mound (for *hula,* chant, storytelling, narrative, and nose flute), a *hale* (house) for "*kapa,* medicine, basket and coconut weaving," and two *lei*-making booths with another entrance between them. There were ten structures indicated on the "other" end of the layout. One is a "plantation façade" stage for music and dance, and the remaining nine were each designated by ethnicity. In addition to Okinawan, Hawaiian, Filipino, Puerto Rican, Chinese, Japanese, and Portuguese, ethnicities selected in the fieldwork review meeting were Southeast Asians and *haole* (misspelled as "Howli"). Chinese and Japanese structures were each attached to a sugarcane patch and an entrance placed between them. The Portuguese and *haole* structures were connected and a *forno* (beehive oven) was placed next to the Portuguese area. The Hawaiian structure was designated for quilting, woodworking, and hat making. Layout notes specified that the Okinawan structure should have a red tin roof.

There are several discrepancies between this design and the recommendations. This plan included features that had been deliberately excluded by Kennedy, Martin, and Moriarty in their effort to avoid primitivizing. For example, they had excluded *kapa* making as a revivalist craft, saying that it would create an anachronistic perception among visitors.[8] Although Smithsonian staff had explained that the focus should be on the present as informed by history and that the purpose of the Festival was not historical reenactment, several of the structures belie that emphasis. In the Hawaiian end of the plan is a *heiau* replete with a hut, a *tiki* (carved wooden deity), and a tower. While a few *heiau* still exist in Hawai'i and some are being restored, they are essentially ruins from an earlier era. Including such structures in the Festival would have symbolically situated Native Hawaiians "out of time."[9]

A plantation façade and the Okinawan red roof suggest that the ambiance sought in this design was an evocation of plantation life.[10] This strategy is understandable given that plantation life was the theme used at the fieldwork review meeting to decide which groups to represent and how to link them into a unified narrative, but it commits the same error of re-creating history instead of representing the present. Some elder tradition bearers did remember plantation life, but what they remembered no longer existed. Nor was the plantation a happy multicultural haven in its time.[11] Furthermore, this design's division of traditions by ethnicity imposed a multicultural template on Hawai'i that had been roundly rejected by the Hawai'i fieldworkers who had preferred to stress shared traditions. The inclusion of *haole* redresses their omission in the concept phase. Lastly, the implicit connection of *haole* and Portuguese groups contradicts the fieldwork review meeting assertion that Portuguese are not considered *haole* in Hawai'i by virtue of their being connected to plantation history.

Seen as a whole, what these early designs reveal is the difficulty of representing multi-layered and hybrid history and culture in any kind of exhibition space and the special challenges of doing so in a festival environment that must convey a great deal through initial impressions. The problem of rendering "authenticity" is reflected in the variations between the designs of two people who attended the same meetings and heard the same discussions, yet interpreted the imperatives in very different ways by infusing them with their own observations and sets of signs.

The final design merged the focuses on ethnicity and hybridity from the two previous designs. It was obviously the result of much rethinking of how to mesh space and concept. This design was integrated into the landscape of the Mall, worked around trees and walkways with an organic flow that the other designs lacked. The plantation narrative was retained as a framing device, but rather than being represented by an assortment of small outbuildings reminiscent of workers' houses evoking the past, it was relegated to two shared structures: a historical exhibit representing shared history and a storefront that would function as a shared performance space.

Although participants had been selected for a balanced representation of ethnic groups, exhibit spaces foregrounded activity rather than ethnicity, stressing shared history and traditions. Expressing this emphasis, an immigrant exhibit with the radial construction suggested in the concept stage housed quilters and a learning center on immigration. On the other hand, the hybrid *paniolo* area was dropped and only a tack shed retained; it appeared near the *hula* performance area rather than at the far end of the program plot, implying its connection to Native Hawaiian culture. Shared traditions such as woodworking, agriculture, maritime practices, weaving, and herbal medicine were each accorded a separate space, and the only spaces designated by ethnicity were distinctly Japanese and Chinese crafts. The *hula* stage was placed at the site end nearest the Washington Monument, and a music stage at the other end, next to the Metro stop. Behind the music stage were the program office and the *pu'uho'omaha* (place of refuge)—a space for staff to escape the crowds. Across from the music stage and at the hub of five exhibit structures was the *yagura*. The overall effect of this site plan was to accomplish what the Hawai'i committee had preferred: instead of a division between ethnicities being foremost, the main division was between Native Hawaiian and "local." Although the term "local" had multiple meanings in Hawai'i, Festival organizers chose to interpret it as a non-racialized and inclusive term emblematic of Hawai'i multiculturalism.[12]

In some ways the Hawai'i program was a site design trendsetter. Festival programs usually have two large stages on which multiple performances take place. The Hawai'i program site design was no exception, but the design was unique. When the division between indigenous and immigrant culture was translated into an actual layout, the result was a designated stage for each group: Hawaiian and Other. Although performance stages in Washington are usually covered and much *hula* in Hawai'i is performed indoors in generic performance spaces, a decision was made to create an outdoor stage for *hula* in order to stress Native Hawaiian connections to the *'āina*. Low bench seating was constructed in rows with grandstand seating farther back. The result was a compromise between a traditional *hula* mound—on which ancient *hula* was (and revival culture is) performed—and the standard arena type of performance space where an audience looks down on the dancers rather than up to or at eye level. The dancers would be symbolically elevated above much of the audience, but the setting would remain intimate and outdoors. Since Washington, D.C., is not the tropics, the plan was to create spatial authenticity by surrounding the structures with flowers and palms rather than with iconic images of an indigenous past. At the other end of the program area, a covered stage with standard bandstand seating was to be shared by the various immigrant groups.

The final site design solidified some of the conceptual debates and shifted the balance in others. For instance, despite discussions in the meetings in which prayer was cited as a unifying force and a church was suggested as a way to visualize missionary influence and incorporate Hawaiian hybrid culture through Christianity and quilting, the church idea was dropped, suggesting that Christianity was associated with hegemonic cultural influences. While a Christian church as a symbol of modern Hawaiianness and synchronicity was eliminated, along with the Portuguese Holy Ghost Festival and Korean Christianity, Japanese Buddhism and Chinese Taoism were deemed acceptable for Festival presentation. In addition to space for Japanese *bon* dance, an area was designated for a Taoist altar.

The compensatory demographics of the selection process played out vertically as well as horizontally in the site design. Neutralizing local Japanese socioeconomic and political power in the islands by representing them only through traditional culture and as equal to less powerful immigrant groups was countered by a spatial domination of the immigrant end of the Festival site. The *yagura* echoed the radial organization of the interdependent immigrant area plan, but it was also the tallest structure. Enhancing this focal point in the site design was the fact that the *yagura* would become an ideal spot for reporters and photographers who wanted a bird's eye view of the site.

The plan featured four entrances to the Hawai'i program's site: the *paniolo, kahili* (feathered standards associated with Hawaiian royalty), *puka kom* ("western gate" in Hawaiian), and *torii* (Japanese gate). Each gate was designed to create an impression for the area into which it led. The *paniolo* gate would look like the entrance to a ranch, the Japanese gate like the entrance to a temple. That left two Hawaiian gates, one of which was to be *kahili,* an image that was later dropped as too elite since it referred to royalty. At the fieldwork review meeting, when Kennedy had asked for a suggestion for a Hawaiian gate, Native Hawaiian historian Nathan Napoka had facetiously suggested, "How about airport greeters?"—implying that commercialized and commodified Hawaiian culture manufactured by the tourist industry was the actual entrance to Hawai'i. Those present at the meeting had enjoyed the joke, but the idea was quickly abandoned for a more serious and picturesque solution: tropical vegetation. Opting for what Helàn Page refers to as "embraceable imagery" (1997, 99–111), they avoided the "real" because it did not match the program-defined notion of authenticity. In the final design, the Japanese gate became the generic symbol for all Asians in Hawai'i, making it, like the *yagura,* another symbolically dominant structure for the immigrant representation. The gates marked the boundaries between the outside and the inside—inviting visitors into Festival time and space and operating as thresholds to the liminal zone of cultural mimesis.

Anachronism was not eluded entirely. The *tiki* and *heiau* were omitted, but the past as a lens on the present was maintained in the immigrant area. A Portuguese *forno* appeared despite its being "extinct" in the words of the fieldworker who had researched Portuguese culture in Hawai'i. The "mom and pop" store became a plantation store, although most of the fieldwork photos used as models for program structures show family-owned stores in Honolulu's economically depressed neighborhoods rather than actual plantation stores. Furthering that irony is the fact that the plantation store was historically a company store that operated in such a way as to keep plantation workers economically dependent rather than simply a gathering place in front of which people could "talk story."

While the store as narrative stage might be seen as breaking the historical reconstruction rule, the Hawai'i curators were deeply concerned about setting the record straight about Hawai'i culture and history. As a result, a learning center was included as a space in which history could be presented as adjacent to the present without compromising performances into anachronistic relics of the past.

Overall, the final site design struck a balance. It granted the majority of the program space and structures to shared traditions, opposing Hawaiian and Japanese structures at their respective ends of the green, with the staff areas hidden behind the immigrant music stage. As in the demographics of the Festival, representational power was effectively masked and hidden to stress participant authority and voice. The result was a compensatory spatial design in which the Japanese and Hawaiians were highly visible, other immigrants appeared in juxtaposition to each other, and *haole* appeared only in the guise of syncretic cultural influences presented through indigenous and immigrant appropriations.

Practical Considerations

No Festival program can be produced without adequate funding, and funding comes most readily from sources that see the program as an investment that will in some direct or indirect way benefit the sponsor. The state of Hawai'i put up a million dollars to promote itself within the Smithsonian frame. The following list of sponsors was repeated in signs and the program book.

> State of Hawai'i, with support from the Office of the Governor, the Hawai'i State Foundation on Culture and the Arts, the Hawai'i Visitor's Bureau, the Hawai'i corporate sponsors: Duty Free Shoppers Inc.,

> Alexander and Baldwin, Aloha Airlines Inc., American Telephone and Telegraph Inc., Bank of Hawai‘i, First Hawaiian Bank, Frito Lay of Hawai‘i Inc., GTE-Hawaiian Telephone, Hawaiian Electric Industries Inc., International Savings/National Mortgage and Finance Co., Japan Travel Bureau, Oceanic Properties, Pacific Resource Inc.

This list includes tourist agencies operating in both Hawai‘i and Japan as well as a number of institutions that stood to benefit from investment and/or expenditures in Hawai‘i. Although the pledges from the state were generous, Kurin's midterm report indicates that the money did not flow as easily as did the promises. In a letter to the state, Kurin jokingly prodded by saying he would be willing to swim to Hawai‘i to get the money if need be. But the money was produced for what was undoubtedly the biggest investment ever in buying a place for Hawai‘i in the national imagination.

The trick to a successful cultural spectacle is to incur such a convincing re-presentation that it never occurs to visitors to peer behind the curtain to see just how the wizard is making it all happen. The audience wants to be convinced by illusions of spontaneity and authenticity, and the technical crew at the Festival is at the working end of producing that magic. In addition to raising tents and constructing structures, the Hawai‘i program tech crew had to set up electrical equipment for everything from microphones to kitchens to refrigerators for *lei* flowers—all run on portable generators. The Smithsonian version of traditional culture is wired to sound systems and recording equipment, and, ironically, it took a lot of technology to engineer a version of Hawai‘i, which, for the most part, fell outside the scope of the modern.

Curators had to decide what supplies were needed, and actually obtaining the supplies required the services of Sallie Brodie, Festival resource coordinator, and Barbara Strickland, Festival purchasing agent. Brodie contacted government and private agencies in her search for plants, rocks, and other supplies, asking for donations to defray Festival costs whenever appropriate: "Since the Smithsonian Institution is non-profit and the Festival is free to the visiting public, we appreciate any contributions which help make the Festival a reality." Making the Festival a reality is exactly what the supply procurement people do, and the reality they create depends on available funding and inspiring generosity in potential sponsors, transportation, and government regulations as well as the coordination of logistics for packing, shipping, and getting everything delivered on time and in acceptable condition.

Practicality and logistics dictated many of the structural choices and anchors the site design for all Festival programs. For reasons of budget and space, most structures for the Hawai'i program were committed to multiple uses—conceptual and actual. The canoe shed could stand for both ocean and maritime traditions, although it would omit past boat building and current voyaging. The stages would be shared and the "store" could serve as a narrative and performance stage. Certain traditions dictated their structural needs, making for logical decisions about the sorts of structures that would be necessary to frame cultural performances and demonstrations: for example, the Korean dancers, who wear multi-layered costumes and masks, requested a dressing area and a shaded performance space so they would not swelter in the heat. Weavers and quilters also needed shelter from the sun while throw nets and active games required large open spaces. *Lei* makers needed tables and nearby refrigeration to protect delicate flowers from wilting. Musical instrument makers, who needed to keep instruments cool, were placed next to the *lei* makers.

Once participants had been selected, queries were sent out to them about the supplies they would need for their cooking and crafts demonstrations. One list in particular highlights the complexity of realizing Hawai'i traditions in a de-contextualized site. Ah Wan and Jane Goo from Kaua'i had been selected to demonstrate *imu* cooking, the traditional method of preparing food for a *lū'au*. The plan was to demonstrate the cooking method by preparing a number of traditional foods. An internal memo from Moriarty to Brodie (1989) contains the following list of required materials.

EQUIPMENT NEEDS:

A. IMU:

1. ONE HOLE: 2½' deep with 4' x 4' dimension, must have good loose dirt to cover
2. WOOD: need two cords for all imus
3. IMU STONES: three wheelbarrows
4. TI LEAF: 8 sacks per imu, 32 sacks for all imus
5. BANANA STUMPS: 7 trunks per imu, 4' long with at least a 6" diameter, 28 stumps for all imus
6. BURLAP BAGS: 10 bags can be reused for each imu
7. CANVAS: 10' x 10' to cover imu
8. CORRUGATED IRON: 3' x 4" to cover kulolo cans
9. SHOVELS: 4 shovels 5' long with all metal base

10. PICK: with a good pointed end to open coconuts with
11. FIRE STARTER: ½ large can wizard charcoal starter
12. CHICKEN WIRE: 1 sq yard of 1" mesh
13. COOKING PANS: 2 disposable aluminum foil turkey pans to fit turkeys in for all imus
14. ALUMINUM FOIL: 1 large width roll for all imus

IMU FOOD NEEDS PER WEEK:

1. PIG: 80 lbs slaughtered and cleaned, will yield 60 lbs of edible pork, need 1 pig per week
2. TURKEY: two 20 lb turkey per week
3. SWEET POTATO: 20 lbs per week
4. 20 lbs of Hawaiian salt per imu

KULOLO FOOD NEED to prepare 1, 4-can imu:

1. TARO: 1 100 lb bag of mature taro corm per imu
2. SUGAR: 15 lbs white granulated per imu
3. COCONUTS: 50 mature coconuts per imu
4. TI LEAVES: 84 leaves per imu, plus leaves needed to cover the imu

Anyone who has ever organized a picnic for a large crowd will appreciate the amount of careful planning this list encompasses. Not only does it anticipate cooking in an environment where none of the usual tools are at hand, but it also estimates quantities for supplies that would have to be brought in from Hawai‘i because they were not readily available on the mainland. The emphasis on authenticity also incorporated new challenges for the production crew. A hole seems a simple enough requirement, but a hole is not easy to come by on the National Mall, where the National Park Service had strict prohibitions against digging.[13] Presentation was also an issue. Traditional rural cooking methods might not be seen in the same way in an urban metropolis where cooking whole pigs risked bringing out the animal rights protesters.[14] Additionally, tropical ingredients had to be secured, and substitution was a last resort. Moriarty had made handwritten notes on the supply list, saying that banana stumps might be a problem although they might be able to replace them with cabbage, and that sweet potatoes did not mean yams. In the case of supplies that had to be the real thing, she identified suppliers for items to be shipped: *ti* leaves, Hawaiian salt, taro, and coconuts. Fifteen hundred *ti* leaves were shipped from Kapa‘a on Kaua‘i, and one hundred coconuts sewn into burlap bags were shipped from Lāʻie on Oʻahu, along with various types of coconut leaves for weaving. The price tag for this small piece of the whole production was $1,445 before shipping (Purchase Order 1989). Supply lists were produced for other participants as well—each entailing their own logistics.

It is one thing to draw up an ideal plan for re-constituting Hawaiʻi in sight of the Capitol Building, but obtaining the materials to do it is sometimes another story altogether, one in which appearance sometimes had to stand in for the real thing. In addition to plant materials needed for cooking, weaving, and herbalists, the site design in all its stages had been conceived with an abundance of tropical plants in mind. However, according to the U.S. Department of Agriculture (USDA) (1980), Hawaiʻi is treated as a foreign location subject to quarantine rules. Importation is limited to only soil-free plants, and some plants are prohibited altogether.[15] This posed a potential problem for overall site enhancement, the taro field, and herbalists who needed plant materials for their demonstrations. Furthermore, the USDA requires that all categories of plants imported into the United States be listed by scientific or accepted names in English (U.S. Department of Agriculture 1980), hence requiring Hawaiian plant names to be translated. An effective demonstration *loʻi* would require taro in various stages of maturation, so Festival staff worked with the Smithsonian Horticulture Division to have them provide plants. From a nursery in Boca Raton, Florida, $8,420 worth of plants for the site was ordered. These ranged in height from the one-inch to two-inch range to 112 palms from four to five feet high. The OFP saved money by ordering "B" grade plants, for, as Lau pointed out in a memo to Kennedy, "considering what 3 weeks on the mall will do to them, 'B' grade is definitely worth the savings."[16]

Papa Auwe, Native Hawaiian *lāʻau lapaʻau* practitioner from the Big Island, needed fresh plants that could be "grown" on the Mall. Ethnobotanists at the Smithsonian were called on for help procuring the plants and providing scientific names for plants known by their Hawaiian names. While Papa Auwe's plants needed to be authentic, the plants for the site were approximated to create the desired site appearance.

The acquisition and transport of some supplies was more labor intensive than for others. Rather than build a facsimile *yagura,* Hawaiʻi organizers located a temple in Honolulu that was willing to lend theirs despite the fact there had been some initial resentment that only a Kauaʻi *bon* dance group would be representing Japanese *bon* dances from Hawaiʻi. The *yagura* had to be disassembled and packed into a twenty-foot shipping container for transport to Washington, D.C. It also had to be returned before *bon* dance season in August.[17] Obtaining lava rocks was another challenge. The plan was for Thomas Kamaka Emmsley, a rock-wall builder from Maui, to arrive early and construct walls on the site. There are many kinds of lava in Hawai'i, and it needed to be *a'a,* the type typically used for walls. Although there are people who maintain that the reason lava rocks were not brought from Hawai'i was because of the commonly held belief that removing rocks from the islands will result in bad luck for the remover, it is much more likely that cost was the major factor in the decision to find suitable lava elsewhere. In fact, *imu* stones, which are a particular kind of lava rock, *were* sent from Hawai'i—by a man in Kāne'ohe (a town on the east side of O'ahu) whose wife happened to be living in Washington, D.C., and who was active in the Hawai'i State Society (HSS). Lava was needed for rock-wall building demonstrations, to surround the hula stage, and "to delineate entrances and program boundaries." Brodie contacted a number of rock wholesalers and through the Bureau of Land Management in Shoshone, Idaho, finally located sufficient lava rock; however, the cost to ship them by rail and truck to D.C. was astronomical. A flurry of correspondence took place as the Festival dates edged closer. The problem was not helped by the fact that none of the rock dealers in the D.C. area was familiar enough with lava to help with estimates. Brodie's letters to Idaho sound like a grade-school word problem: "A few questions—what is the ratio of lava rock in volume to weight? If we ship by rail, how may tons will a rail car hold?"[18]

Brodie also had the task of procuring people and horses for a *pā'ū* parade—a form of parade pageantry in Hawai'i in which a court of female riders dress in elaborate skirts made from many yards of fabric wrapped to look like a skirt and riders and horses are decked out in beautiful *lei.* This hybrid tradition, which had emerged out of a Hawaiian practice and been adapted into a local and tourist spectacle, was included after the fieldwork meetings. The equestrian riding unit, a standard feature in Hawai'i parades since at least 1903, was a portion of the program recommended by Martin and was included when a donor had designated funds to send six island *pā'ū* princesses and their costumes to the Festival. Each princess would represent a major island in its traditional colors: Hawai'i, red; Maui, pink; O'ahu, black and gold; Kaua'i, purple; Moloka'i, green; and Lāna'i, orange.[19] To cut costs, Martin had suggested that escorts could be recruited from the D.C.-area HSS.[20] Horses were secured from Tyler, Texas. Twelve male riders were to be identified and coached in their responsibilities so that they would be able to appropriately play their roles as escorts. Again, authenticity was a relative issue. Hawai'i pageantry would be performed by the female riders, and the borrowed props—in this case the male riders and the horses—would support their performance in a practice that owed its continued existence to tourism.

Concessions

Since medieval times, the fair has been a space where goods are sold or bartered, and the Festival does its best to avoid this kind of image, yet it contains concessions reminiscent of the fair and crucial to its economic survival. National Park Service regulations now prohibit buying and selling on the Mall proper, and the sale of crafts and other program-related items is relegated to designated areas on the sidewalks in front of the Smithsonian museums. In 1989 the rules were not so strict. Program coordinators recognized the profit potential if they could sell flower *lei* and other items during the Festival and considered the museum shops and the HSS as possible vendors. Folkways Records, headed by Anthony Seeger, proposed an audiocassette tape anthology of Hawai'i performers that would be available for sale during the Hawai'i program. To this end, Folkways contacted performers from Hawai'i to ask if they would be willing to contribute pre-recorded pieces to such an enterprise. Performers were told that Folkways did not expect to make much money off of the tape but that they would give each of them fifty copies. Musicians were asked to select their favorite recordings and send them to Seeger. The idea was to produce a tape that fit the ideals of the Festival, "a double cultural creation" that was a collaboration between performers and producers, although any profits would be channeled back to Folkways, a nonprofit agency, for its projects (Seeger 1988).

Traditionality and marketability conflicted in plans for Festival concessions. The Smithsonian museum shops were in charge of the marketplace, and a representative had made a trip to Hawai'i to determine what goods could be sold during the Festival.[21] He made the rounds of the shops in Hawai'i and came up with a list of items that he sent to Martin. In her letter to him, she tactfully told him that none of the things he had listed were folk or traditional arts of Hawai'i and suggested that he contact the Pacific Handcrafters Guild if he was interested in contemporary crafts such as wind chimes, stuffed animals, and jewelry rather than limiting himself to commercial enterprises. Clearly, he had been looking for small items that could be sold as souvenirs (a word that is never used at the Festival) rather than handicrafts made by the craftspeople who would be participating in the Festival. While there are many craftspeople in the islands, they generally do not sell through the tourist-oriented shops, many of which carry low-priced items made in the Philippines and Asia. Most traditional Hawaiʻi handicrafts, such as quilting and *lau-hala* hats, are labor intensive, and the products can be quite expensive. Martin recommended that the museum representative talk with Moriarty, who had operated a Pacific import business, and sent him a list of craftspeople he could contact directly. As an advocate for traditional artists, she pointed out that traditional handicrafts are produced in limited quantities but that many people would be proud to have their work sold through the Smithsonian shops. As a businessperson, the buyer was most concerned with cost effectiveness and marketability.

Food concessions were considerably easier. With a direct tie to the multicultural emphasis of the Festival, the decision was made to serve a version of the local "mixed plate," heavy on the Hawaiian food. The mixed plate—usually a combination of ethnic foods accompanied by rice—had entered the planning through fieldwork discussions as a metaphor for cultural sharing, so the concept was generally accepted as being a practical alternative to choosing which foods to feature for nine ethnic groups. Unfortunately, all anyone remembers is that the food sold by the concessions was universally bad. Due to health department regulations that prohibit demonstration food from being served to the public, visitors were able to watch delicious ethnic foods being prepared but then had to eat a tasteless facsimile at the food concessions.

Textual Productions

Although most visitors experience the Folklife Festival as performance, interpretation of that performance is not left to chance. The Festival is heavily "captioned"—by promotional materials, signs, program books, and even structures. These captions are never simply informational; they are crucial to executing the Festival's educational mission and telling visitors how to filter Festival sites and sights; they form a narrative through which a variety of performances are strung together into a coherent whole. Formulation of Festival text and subtext begins in the planning phase, when the overarching theme for a particular program is hammered out. It is put into actual production when the fieldwork phase is completed and the curator has a corpus of materials and ideas from which to work. The Festival itself is a discursive field, and the textual materials for any program are fitted within the template of the general Festival concept, which has its own carefully constructed jargon to symbolically differentiate it from tourism. It is crafted with care as neighborly, intimate, and inclusive; people in the audience are referred to as "visitors" and never tourists, and tradition bearers are called "participants" to stress their active involvement in presenting their cultural processes. Tourism implies outsiders and insiders, viewers and viewed. The Festival is about "us," so there can be no such easy divisions. In the literature, the interactions between those onstage and off are described as "sharing" and "conversation." In the words of OFP director Richard Kurin, "the festival cultivates dialogue, not didacticism" (1989, 15). Promotional literature states that the purpose is "to celebrate," and the atmosphere is described as "spontaneous" and "festive." These parameters framed and guided the textual productions for the Hawai'i program from signs to the program book.

Signs at the Festival, like the godlike omniscient narrator in a novel, are a framing device, the disembodied voice of cultural authority. As emissaries for Festival ideals, they narrate the philosophy on which the Festival turns: that cultural diversity is superior to cultural hegemony and necessary to national health, that there is social value in communities learning from each other, that there is vast creativity in the ways that communities craft identity and adapt to change. As program markers, signs articulate the narrative honed by the organizers to frame performance and display.

Hawai'i program signs relied on three forms: maps, text, and photographs.[22] Maps of the Hawaiian Islands were prominently displayed throughout the program. They operated as reminders that Hawai'i is a collection of islands in the Pacific and that what visitors were seeing was culture de-contextualized despite the care given to creating illusions of reality. Historical and contemporary photographs were juxtaposed with texts wherever appropriate. Photographs were especially effective, along with maps, as a means for re-contextualizing de-contextualized performance. Six signs were devoted entirely to photographs of spectacular land and waterscapes. Other photos showed the vegetation, structures in situ, dancers on a *hula* mound, and traditional arts in their home contexts. Historical photos provided a visual link to the past by presenting the Hawaiian monarchy, plantation work and housing, early immigrants in attire from their homelands, and the before and after views of development.

In addition to depicting instruments, occupations, and native plants, images advocated conservation of both natural and cultural resources. Maps and photographs did this visually while narrative knit images to ideas. Textual captions for the Hawai‘i program filled in gaps, explained processes, and represented the otherwise un-representable. Signs informed performance by presenting history and cultural information that could not be made readily apparent through performance. Signage served as a corrective and supplement to dominant histories by inserting immigrants into Hawai‘i's cultural landscape and correcting colonially inflected accounts of indigenous history. For instance, a sign on *hula* and chant explained that missionaries "managed to ban it for at least 50 years." This sign and one on the Hawaiian renaissance inserted discordant notes into the generally benign multicultural presentation, albeit relegated to a footnote on the past.[23] Ironically, signs were needed to flesh out the live exhibits, and occasionally offered the possibility to move beyond Festival parameters. For instance, a sign explaining the concept of *‘ohana* featured an actual genealogy for a presenter who had multiple ancestries. On the one hand, this sign recognized the widespread practice of miscegenation in Hawai‘i and problematized the mainland and Festival multicultural paradigms. On the other hand, it reiterated the "unity in diversity" theme of the Festival ideology.

Sign texts addressed what could not easily be displayed on the Mall, such as fishing, canoe racing, *pā‘ū* riding, and surfing. Information that fell outside program definitions also appeared in signage, such as the reinvention of Polynesian navigation and voyaging (without mentioning that the teacher had been a Micronesian or that the art had been lost and re-taught) and the development of *hapa-haole* music (which had been banned from performance at the Hawai‘i program). Signs made space for some conflict to be voiced; however, most sign texts operated to reinforce the Festival theme, to note cultural contributions of the various ethnic groups to the whole, and, by extension, to underscore the Festival mission of valorizing democratic culture through folklife. These signs spoke to concepts adopted by the program as iconic of a Hawai‘i ethos: *‘ohana*, *aloha*, and reciprocity symbolized through flower *lei* exchange.

Twelve signs in the learning center were allotted to individual ethnic groups and filled in gaps by adding immigrant histories and information about immigration. While they made room for accounts of U.S. immigration restrictions, in places they sounded suspiciously like the format of good news/bad news jokes where positive and negative messages are always presented in tandem. The introductory sign to this exhibit read "They Settled in Hawai'i," and the text relates that "new visitors, mass media and foreign investment are altering the landscape of Hawai'i, but communities are responding to the changes with a renewed pride in their own cultures and in the unique, multi-ethnic heritage of their state." This rhetoric set the tone for the remaining panels by presenting an idyllic view that precluded any glimpses of the massive out-migration and displacement or ecological costs of immigration and infiltration; in the signage, damaging forces are pleasantly trumped by islander flexibility and pride of place. The effect of this presentation was double-edged: in one breath a reader was informed of the existence of a problem, and in the next that a solution was already in progress.

Haole had been omitted from performance but were included in a sign that read "Europeans and Americans" identifying them as skilled workers in various occupations and tracing their presence from early immigration to economic domination. This sign also noted that 25 percent of the population were recent European and American immigrants from the military, business transplants, retirees, and former tourists who, it went on to say, were arriving in the islands at the rate of five million a year. "Hawai'i is the most militarized state in the United States" (Ferguson and Turnbull 1999, 1), yet this sign is the only place in which the military is mentioned in the Hawai'i program information. Likewise, Mormons, a strong presence in the islands since the early 1900s, were mentioned only as an aside on the Samoan sign and elsewhere omitted. What these omissions indicate is that in a venue dedicated to championing under-represented populations, there is little room in which to expose or discuss the hegemonies that govern their daily existence.

The sign for "The Hawaiians" related how powerful foreigners drastically altered Hawaiian traditions and stated that half of the population died from disease after contact, but also stated that "the influence of Hawaiian culture pervades all aspects of contemporary island society even though the original Hawaiian population continued to decrease in number." It concluded on a positive note by talking about the Hawaiian cultural renaissance as a movement in which people from other groups who were "Hawaiian in spirit" participated and did not mention demographics or socioeconomics for Native Hawaiians in the present. Hawaiian activists were mentioned in the "Hawaiian Renaissance" sign, but the focus on traditionality contained and dismissed them by associating them solely with universities, implying that they were disconnected from "real" Hawaiians—those at the Festival. The result of these portrayals was a narrative that honored cultural resurgence while preempting political activism and identity.

Overall, the signs for ethnic groups followed a recognizable formula that served to structure a collective national and regional identity by inserting immigrant histories into the quintessential American "rags to riches" narrative form (Boatright 1958, 1–19) by posing conditions in the home country against immigrant success stories. The focus throughout the learning center display was on survival, continuity, and creativity—a combination that relegated conflict to the past in order to reinforce unity in the present. The Chinese sign mentioned that Chinese were currently only 5 percent of the population but that they "play an important role in the economic and social life of the islands." This is quite an understatement compared to perceptions discussed openly in the fieldwork review meeting that the Chinese had become rich on real estate in Hawai'i and continued to be very insular in relation to other communities. Nor does it recognize that many of the Chinese in Hawai'i in 1989 had recently come from Taiwan or Hong Kong and were not necessarily affiliated with those who came to the islands from the Guangdong region as plantation laborers. The sign about local Japanese mentioned that the Japanese had been the largest immigrant group until the 1960s but did not mention their economic or political success in Hawai'i after World War II. Instead, it portrayed the history of picture brides and the active preservation of court dance and music. The Okinawan sign discussed how Okinawans identify as separate from the Japanese, and the Korean sign mentioned that they had boycotted Japanese goods at one time, but neither made mention of Japanese colonialism in the Pacific, and nowhere was Japanese investment in the islands engaged, although the Hawai'i economy was painfully inflated at the time due to the speculative investments of Japanese nationals (Okamura 1994, 161–178). Issues of tourism and development were treated in much the same benign manner.

Some signs were tied to special interests. The history of the sugar plantations in Hawai'i was told through the lending of a special exhibit called "Paia: Looking Back," produced by Gaylord C. Kubota for the Alexander and Baldwin Sugar Museum, a facility that commemorates one of the major sugar producers in the islands. This exhibit, produced for a plantation worker reunion sponsored by the company, did reveal a great deal about plantation life, but the history was focused entirely on the cultural experience of workers. While the text accompanying photos acknowledged that laborers were placed in separate camps according to ethnicity "to discourage cooperation among ethnic groups in the event of labor dissatisfaction," it submerged this information by privileging positives: that this separation fostered the perpetuation of language and custom, eased transition from the homeland to the plantation environment, and fostered "a natural interaction."

This account omitted the role of harsh conditions and unequal wages in these happy outcomes. The resulting image of plantation life was a biased view in which Alexander and Baldwin are touted as "pioneers" and in which "plantation camps melded into interracial communities whose members shared a common spirit and experiences." This view may reflect an outcome in accord with the desire of former workers to remember their experiences through a lens of nostalgia rather than victimization; however, it omitted key elements in any melding that did take place, such as unionization and labor strikes and universal opposition to company abuses of plantation workers. A brief critical view of the plantation system appeared on the signs for Portuguese immigrants. It mentioned only that they had received higher wages and been made *luna*s, or labor bosses. These signs left it to visitors to read the unstated subtexts hinted at in these interpretations of the plantation experience.

Signage formed a critical link between concept and visual spectacle. In tandem with live exhibition, the signage conjured missing places and narrativized cultural/historical continuity. It also served as the insertion point for the political, albeit a contained, historicized version that, on the surface, reduced debates over citizenship and identity to past issues that had been seemingly resolved by statehood. Still, the insertion of multiple local histories into national space, and by extension the national narrative, might be seen to constitute debate in a reformulated context and underline the Festival's mission to be, as much as possible, a setting for dialogue. If the dominant discourse is seen as an erasure of Hawai'i's multi-ethnic population, its plantation history, its seizure and control by the U.S., and the transformations to a tourist economy, then the narrative constructed by the signage is progressive even if muted and apologetic in places. From this perspective, the Hawai'i program signage was one half of a conversation conceived in opposition to the dominant discourse, an intervention in hegemonic discourse.

An impressive amount of ethnographic, botanical, and historical information was packed into the Hawai'i program signs, despite the limitations of space, but visitors can neither be led to signs nor made to read them; audience absorption of the information offered by signs is an uncontrollable element. Their creation is an act of faith in the patience, literacy, and intellectual curiosity of the festival-going audience. Making signs attractive and brief and placing them at eye level, in the shade, and contiguous to live exhibits were strategies that sharpened the possibility that they would be perused, but thorough reading is never assured and digestion difficult to assess.[24] The question also remains as to whether in a festival that proclaims to give voice to its participants signage acts as amplification or obfuscation. In whose voice(s) do the signs speak? Do they replace one official paradigm with another? The ideal is that they represent an incorporation of the research, planning, and fieldwork processes; however, textual productions distill the many voices of the information-gathering process into one singularly authoritative voice. In Festival signs, the Smithsonian Institution, itself a discursive field in which the OFP is a small and often aberrant agency, fulfills the role of omniscient narrator and ultimate cultural authority.

Program Book

Whereas signage is necessarily a hit-and-miss, patchwork sort of educational enterprise, the annual Festival program book is an opportunity to package the Festival concept into a coherent and portable product. If the consumption of signage is limited to the reading public (i.e., those who would take the time to read a sign and measure its meaning and impact in relation to performance), the audience for the program book is further constricted by being limited first to those who would and could afford to buy it and, second, to those who would actually read it rather than simply use it for the maps and daily schedules and/or take it home as a souvenir. A dim and hopeful third would be people who bought it, took it home, and read it cover to cover rather than skimming and looking at pictures. Program books, which over the years have become attractive 8½ x 11 catalogs filled with photographs and brief scholarly articles, are produced in advance to be sold at the Festival. Cleverly, the CFCH has determined that placing the daily performance schedules and maps in the program book encourages sales and allows for piggybacking scholarly perspectives on practical information.[25]

Although the program book for the 1989 Festival encompasses all four programs for the year—Caribbean, Native American, French Traditions, and Hawai‘i—the cover of the program clearly indicates that

Hawai'i was the centerpiece of the Festival. A color photograph by Martin of two *pā'ū* riders appears on the cover. One rider faces forward and one to the side. Both women and their horses are wearing elaborate flower and foliage *lei* and the standard costume comprising many yards of fabric. The woman in the foreground wears a flower headpiece and a velvet cape. An observant viewer in Hawai'i might notice that the photo was taken during the Merrie Monarch Festival in Hilo and that the rider in the foreground appears to be *hapa*. The choice of this photo invites contradictory interpretations. It rejects the familiar tourist industry iconicization of the *hula* girl, yet it reiterates the use of a flower-bedecked, brown-skinned, and racially ambiguous woman to signify Hawai'i. Embracing all sides of the authenticity debates from the fieldwork and productions processes, it foregrounds an image of creolized tradition—horses and Western dress adapted to a Hawaiian aesthetic and representing royalty that no longer exist—that emerged out of colonialism and has become central to pageantry performed for both local communities and tourists.

The program book became the one site in which otherwise invisible frames of authority were made unmistakably visible. Each book begins with statements from those in charge arranged in order of their level of relative power. The 1989 book contains grand conceptual statements from secretary of the Smithsonian Robert McCormick Adams, "Celebrating Freedom"; director of the National Park Service James M. Riddenour, "Our Shared Cultural Resources"; and director of the OFP Richard Kurin, "Why We Do the Festival." Each of these articles addresses the Festival in terms of how it enriches national identity. Following the directorial addresses are scholarly articles, one per program, that serve to frame each of the Festival programs.[26] In the back of the book are, in order, general information, a list of Festival participants, site maps and schedules for each of the programs, sponsor lists, and the names of Festival staff. Contrary to Festival rhetoric, which inverts power by placing participants on top, it is worth noting that Festival participants—the central attractions—are centrally embedded in the book, midway between directors and scholars and sponsors and staff. In other words, participants are encountered through the legitimizing voices of officials and culture scholars but supported by the sponsors and staff—an accurate mini-model of Festival hierarchy and institutional protocol.

Underlining a focus on cultural blending and adaptation in the scholarly articles and on links between groups and ethnic practices in the signs and site, participants are listed by traditional practices rather than by ethnicity. Cultural practices, on the other hand, are listed by ethnicity except in the genres of occupational traditions and crafts. The result is that ethnicizing traditions rather than people served to distinguish ethnic groups without privileging the distinction.

The program book was also the one site in which the entire Festival was presented as a whole since despite the juxtaposition of programs on the Mall, even site designs are individually orchestrated within programs and by program-specific staffs. In the 1989 program book the programs seem conceptually linked through article titles (in order): "American Indian Problems of Access and Cultural Continuity," by Thomas Vennum, Jr.; "Hawai'i: Cosmopolitan Culture at the Crossroads of the Pacific," by Richard Kennedy with Lynn Martin; "French Traditions: Their History and Continuity in North America," by Winnie Lambrecht; and "Creolization in the Caribbean," by Helena Portes de Roux.

The last two articles are preceded by a page in French. Hawai'i and Native Americans are not accorded an alternative language space, presumably because they are polyglot entities and American. The 1989 articles thematically linked four programs that came together as accidents of history and funding.[27] They cohered remarkably well, but it must be remembered that an editing and design team was given the job of producing a unified product out of seemingly disparate parts—imposing yet another lens on the Festival concept. The key operative words were "creolization" and "continuity," and together they were applied to dislodge tradition from the backwoods of the past and project it into modernity while animating it with creativity in the face of change. This dialogic dynamism is especially apparent in the article written by Kennedy with Martin.

Kennedy's article is presented in four parts that highlight the program themes in Martin's signage: "sense of place," hospitality, continuity, adaptation, cultural integrity, and creolization. The use of creolization as a keyword to describe Hawai'i culture focuses on cultural processes rather than on hybrid products and emphasizes the adaptation and agency themes privileged in the signage. Hawaiian words with diacritical marks are used throughout the article, a symbolic gesture that recognizes the resurgence and politicization of Hawaiian language by trying to present it authentically and with cultural sensitivity. (Although today readers would note that the *okina,* or glottal stop, was typed backwards, the use of diacriticals was still new at the time and not yet standardized.)[28] Because the program book needed to link the four programs, the article needed to link nine ethnicities as well as tie the past to the present and fill in historical gaps. The title, "Hawai'i: Cosmopolitan Culture at the Crossroads of the Pacific," is already a counterstatement to tourist imaginings of Hawai'i as an atemporal American playground. A look at a denotation of cosmopolitanism illustrates what a radical departure this article takes from tourist productions in utilizing this term as a label:

1. having worldwide rather than limited or provincial scope or bearing.
2. having wide international sophistication: worldly.
3. composed of persons, constituents, or elements from all or many parts of the world.[29]

In his introduction about the importance of the Hawaiian Islands' isolated but central geographical location, Kennedy invokes all of these meanings as a way of introducing Hawai'i cultural dynamics. All four sections are focused on a "sense of place." In the first section, which covers Polynesian migration, Kennedy historicizes and explains an often appropriated and misunderstood phrase meaning love of the land that had become a slogan of the Hawaiian renaissance: "*Aloha 'āina* is not a romantic concept arising out of a need to reestablish roots in the soil; it is rather, a ecological necessity born of people who had no choice but to accommodate themselves to the islands that became their home." Kennedy makes this point in order to contrast early Hawaiian ecologically sound land use with the ecological devastation wrought by immigration and development. His discussion reiterates the bifurcation between a "sense of place" and a "sense of displace" introduced in the fieldwork meetings and represented in the earliest site design. He inserts the ravages of disease and colonization to applaud Hawaiian adaptability: "Hawaiians today may appear to be more acculturated, but perhaps less concerned with their origins than their Polynesian neighbors in the South, but this implies no inherent weakness in Hawaiian culture. In fact, Hawaiian cultural accommodation over the years can be attributed to the strategic position of the islands in the center of the Pacific and their colonization by European and American powers."

Kennedy characterizes European and American colonization as an unparalleled invasion that caused massive dislocation and reduced Hawaiians to "a minority in their own land." But the Festival is about empowerment, continuity, and creativity, so even here this unhappy history is subjugated to a good news/bad news formula that emphasizes cultural survival, invention, and amalgamation. Thus the attachment to place is presented as a remarkable achievement in itself given the theft of Hawaiian land by outsiders, and the evidence given is a thread of continuity that is woven through Hawaiian music, dance, and crafts. The good news is that Hawaiians emerge from this treatment as heroic survivors to be respected and admired for their creativity. The bad news is that the message of the Hawaiian movement—that ongoing neo-colonialism still exists in Hawai'i—is eclipsed.

This contrast, in turn, works as a foundation for a discussion of the soundness of Hawaiian values and the ecological devastation wrought by contact. The second section, "Āpuka 'Āina: The Desire for Land," continues this direction by contrasting the suppression of traditional culture in the missionary era with the creativity of Hawaiian quilting, and the third section, "Ho'olioli 'Āina: Transformation of the Land," juxtaposes the dislocations and harshness of immigration and plantation life with intermarriage and cultural borrowing with other ethnic groups. The final section, "Lu'au, Lei, and Plate Lunch: Culture in Hawai'i," contrasts cultural loss with cultural revival for Hawaiians and cultural adaptation and continuity for former immigrant communities. The *lei*, the *lū'au*, and the plate lunch are then each explored as symbols of how the host and guest cultures have intermingled and emerged as local culture. Kennedy momentarily mentions current socioeconomic reality in his conclusion, saying,

> Hawai'i is a complex state that is home to an incredible array of ethnic groups and cultures. Each of these groups has maintained its unique identity and at the same time blended to create "local" traditions that are expressive of the community as a whole. However, increasing pressures from foreign investment and mass media are today further disenfranchising native Hawaiians and threatening the stability of several generations of other cultures in the islands. (1989, 36–49)

Throughout this piece, ugly counter-histories are introduced. Each time they are offset by the agency of the victimized. While the goal is precisely that—to accord agency to victims of oppression and/or dislocation and hardship—the effect tends to blunt any message about ongoing effects of oppression. At no point is America held responsible for current socioeconomic disparities in Hawai'i. In the present, it is the nebulous forces of foreign investment and mass media that are presented as a threat, one aimed at traditional culture and to which cultural preservation is posed as the solution: "Hawai'i's characteristic attitude of tolerance and acceptance, molded in part by centuries of isolation, may be compromised by such pressures. Preserving these arts is crucial, for a community's psychic well-being is only as strong as its commitment to protecting its traditions." Although the intent may have been to stir potential donors and perhaps government agencies to the task of cultural preservation, the charge to preserve tradition seems to be laid on the doorstep of tradition bearers, perhaps with the help of cultural agencies like the Smithsonian and the HSFCA.

Overall, the Kennedy article appears to be an attempt to resolve differences between at least two Hawai'i narratives: a post-colonial Pacific narrative that exposes the ravages of colonialism and a multicultural one that posits cultural preservation programs as the solution. It is unique in the textual production of the program in that it presents sociocultural issues and warnings in the present, but these are topics neatly balanced with a naturalization of the host culture's hospitality, made legendary by the tourist industry.

* * *

Paying attention to the spatial logic that shapes and constrains performance raises questions about the ways in which performance is directed by site design, and examining the program's textual productions sheds light on how master narratives direct the festivalgoer's gaze. For the Hawai'i program, "A Sense of Place" was a spatial strategy and guiding principle shaped and reshaped between local and national interests and within Festival parameters. The result was a stage set for a re-imagined Hawai'i that would stretch festivalgoers' preconceptions, an expanded but localized Hawai'i fitted within both a national narrative and a national space. In keeping with this paradox, before the opening of the Hawai'i program, when the behind-the-scenes production phase was about to transform into public performance, organizers gathered the participants for a preparatory speech in which they told participants "to take ownership of the space and make it their own." That this expansive directive was immediately trumped by a list of National Park Service rules highlights the difficulties implicit in creating Festival space on the nation's front lawn.[30]

Two anecdotes in conversation with each other speak to the complexity of the production process and suggest a way of viewing how it was instrumental in articulating a narrative of the "real Hawai'i" that reflected a debate over authenticity.

The first anecdote demonstrates how interpretation of textual production depends on the ideological bents of the writers and readers. During the fieldwork phase, Kennedy chose a quote that he felt poignantly expressed the ethos of the Hawai'i program and used it on the first page of his in-house production report:

> A'ohe o kāhi nānā o luna o ka pali; iho mai a lalo nei; 'ike i ke au nui ke au iki, he alo a he alo.
>
> The top of the cliff isn't the place to look at us; come down here and learn of the big and little currents, face to face.[31]

Kennedy said he was drawn to the quote because he felt that it spoke in an indigenous voice to invite those who held themselves apart or aloft to a closer view of culture, one that would demystify stereotypes and debunk hype. In that sense, it encapsulated the ethos of the Festival, the mission to valorize the creativity and tenacity of traditional practices. He planned to use the quote in the program book to set the program theme. When Napoka saw the quote, however, he laughed and said Kennedy had it all wrong. In its Hawaiian context, Napoka said, the quote was actually a challenge inviting warriors to come down and fight, an invitation to battle to the death.[32] The implicit lesson is that culture broker perceptions are often not all that is needed for the interpretation task.

The second story takes place in Volcanoes National Park on the Big Island. A short hiking trail leads onto a lava field dotted by petroglyphs where a small sign is a striking example of the power of contestations underlying sites and signage. Most of the petroglyphs at this location are small, round depressions in the lava with circles carved around them. A circular boardwalk is suspended above them so that visitors can view the petroglyphs but not walk directly on the lava bed. A sign on the wooden railing explains that this place was once considered powerful and sacred enough that Hawaiians came here to bury the umbilical cords of their newborns to ensure the protection of the gods. Another sign asks visitors to stay on the walkway to help preserve the heritage of the "Hawaiians who lived here." But the sign's meaning has been altered. An anonymous editor boldly crossed out the "d" in "lived," and the sign now reads as a protest against the museumization of Hawai'i's indigenous people: Hawaiians LIVE here.

Together these two stories, one writ by a culture broker's hand and one by an anonymous cultural subject, emphasize the gap between lived cultural experience and cultural interpretation. The challenge in producing the Hawai'i program was to move beyond museumization using ordering strategies that framed, categorized, and narrativized the workings of Hawai'i folklife, while using the tools central to museum production processes. The materials created in the production phase—the site design and structures, the signs, the book of the program—became part of the loop of meaning making in the discursive field of the Festival's culture industry.

Chapter 4

Performing "The Other Side of the Island"

Hawai'i is unique in our nation in that its indigenous culture suffuses its society as a whole, giving nuance to the forms of immigrant cultures that came there.

—Robert McCormick Adams, *Festival of American Folklife Program Book*

Prior to the opening of the 1989 Festival, the Hawai'i program production crew had worked hard to transform the physical site into a sensory experience that evoked the islands, and the results must have been effective. One longtime Festival volunteer reminiscing fourteen years later recalled that "it looked like Hawai'i," although Hawai'i was a destination he had never visited.[1] And in many ways the site must have evoked Hawai'i for arriving participants as well as visitors. Potted palms and the sight and scent of tropical flowers were everywhere. Despite its location in the middle of an area that stretched from 10th to 14th Streets, the Festival site included an open canoe shed. The Hawaiian music stage was open-air with low lava-rock walls and benches for the audience. Nearby was a small, water-filled *lo'i* with young taro plants. Opposite the Hawaiian stage stood the *yagura* with strings of colorful paper lanterns festooned from the top of the tower to the crafts booths arranged around its perimeter. Between these Native Hawaiian and Asian attractions were booths for indigenous and immigrant occupations and crafts, a demonstration kitchen, a shave-ice stand, and a narrative stage disguised as an old-time store. Missing from this carefully selected assortment of sights, sounds, and smells of Hawai'i was the ocean, but there were photographs posted throughout the site to evoke even that. Also missing were the participants who would populate the site and, in their interchanges with each other and with visitors, bring the Festival to life with their performance within and around the program's physical location over the next two weeks.

The performance phase of the Hawai'i program complicates questions about cultural authority, the ethics of representation, authenticity, and tradition by adding the wild card of participant agency. Pulling off a program of this magnitude is predicated on the deliberate erasure of its institutional frames, so what visitors to the Mall see, when things go right, is either orchestration that appears to be spontaneity or spontaneity that happens in spite of orchestration. What participants experience, when things proceed according to plan, is the imagined community of the Festival and connection with the festivalgoers. However, institutional representation of folklife raises questions about whether spontaneity and community can really be nudged into being by careful production. Can "festival"—in the sense of a liminal zone that transcends the everyday (Falassi 1987, 1)—actually combust in what organizers admit is really not a festival at all, but rather a museum masquerading as a festival?[2] Most important, how does performance mediate festival ethos and design?

This chapter looks at how performance became a site of contestation and negotiation once performers inhabited the carefully crafted site and narrative of the Hawai'i program. The planning through production phases of the Festival determined its casting, staging, and choreography and culminated in the performance phase, at which point the program took on a life of its own as a multi-sited, multi-vocal public spectacle. The first section of this chapter examines the preparation of performers (both presenters and participants) for their roles in the Hawai'i program. Subsequent sections consider how the program concept was transformed by being embodied and negotiated through and within the multiple programmatic frames. By considering performers' experiences in and perceptions of the Hawai'i program, this chapter considers how the dynamics of resistance, complicity, and collaboration play out in institutionally backed ethnographic display.

Framing Performance

One Native Hawaiian woman's reply to the letter she had received in April 1989 inviting her to be a participant in the Hawai'i program speaks for many and suggests that the OFP's position as respectful cultural advocate had been effectively communicated through the efforts of Kennedy and Moriarty. In her letter, future participant Pearl Garmon wrote, "It is with great honor and gratitude that I look forward to the 1989 Festival of American Folklife in Washington, D.C. I will do whatever is expected of me with great pride in my culture and the heritage of my past."[3] For her and others who agreed to go, the invitation was an honor and an opportunity, and because Hawai'i participants were to be treated as the nation's guests, the process of caring for them began well in advance of their late June arrival in Washington, D.C., and continued throughout their stay. Special attention was paid to preparing the Hawai'i crew before departure. Ironically, preliminary efforts to meld a cohesive community and avoid conflict at the Festival highlight the amount of negotiation required to achieve that end.

Although organizers claim that the Festival is relatively informal and emphasize that it is unscripted, a great deal of control must be exercised over Festival frames in order to produce a product that is in accord with its educational philosophy as well as to coordinate the logistics for such a large production. In particular, producing an image of harmonious diversity for Hawai'i, despite claims that this image represented reality, required pre-Festival coaching. Martin was aware of this need early on when she tactfully wrote in her 1988 survey document to Kennedy that it would be important to select congenial personalities: "When selecting the participants for the festival, we should look for not only the best representatives of each tradition, but the best 'mix' of representatives and how their individual spirits, skills, and personalities will harmonize with one another."

She also stressed that it was imperative to provide ample opportunities for participants to bond prior to departure.

> Once the participants are selected, it is very important to encourage a "team" or "'*ohana*" feeling among them prior to the departure to Washington, D.C. . . . Once in Washington, it is very important to set up opportunities for some bonding of the Hawai'i group to take place. At the orientation meeting, time should be set aside . . . for an elder Hawaiian to say a prayer in Hawaiian and/or English. There should also be an opportunity for an elder to bless the site of the festival and for everyone there to have at least one opportunity before opening day to gather together, hold hands, and unify their intent to share the best of Hawai'i through a prayer. My experience has been that doing these things assures the group that the organizers are respectful and sensitive to their traditional spiritual concerns. It also helps keep everyone

focused on the higher purpose of their presentation, keeps stamina up, frictions to a minimum, and charm at a maximum![4]

It is clear from Martin's directives to Kennedy that the desired outcome of pre-departure meetings was the molding of consensus among the staff and participants with regard to the state's Festival mission, so that Hawai'i could be represented as a unified entity. In other words, representing Hawai'i as a model community meant first transforming its delegation into one. Primed by the program themes conceived in the planning and fieldwork phases—the inclusive notions of *aloha,* "a sense of place," and *'ohana*—participants were being asked to serve as state delegates whose task, as the planning committees had agreed, would be putting "Hawai'i's best foot forward."

Keeping 136 participants—not counting the many family members accompanying them and the 21 presenters from Hawai'i—happy on a trans-Pacific, transcontinental journey was a formidable challenge, but the experienced Smithsonian staff handled the majority of the housekeeping details. The task facing Kennedy and Moriarty was forging the participants into a coherent yet diverse whole for performance in a new environment. This required meeting with them before departure and inculcating them with an attitude of ambassadorial teamwork as well as enabling as many of them as possible to meet each other, for although they were to be presented as a unified entity, most of them had not previously met. To this end, the OFP sent out pre-Festival packets and inquiries, and Moriarty and Kennedy hosted separate meetings for presenters and participants prior to departure.

Training presenters was an important component of the mission to care for the participants, so Kurin and Parker flew in from Washington, D.C., to represent the Smithsonian at the presenters' meeting. On April 29, 1989, the Smithsonian directors, Moriarty, and Kennedy met with presenters at the East-West Center from 9:30 A.M. to 5:00 P.M. to discuss the Festival program and the presenter role. Seventeen individuals—cultural specialists, community or academic scholars, and at least two craftspeople—had been selected to act as Festival presenters. Their job would be to give background information and facilitate interactions between participants and audiences as well as serve as liaisons between Festival staff and participants. All but one of the selected presenters were already familiar with the project because they had also been contracted as fieldworkers in the early phases of the program planning and had participated in the selection process. The additional presenter was Marie McDonald, a *lei* maker and former educator who had written a definitive book on Hawai'i *lei*. Wherever possible, presenters were matched with communities where they had previous dealings. Four more people, including Martin, who had been on maternity leave but had continued to work with the Festival as an advisor, and Moriarty, the Hawai'i coordinator, were also added to the presenting schedule.

More so than signage and the program book, presenters are the key component in program interpretation. They are the critical liaison to participants and a communication and information link between participants and audiences. They are charged with framing performances, inviting and fielding questions, interpreting cultural practices, and assisting with interactions between participants and visitors. At the preparatory meeting, they were told that presentation is another form of public performance: "Presenters are [a] special kind of performers at the Festival. Their performance is to communicate a face through which the audience can understand the performances of tradition-bearers."[5] Along with in-depth knowledge of a topic and its contexts, presenters were expected to have the ability to speak articulately and comfortably with a microphone to a large audience. Although Festival philosophy is mediated through signage and other textual productions, it is disseminated most directly by presenters, who form a visual and aural link to the Smithsonian (Kurin 1998, 85).

The need for presenters is predicated on the very nature of Festival performance. Although tradition bearers were experts in their respective traditions, possessing expertise did not guarantee that a participant was prepared for the public demands of Festival performance. Among the implicit criteria used in the fieldwork phase for selecting participants was the ability to communicate a traditional practice to the public and to answer any questions they might have about cultural practices. In other words, the educational facet of the Festival required that participants possess a degree of meta-consciousness about their skills and be able to articulate as well as perform them. For seasoned public performers accustomed to bantering with an audience in tourist venues, the presenter's challenge was sometimes to persuade them to trade disingenuous patter for a Festival ambience grounded in ideals of authenticity, informality, candor, and relative intimacy.[6]

Preparing the many people who were not performers presented a different set of challenges. Tradition bearers were selected because they had learned their craft through informal rather than academic transmission, and for this reason many of them did not have the sort of historical or scholarly information required to situate their cultural practices in an academically informed educational context. Language issues and lack of experience with crowds were other foreseeable obstacles. Although all of the participants were American citizens who were residents of the state of Hawai'i, for some of them, like the Hawaiians from Ni'ihau, English was a second language and one in which they were less comfortable.[7] Other participants were more conversant in pidgin than standardized English.[8] In addition to facilitating and interpreting performance, presenters were told they should look out for participants outside of performance times. Organizers were especially worried that participants who were traveling from relative isolation in rural areas would experience culture shock in an urban environment and in front of the huge crowds on the Mall.[9]

To enable the presenters to answer all questions in an ethnographically informed way and ensure the presentation of a more coherent and seamless program narrative to the public, presenters had been given packets prior to the April meeting that familiarized them with the Festival and outlined their duties. The guide presenters received contained the following subsections delineating their role and providing information pertinent to specific traditions that they might present. The contents, which follow, detail the expected scope of presenter knowledge and responsibility as well as emphasize that presenting is also performance: Informing Yourself and Your Audience; Participant Ease; Repertoire: Individuals, Contexts, Communities; Recontextualization; Performance Traditions; Material and Occupational Traditions; Presenting as Performance; 1989 Programs. In order for the presenters to become familiar with a specific tradition, an information loop was prescribed in which presenters were asked to inform themselves by reading the curatorial statement for the program; program-related articles written for the book, including bibliographic references; text of signs for the area in which they would be working; participant biographies or interview field reports; and the promotional pamphlet and press releases. They were also instructed to discuss repertoires with participants. As a baseline, the guide informed them of the program's inclusive stance on creolization and cultural adaptation while reminding them that the Festival's primary goal was *"to present exemplary representatives of specific folk traditions from particular communities through repertoires that reflect a community aesthetic"* [emphasis in original].[10] In other words, they were to assist participants in making selections that would be recognized as valid within their community aesthetics and would fit within the Festival definitions of folklife. The two were not always compatible.

One of the most important tasks addressed at the daylong presenter meeting was the selection of topics for narrative stages, since they are one of the interactive spaces in a program where topics that do not otherwise fit into the visual and performative aspects of the Festival can be placed. Suggestions had been made throughout the planning and fieldwork phases for topics and included such ideas as immigration histories, plantation experiences, tourism and development, and *hula* traditions, and the process undertaken in the presenter meetings was to refine the list already compiled by organizers from issues raised in the fieldwork process. Scholars and culture workers, who had been prominent in the conceptualization and fieldwork phases of the program but otherwise peripheral to the performances and demonstrations, would conduct and participate in some of the discussions. These culture experts determined the topics for the relatively small portion of the Festival devoted to "talk story."

Careful attention was also given to preparing Hawai'i participants for their roles in the Festival. Much of this preparation was designed to cover the various logistical requirements of OFP administration for legal and commercial purposes. In addition to invitational letters, participants who had accepted received travel questionnaires so that the Smithsonian could coordinate their travel plans, including assistance with additional family members (at participant expense). Besides attending to practical cohesion for the group, organizers were concerned about psychological cohesion.[11] Moriarty coordinated meetings on four islands—O'ahu, Maui, Kaua'i, and Hawai'i—so that at least some of the participants could meet each other and review programmatic, travel, and housing arrangements. Pre-Festival packets were distributed that contained a participant handbook (medical services, meals, transportation, maps, clothes and climate, etc.), an introduction letter from the participant coordinator, a letter from Folkways Music pertaining to music rights,[12] a release letter from Richard Kurin, a small pamphlet on the Festival, a museum shop sales questionnaire, a "Planning Your Smithsonian Visit" guide, hotel information, a name badge, and a contract letter. In a follow-up mailing, participants received a special events calendar, a guide to the nation's capital, a critical information checklist, orientation walk-through schedules, a Metro system guide, a map of Washington, D.C., meal tickets, a program book, release forms, an invitation to an opening reception at the Arts and Industries Building of the Smithsonian, and specific program information. Participants were definitely not going to Washington, D.C., uninformed, and once the forms were signed, the OFP was ensured of having the production and reproduction rights to performance.

Much of the information exchanged in pre-Festival correspondence and meetings was practical and concerned performance logistics. People were introduced to each other and the role of presenters was explained. Cooks were advised to consult with their presenters about which recipes would be most appropriate for Festival presentation and advised about what kinds of equipment would be available in the on-site kitchen. Like the cooks, the craftspeople worked with their presenters to produce lists of supplies and tools to be shipped or acquired in Washington, D.C. Musicians were instructed to discuss their repertoires with their presenters, and those who wanted to be anthologized on a Folkways recording to be sold on site were advised to provide prerecorded material and releases. Artists who produced anything, be it music or craft, were instructed to communicate with the museum shops in charge of concessions if they wished to have their products sold on site.

In spite of being provided with local presenters who would serve as stage managers and facilitators, many participants were still nervous about the idea of performing for the nation. According to one presenter, the group of musicians with whom he was matched did not feel confident that they were good enough to represent their community. Although they were excited about the trip and honored by the invitation, they privately asked their presenter if they might be asked to play less than others.[13] Some of the participants, faced with being labeled experts in the Smithsonian context, suddenly felt the need to learn more about their craft. Robert Ruiz, a saddle maker and fireman who lives in Waimea, Kaua'i, said that although he is a very proficient leather worker, he didn't know anything about the history of *paniolo* in Hawai'i and felt compelled to do research before going to Washington.[14] As a result, what he eventually transmitted as his tradition became a mixture of unofficially and officially garnered information. Invested with a sense of mission, participants felt they were carrying a great deal of responsibility to represent their groups and traditions.

The organizers from Hawai'i felt this responsibility as well. Once live people inhabit a program, an uncontrollable factor is added, and the fostering of spontaneity and multi-vocality puts organizer credibility at stake in the most public of American public places. Kennedy observed that although the Festival staff continually tells program organizers to "blame it on the Smithsonian" if anything goes wrong (the idea being that the Smithsonian is big enough to take it on the chin), state agencies and program organizers do not have that kind of legitimacy buffer.[15] In the case of the Hawai'i program, the result was that little was left to chance. For example, prior to going to D.C., performance groups selected, ideally in conversation with presenters, the repertoires they would present. In the process of negotiation, vertical and horizontal lines of authority intersected. At the pre-Festival meetings, presenters helped craft the interpretive elements of the Festival frame and helped participants shape the parameters of performance. At the same time, pre-Festival literature set guidelines for Festival thinking and behavior, and presenters were inculcated with their station as "ambassadors of *aloha*" (Imada 2004).[16]

The actual social diversity among participants could not be contained in the broad sweeps of the nine ethnic categories derived from the fieldwork process and was, in fact, much more textured and varied than the multicultural model planners had designed for the Festival environment. For example, many members of designated ethnic groups actually claimed multiple ethnic ancestries. Participants also hailed from different communities and islands, rural and urban environments, different socioeconomic levels, different immigration histories, and varied educational backgrounds. Although Festival signage and literature stressed shared backgrounds and traditions, in many cases participants' paths had not previously crossed. Many people on the same island and in the same towns had never met and were quite unfamiliar with the cultural practices of other ethnic groups or even some practices of their own ethnic group. This unfamiliarity is understandable given that the program was constellated around indigenous and plantation histories; the plantation history that had been the foundational concept for ethnic group selection and site design was an abstraction for many of the actual participants who were at least a generation removed from that history, if they had any ancestral connection to it at all. To overcome these obstacles presented by Hawai'i's actual pluralism, the organizers prepared the Hawai'i delegation by stressing the same overarching cultural themes that have been appropriated by the tourist industry—*aloha, 'ohana,* mixed-plate—in the repackaged forms crafted in the fieldwork and early production phases. Boosterizing these themes was a strategy to unify the participants and presenters into an island delegation that would fit the program's carefully crafted "big idea" of Hawai'i as a model of utopian multiculturalism.[17]

In much the same way that the Hawai'i contingent was shaped into a diplomatic unit, the Festival itself is held together by a sense of purpose that permeates all levels of operation. A multi-sited public program of this magnitude could not be accomplished without a huge and efficient staff. The supporting cast of the Festival involves many more people than just the CFCH paid staff, the presenters, and the participants. Tuned to the seasonal schedule of festival making, every year the CFCH swells in size and springs into a frenzy of pre-Festival activity approximately two months prior to arrival of the participants. As soon as college classes let out, interns conveniently arrive from various places and programs and are put to work under staff persons in charge of Festival tasks. Past volunteers, many of them regulars, are recruited, and as the date of the Festival approaches, hundreds of volunteers are signed up and assigned to the volunteer coordinator.[18] Interns and volunteers are apportioned according to their interests and staff needs. They work on everything from correspondence, to travel coordination, to site construction.[19]

During the Festival, temporary staff are deployed to the participant hotel, the participant hospitality area, and throughout the Festival site. Volunteers come in a wide range of ages but are overwhelmingly middle-class, educated, white, and politically left.[20] Many of them are professionals who take time off from their jobs each year in order to work at the Festival. In written materials and orientation sessions, volunteers are primed with the Festival mission of social democracy and advocacy and pumped with a sense of responsibility by being reminded that they are often the first contact a visitor has with the Festival and that they are representing it and the Smithsonian. For hours of often demanding duty under the hot sun and pouring rain, they get free lunches, recognition from Festival staff, and a chance to work with "the folk." Longtime volunteers with whom I talked verified that Festival volunteering was, indeed, a labor of love for which they feel amply rewarded. For them the Festival serves the dual purpose of social activism and contact with interesting "others." It is travel without going out of town—in the case of the Hawai'i program, it was a tropical (working) vacation for free.[21]

Community groups also get involved, although Kurin admits that such involvement can be a "mixed bag" that can derail or abet Festival goals.[22] The Hawai'i program was fortunate to be aided by members of the Hawai'i State Society in Washington, D.C., a group comprising former Hawai'i residents of various ethnicities. This group had been the resource through which the landscape architect for the Hawai'i program, Gordon Velasco, as well as the *imu* stones, had been located. When this organization approached the OFP about volunteering and conducting flower *lei* sales on site, the OFP asked HSS members to help in areas where familiarity with Hawai'i would be especially useful: decorating horses and trucks for the *pā'ū* parade, showing up as spectators for the parade, and hosting families and individuals from Hawai'i. Delighted to be connected to the Hawai'i program, the group enthusiastically complied with these requests and voluntarily hosted a *lū'au* for Hawai'i participants and staff prior to the Festival.

Getting media involved is critical to the ongoing success of the Festival, and the media are yet another performance venue in which cultural meanings are interpreted and negotiated. News agencies receive press releases imbued with the Smithsonian's credibility as a cultural and historical authority, leaving little need for journalists do background research. To ensure intriguing and appropriate coverage of the Hawai'i program, journalists familiar with the Festival were given lists of participants within the Hawai'i program who were considered particularly articulate and colorful. To publicize the 1989 Festival, a segment of the *Today Show* was carefully planned to maximize coverage of all the Festival programs but with most of the interviews to take place in the midst of the Hawai'i site, specifically in and around the *yagura,* which would give the camera people a visual vantage point. The show was filmed between 7:00 A.M. and 8:30 A.M., before the grounds were open to the public. Participants and staff were asked to populate the grounds to make the Festival look "alive" without the liability of dealing with an unpredictable real audience. To ensure the Hawai'i program's memorableness, Moriarty had been asked to find "a humungous *aloha* shirt" to present to the television interviewer. On camera, the interviewer actually received a T-shirt with a Hawaiian quilt pattern; Marie McDonald, a flower *lei* maker from the Big Island, presented him with a *lei* while Elaine Kaopuiki's *hālau* danced.[23] These scripted scenes of gifting underlined the themes of hospitality, generosity, sharing, and *aloha,* themes established in the program's earlier phases and publicized through nationwide Smithsonian press releases focused on *lei* making as symbolic of Hawai'i hospitality.[24]

Media are also forces to be controlled, especially in an environment in which nonprofessionals are performing and cultural divides might lead to misinterpretation or perceptions of harassment. Hawai'i participants and presenters received guidelines in their preliminary packets to prepare them for handling journalists. An internal OFP memo on media stated that "*the Festival is for participants and visitors*" [emphasis in original] and indicated that participants were to be protected in relation to the media and that journalists and photographers, required to sign in at the press tent, were not allowed to block the audience's view or go "behind the scenes" without the permission of the program coordinator. A press officer, Mary Combs, was designated for the Festival, and a chain of command was established for interview requests. Participants were assured that interviews were a matter of choice and told that they had the right to say "No, thank you" to interviews as well as photographs. A humorous anecdote about a former participant who had preferred not to be photographed was included; that incident was handled with the erection of a "No Photographs, Please" exhibit sign, with the understanding that if photographs were taken, they would be unpublishable due to the presence of the sign.[25] Despite efforts to impose ethnographic ethics and respect participant ownership of culture, the document acknowledges that in a crowd of a million people waving cameras, photography was a difficult activity to control.

Another media-related memorandum circulated to all OFP staff prior to the 1989 Festival boldly proclaims, "*The Festival concerns culture, not politics*" [emphasis in original]. Although this statement appears to take a stance that is antithetical to much of what the Festival literature professes, its practical purpose is to maintain Festival goodwill by dissociating it from politics "on the Hill" in Washington, D.C. The memo anticipates various topics of a "sensitive nature" that might be brought up by the media and reiterates the chain of command with regard to Festival policy and philosophy, with Kurin at the political question-deflecting helm. Interestingly, all of the anticipated questions refer to the adjacent Caribbean and Native American programs, and none to the two American programs. Questions about the presence of Cuba on the Mall were to be fielded by making a clear demarcation between politics and culture and insisting that the Festival was apolitical and that the Cuban participants were not government officials. Questions about the performance of Haitian Voudon and Cuban Santerìa as "black magic" were to be used as opportunities to debunk misinformation and educate by making reference to a scholarly article in the program book that explained these practices as folklife. Likewise, allegations of animal mistreatment on the Mall (buffalo, horses, and fowl in 1989) were to be met with information about expert veterinary care as well as the animals' respected status within the cultural groups to whom they were being attached.[26] (In fact, although the OFP had jumped through cultural sensitivity hoops to be able to have buffalo on the Mall, petitioning Native

American elders about their feelings on the matter,[27] the experts cited in the memo somehow did not anticipate the surprise arrival of a buffalo calf during the Festival.) That there were no "sensitive questions" anticipated for the Hawai'i program, despite the local sociopolitical ferment of the 1980s and Martin's alert to Kennedy about "sensitive issues," points to the assumed domestication of Hawai'i within American discourse and the elimination of controversy from the Hawai'i program.

The Festival, like the national museum, guards its particular vision of culture against distortion from within and without, and staff at all levels are charged with image management, particularly with regards to the media. All questions about Festival policy and philosophy were to be referred to the directors. Participants were politely but firmly asked not to respond to questions about Festival concept. There were also prohibitions against individual participants using the Festival for self-promotion. The notes explain that the Festival would not permit "'do-it-yourself' publicity," nor would it distribute its press kits to participants, although it could provide them directly to journalist contacts back home. Tradition bearers were encouraged to conduct interviews about their skills and experience, but they were not to transgress the institutional frame by acting as program experts. Ironically, maintaining the democratic image and feel of the Festival required a clear chain of command with hierarchical roles and institutional control over information and behavior.

For all the talk about Festival spontaneity, most true spontaneity must be timed to happen within a very rigid schedule. Before the Festival officially opens, there are program orientations, site walkthroughs, daily staff meetings, and special events for participants and VIPs. Once the Festival is open to the public, there are multiple events scheduled for each day and special events, such as concerts and dance parties, for most evenings. Some of these evening events are scheduled for the Mall and others for the hotel where the participants stay. The former is designed to maximize audience participation and the latter to maximize a sense of community for the participants within programs and provide opportunities for contact between participants in different programs.

The Festival is kaleidoscopic once it is set in motion. In 1989, on each operating day, the Hawai'i program had between five and six stages in simultaneous performance—11:00 A.M. to 5:00 P.M., with anywhere from four to eight performance slots per day. These performances took place in several locations: the music stage, *hula* stage, narrative stage, foodways kitchen, children's area, and special demonstrations areas (involving such things as *lū'au* cooking, canoe building, *paniolo* crafts, net throwing, and *bon* dance, each in its particular area). Each of these areas had to be staffed with a presenter and volunteers. Stages required additional volunteers to run audio equipment, since stage performances were to be audiotaped for the OFP archives. In addition to performing within the Hawai'i program site, some Hawai'i participants were asked to participate in cross-cultural workshops held on the narrative stages of the adjacent programs. There were eighteen of these cross-cultural workshops altogether, with topics like tourism, water rights, cultural revival and folkloristics, and access to natural resources slated for discussion. Of course, the program in action could not be seen from any one vantage point, so I have taken the liberty of imposing my own order in the three sections that follow. "Consecrations" covers ceremonies and rituals, "Performance" covers the program stages, and "Backstage and Behind the Scenes" covers events and areas out of view of the public.

Consecrations

The Mall is repeatedly referred to in Festival literature as "sacred ground," and although it has been the site of many political protests, for the purposes of the Festival it is treated reverently but apolitically, except with regards to the politics of culture (Kurin 1998, 18–27). Politicians attend, but their presence is considered to be in an altered, ambassadorial capacity. The 1989 Festival itself lent an air of religiosity through organizers' use of ritual to define and sanctify temporal space through opening and closing ceremonies. Although the focus of the 1989 program was on valorizing Hawai'i culture, it was inserted within the culture of Washington, and a round of standard Washington-style formal events marked its opening day. There were three such events: a luncheon at the American History Museum to thank the Hawai'i governor, the French ambassador, the Hawai'i congressional delegation, and sponsoring organizations; an opening ceremony and tour of the Festival site involving delegates of all four of the programs; and an evening reception for participants at the Arts and Industries Museum and co-hosted by Hawai'i congressional delegates. The latter reception invitation was sent out from the secretary of the Smithsonian, the governor of Hawai'i, and the Hawai'i congressional delegation, and an earlier memo to the administrative assistants for each of these political figures attests to the Smithsonian's delicate position vis-à-vis politics.[28] To preclude any charges of sponsoring an event of a political nature, the individual names of the congressional delegation could not be printed on invitations; however, they were printed on an acknowledgment card enclosed with the invitation.[29] This card did not have the Smithsonian seal and, presumably, exonerated the Smithsonian of political dealings through its mysterious appearance in the envelope.

The kick-off opening ceremony is generally held in one of the big-top-style tents on the Mall, but unlike the rest of the Festival, it is conducted under conditions of higher security.[30] Despite the tent, it is a formal VIP event that shows off the Festival to the powers behind and connected to each program: politicians, dignitaries, and Smithsonian and National Park Service directors.[31] It is a platform from which the mission of the Festival is advertised, where curators and coordinators receive their laurels, and where subalterns are momentarily recognized by the elite and the standard hierarchies of power momentarily undergo what Barbara Babcock refers to as a "symbolic inversion." Still, it should not be overlooked that it is the officials who occupy the platform and make the addresses (Babcock 1978). It is in the opening ceremony where cultural advocacy is showcased and voiced to a captive audience, although the assemblage might arguably be seen as a choir of the converted. Participants do not speak; instead, they are honored by the presence of the officials occupying the same space and talking about the value of the participants' folklife.

In the opening-ceremony speeches, not heard by the general public, the official platforms of the various programs are voiced. At the 1989 opening ceremony, speeches about nationalism and resistance figured prominently, despite the Smithsonian's position on separation of politics from culture. Governor Waihee, Senators Matsunaga and Inouye, and Congresswoman Patricia Saiki and Congressman Akaka from Hawai'i sat alongside ambassadors from France, Haiti, and Jamaica and representatives of the Aandaga, Creek, and Shoshone nations. Folklorist Nick Spitzer, in his introductory address to the assembly, pointed out that the four programs were linked through a common theme of creolization.[32] Ray and Elodia Kane, two of the Hawai'i participants, then gave the standard tourist industry–inspired greeting in Hawai'i, yelling, "Aloooooooooooo-*ha!*" and eliciting an echoing response.[33] This rowdy greeting was followed by Pualani Kanaka'ole, from the island of Hawai'i, who offered a traditional Hawaiian chant as a blessing.[34] After a list of the corporate sponsors for the Festival, Ralph Rinzler, assistant secretary of the Smithsonian and the Festival founder, officiated over a series of speeches. First, the anniversary of the French Revolution was used to remark on the history of French-American alliance, and French-American friendship was used to segue into linked traditions. The U.S. national motto—E Pluribus Unum—was cited as a preface to honoring the occasion of the thirtieth anniversary of Hawai'i statehood, and Smithsonian secretary Robert McCormick Adams discussed the various programs, citing Hawai'i as uniquely multicultural and connecting it to Pacific Rim diversity. He discussed France as more than a continent, credited the role of the Festival in demystifying stereotypes of Caribbean beliefs and rituals, and connected the American programs of 1989 to future Smithsonian projects: the American Indian Museum and a proposed Hawai'i restaging. Adams ended his speech by lauding America for understanding the importance of using public space for dialogue, as opposed to the dark histories of public spaces like Red Square, Tiananmen Square, and the Bastille. In an "apolitical" Festival celebrating America, the politics of other nations made for useful contrast.

Before the representatives of the various programs spoke, Rinzler made a statement that illustrated the OFP's admirable capacity for self-editing. He apologized for the 1989 Festival's title, "Encounters in the New World," noting that it was Eurocentric and should be avoided in the future. This self-correction, as well as calling attention to the constructedness of the rhetorical frame, also served to background the OFP and foreground the program officials who spoke next. Hawai'i had the most politicians at the Festival, yet the state's message, sandwiched midway between Caribbean and Native American speeches, was the least political. The French ambassador spoke to the occasion of the bicentennial commemoration of the French Revolution and Declaration of the Rights of Men and Citizens. The ambassadors from Haiti and Jamaica[35] used the opportunity of the Caribbean program's focus on religious creolization to stress their desire to see uninformed third-world stereotypes corrected as well as to speak about cultural adaptation as resistance. Oren Lyons, Aandaga elder, greeted the assembly "from our country" and talked about how the continent was free before the white man came. Susan Carjoe, representing the Cheyenne and Creek nations, used the anniversary of Little Bighorn the next day to emphasize the egalitarian values of native peoples. She and Lyons both recognized Inouye for his help on Native American policies, and she honored Inouye, Rinzler, Adams, and Lyons as "great men." Carjoe ended by saying, "Like the buffalo, we're coming back!"

In contrast to these speeches that overtly linked culture to politics, the Hawai'i segment of the program concentrated on Hawai'i as a model of successful multiculturalism. Senator Inouye introduced Governor Waihee with a compacted history of Hawai'i immigration in which Hawai'i served both as a destination and as a metaphor for "the good life" that all the trouble spots in the world are desperately seeking. The question he raised was, "How did they live together?" The answer from the *kupuna* (elders), he said, was the Polynesian gift of *aloha*. He then introduced the governor as the "son of Hawai'i." In his speech, Waihee reminisced about being let out of schools and the dancing in the streets when Hawai'i became a state. He built on Inouye's introduction when he talked about "those that came later for a better life, reaching out so that their children's future would be secure." Twice he repeated the national motto, but once in reference to Hawai'i multiculturalism, claiming it as "our E Pluribus Unum," and then asserting that Hawai'i's presence at the Festival was a gift to the nation: "To reinforce our nation's motto: E Pluribus Unum. Out of the many, one. You see, to you, from the community of communities to the nation of nations, we bring you our spirit of *aloha*." Waihee's eloquent speech was an emotional endorsement of multiculturalism, but it also combined national and touristic boosterism. Hawai'i could be seen, thanks to its being showcased in the Festival, as having even more to offer in a tourist economy. Despite the governor's indigenous roots, Hawai'i concerns, such as dependence on tourism, indigenous protests over colonial legacies, ecological problems, and economic disparities—issues that might have been linked with Caribbean and Native American concerns raised in the opening ceremony—were subordinated to advertising Hawai'i's multiculturalism along with its "beautiful beaches and wonderful weather." Hawai'i was/is a remote American constituency, and Waihee's speech was necessarily tuned to politicking. Bidding for greater national recognition, he expanded on the image of the islands as a model of harmoniousness, a tack that left no room for local resistances past or present. Like the other contingents of the Festival, Hawai'i politicians utilized the ceremony as a platform to, as Martin had instigated in the early stages of Festival planning, put Hawai'i's "best foot forward" in the national arena. Senator Matsunaga was the last of the Hawai'i politicians to speak, and he claimed that Hawai'i was "what the rest of the world was striving to be" before he declared the Festival officially open.[36]

After the opening ceremony, other ceremonies were performed to authenticate and activate the program. Within the Hawai'i program, organizers requested participants to perform their own rituals in activities quite different from the formal events held within the confines of the Smithsonian museums. Early in the Festival planning, when unifying themes had been sought, Martin had suggested prayer as a force that spanned island heterogeneity. Following that line of thinking, the Hawai'i program was sanctified and invigorated through the use of multicultural blessings. One opening ritual was performed to symbolically open the program gates. In Chinese communities throughout the world, lion dances are a noisy and festive ritual used to bring good fortune to new businesses and events. A new lion head had been ordered from Taiwan for the dance to be performed by participants Kelford Chang and Clement Lum, and when it arrived, a ritual was required to "quicken" it, or give it life. The ritual, similar to those performed in temples for Chinese deities, was enacted by Reverend Duane Pang, a Taoist priest from Honolulu. It involved invocations, prayers, and some chicken blood (symbolic in this case) prior to painting in the eyes of the lion so that it would be deemed "alive." The ritual and the lion dance that ensued became part of the Festival pageantry—"spectacularizing culture" and in line with the Hawai'i program's complex ethnic makeup, a Chinese ceremony opened the Japanese gate.[37]

Hawaiian and Samoan groups held other kinds of opening ceremonies. Based on Martin's directive, a Hawaiian blessing had been requested for the Hawai'i program as a whole.[38] The idea was very much the same as that of dotting the lion's eyes—to bring life to performance as well as to symbolically consecrate the space the program would inhabit. The use of Hawaiian prayers for a multicultural program also reiterated the planning-phase decision to present Hawaiian culture as predominant in the islands. The Samoan group chose to perform their own ceremony outside of program framing.[39] The Samoan delegation was somewhat disconnected from the rest of the program concept; as recent immigrants to Hawai'i they did not easily fit within the program paradigm based on a shared local identity grounded in indigeneity, plantation history, and creolization. Their separate ceremony suggests they may have felt separate as well. Organizers had decided that it was politically expedient to include Samoans because of their political presence in Washington, D.C., and had thematically linked Samoans to Hawaiians through shared Polynesianness. The Samoan program presenter, Simeamativa Aga, invited Hawai'i congressional delegates to attend a traditional *ava* ceremony to mark Samoan participation in the Hawai'i program.[40]

The Chinese and Hawaiian rituals might be seen to have spectacularized sacred practices in the sense that they were performing them for spectators, but in each case the groups also maintained control over the content and used the ritual for their own purposes as well. In the Hawaiian and Samoan ceremonies, visitors were invited to participate by praying or drinking, and thus were recruited to be supporting actors reifying and sacralizing re-contextualized performance.

Not all ceremony was sacred. The Festival often incorporates the pageantry of parades that move through the Festival grounds, and one of the key events planned for the Hawai'i program was an evocation of Hawai'i pageantry in the form of a *pā'ū* parade. The parade, with eighteen to twenty horses bedecked with floral and greenery *lei,* a lowboy trailer drawn by a truck, and a flatbed truck that would carry dancers and musicians, was scheduled for June 24, 1989. It would start at 14th Street on the south end of the Mall paralleling Jefferson Avenue and make a circuit of the Mall, with stops for two more rituals. At the statue of Joseph Henry, first secretary of the Smithsonian, in front of the Smithsonian Castle, the parade would stop long enough for a large *lei* to be placed on the statue. Putting *lei* on statues on special anniversaries is a common practice in Hawai'i, and this gesture would be a symbolic thank-you to the Smithsonian for its sponsorship. When the parade reached 3rd Street, the governor would leave the parade and get into a limousine with other dignitaries and be driven to the Capitol Building. There he would place a *lei* on the statue of King Kamehameha the Great in the Capitol rotunda.[41] These scripted rituals appropriated a local practice and elevated it to a state spectacle.[42] Contrarily, these actions also asserted a playful post-colonial flair by symbolically superimposing Hawai'i culture onto two national icons.

What was planned ritual and what actually happened on the Mall were two different things, for as anyone who has spent the summer in Washington, D.C., knows, the weather is unpredictable, and no amount of scripting could control how the forces of nature would treat the Hawai'i program. The parade began as scheduled on June 24 with Governor Waihee, in a *palaka* shirt, riding in a convertible and Senator Akaka on a horse.[43] And then the rain came. People from Hawai'i are not easily daunted by rain since unpredictable showers are a regular occurrence in the islands, so they good-naturedly continued the parade. By halfway through, however, they had lost quite a few bodies, and everyone was soaked. Someone found plastic bags for the musicians to protect their instruments, and they continued to play—hands inside the bags.[44] The statues received their *lei,* but McDonald wryly noted years later that they must have been against National Park Service regulations since the *lei* she had made and placed on John Henry, an extra

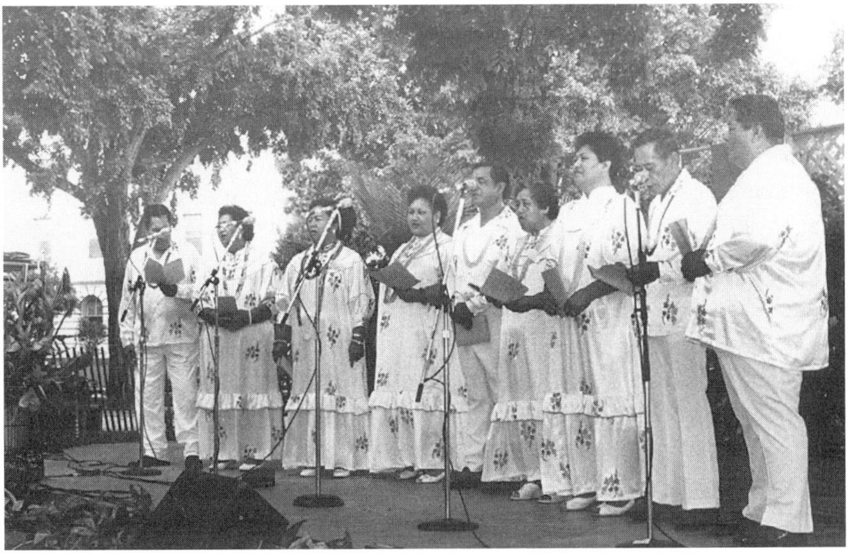

Fig. 1. Waimea Hawaiian Church Choir. (Courtesy of the Center for Folklife and Cultural Heritage, Smithsonian Institution, Washington, D.C.)

long one at that, quickly disappeared.[45] The staged ritual was sodden but redeemed by the good humor of the Hawai'i participants, who are used to carrying on daily activities despite frequent showers and who interpreted what seemed a minor disaster for the organizers as a good omen for the program. Governor Waihee said of the rain, "It started as a blessing, but we turned it into a celebration" (Brislin 1989, A1). Furthermore, the *pā'ū* riders had ritual plans of their own. After the parade, they took their elaborate horse and rider *lei* to the Vietnam memorial and offered them there to commemorate Hawai'i war dead, for as Moriarty said, "There were a lot of soldiers from Hawai'i, and everybody knew somebody whose name was on the Wall."[46]

Unless it is suffused with an ambiance of festiveness, the Festival is merely a live museum exhibit. Pageantry and ritual are techniques that organizers use to strike a match to a program, in hopes that it will spark a program to life and transport it beyond mere mimesis. Beyond the carefully orchestrated parade pageantry, the rain and the spontaneous gesture of the *pā'ū* riders opened new spaces for meaning-making outside institutionalized structures of feeling, even though those spaces were still contained within the frames of asymmetric power relations and tourism on which the Hawai'i program was predicated.

Performance

As I have noted in earlier chapters, mainland and Hawai'i program planners spent a great deal of time negotiating and selecting the categorizations that would be used to represent Hawai'i participants. In the interests of communicability and presentability in a festival format, the OFP preferred clearly differentiated ethnic categories that juxtaposed root traditions. Hawai'i advisors argued that blurred ethnic boundaries were the norm in Hawai'i. The compromise result was a multicultural

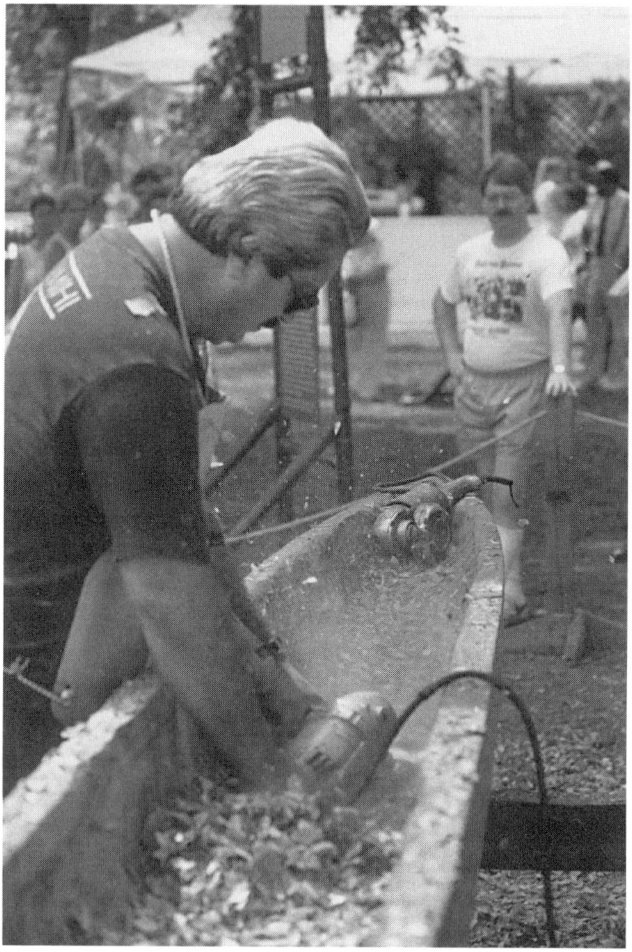

Fig. 2. Kent Bowman building a traditional canoe with power tools. (Courtesy of the Center for Folklife and Cultural Heritage, Smithsonian Institution, Washington, D.C.)

paradigm in which juxtaposed ethnic groups were offset by creolized and shared cultural practices. This conceptual frame permeated the program literature and site design, but the proof of its efficacy remained to be determined in the program's unfolding. How would participants interact with the site and the constructed categories? Would performance coincide with or produce fissures in the carefully constructed frames?

MacCannell's notions of "zones of authenticity" and "staged back regions" in tourist productions are particularly useful in looking at the Hawai'i program performance phase. According to MacCannell, "staged back regions" are crafted to remove barriers and facilitate access to what or who is being viewed and are a calculated response to what he sees as tourist desire to encounter and experience authenticity rather than simulation (1976, 99). The Festival is essentially institutionally rendered ethnography designed to foster intimacy between audiences and participants in the form of dialogue. This is accomplished by inserting cultural practitioners into ethnographically informed spaces crafted to break down barriers and prompt conversation.

As with any environment inhabited day after day, even a stage set can become an alternative version of home. Kennedy fondly remembers

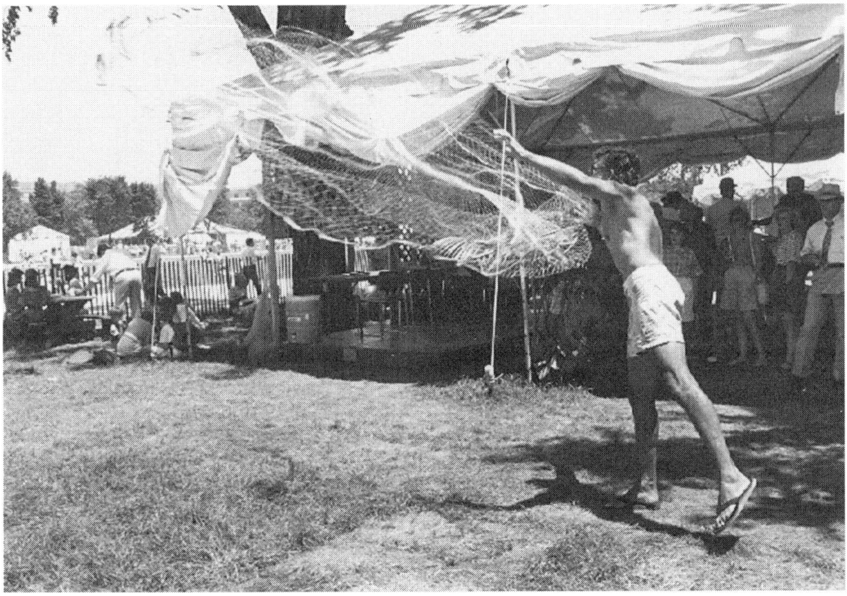

Fig. 3. Chauncey Pa demonstrating net throwing. (Courtesy of the Center for Folklife and Cultural Heritage, Smithsonian Institution, Washington, D.C.)

running into one of the participants on site during the Festival and asking her where she was headed. She replied that she was "going to the store." He realized with amusement that she was referring to K. Awa Grocery, the narrative stage designed to look like a store, and he told this story as evidence of the site's animation as a quasi-believable environment.[47] Benjie Bennington, an arts curator from the East-West Center in Honolulu who was the presenter for the cooking demonstration area, said the foodways stage turned into "a real kitchen." Although they had meal tickets that allowed them to eat at the concessions for free, many Hawai'i participants thought the food sold there was terrible and instead frequented the back of the demonstration area, where more delectable and familiar dishes were being prepared. Bennington remembered that on many occasions she had to shoo extra bodies out of the demonstration area, and once she pointed out to the audience that the governor was "doing what we call cock-a-roaching," or stealing food from the back.[48] Beverly Simons, OFP coordinator for the foodways stage, remembered that cooks were very interested in each other's cooking and used the stage as a place to exchange recipes and observe techniques. Some, like Chinese participant and cookbook author June Tong, had several family members along who tended to congregate in the "kitchen." Conceived of in terms of occupational and regional affinities, the foodways stage became very "communal" and was transposed from a demonstration area directed at audiences into an activity area directed toward participants, friends, and family behind the scenes.[49]

Despite the organizers' desire to produce authentic folklife, official rules and regulations put uncharacteristic restrictions on some of the participants' activities—changing them from what they would be in a home environment and drawing a strict line between actual practice and performed reality. Health department regulations did not permit the distribution of demonstration cooking to the public, so food could be seen and smelled but not eaten by visitors to the foodways stage or observers at the *lū'au*. For Hawai'i cooks who pride themselves on hospitality, this showing without sharing was antithetical to customs at home. Likewise, herbal healers could talk about herbal remedies but could not prescribe on the Mall. For Papa Auwe, a *lapa'au* (traditional Hawaiian healer) who could intuitively detect physical or psychological ailments, it was difficult to refuse to help people, especially since he believed his healing ability to be a spiritual gift and a duty to be bestowed, gratis, on others. Nathan Napoka, a presenter and local historian, recalled one day when cultural imperatives took precedence over Festival rules: one of the participants was so ill that she needed to leave the site, and organizers discussed sending her to the hospital. Papa Auwe looked at her and immediately determined that she was severely constipated. He gave her a remedy, she went back to the hotel, and she recovered completely by the next day.[50]

Audiences and participants especially felt the lack of children as a reality gap in the program. The regulation that the participants not bring children, no doubt due to logistical and legal concerns, was particularly ironic given that so much of the Hawai'i program concept hinged on the *'ohana* theme and that children are ever present in Hawai'i celebrations. Furthermore, implicit in the Festival emphasis on traditional arts is a focus on intergenerational connections. Both the OFP and the participants had addressed this concern as best they could. Many of the participants brought family members (adults) with them who became part of the Festival, and in cases of particularly frail participants, the OFP paid for a family member to accompany and assist a presenter. One intergenerational family of dancers—the Zuttermeisters—performed *hula.* Visitors to the Mall still asked, "Where are the kids?" One of the Hawaiian musicians grumbled about the children's activity area segregating the children when they should be integrated.[51] For participants and visitors, the lack of children created a glaring lack of authenticity.

Perhaps the most difficult factor to assess in any program constellation is visitors/tourists—who they are and how they respond to programs and participants. Yet they are perhaps the most critical frame in Festival production, since without them there is no event, no spectacle, and no dialogue. The OFP mission of educating the public allows for the promotion of traditional culture and the recognition of tradition bearers. The demography of audiences is difficult to determine since the event is free and in public space. The OFP is continually developing new tools for assessing audience response and audience profiles, but the staff admits that so far they can come up only with random samplings. My own observation, shared by others, is that the majority of visitors to the Festival are white, well-off, well traveled, well educated, and interested in learning about other cultures. They include people who reside in the surrounding metropolis as well as domestic and international tourists.[52]

Whether arriving from the surrounding streets or from the adjacent programs, visitors to the Hawai'i program first encountered it by stepping through one of the four gates (two Hawaiian, one *paniolo,* one Japanese *torii*) constructed as part of the site design. However, different from entries to a theme park, these gates did not mark a threshold between worlds of fantasy and reality. Instead, they invited visitors into a setting that evoked but did not constitute another temporal or physical zone. It was a mediated space and experience that constantly called attention to its constructedness at the same time that participants communicated their contemporaneousness with that of the visitors. The Hawai'i program was a multi-sited ethnographic display, but unlike such displays of the past (e.g., the world's fairs), it was designed to be an intimate spectacle that was primarily interactive and that would, wherever possible, invert the roles of viewers and viewed.

Rather than being educational curiosities, participants were given the role of educators. This role was reinforced by site design, presenters, and Festival literature. The most direct form of educational interactions took place at the foodways and narrative stages and at crafts and occupational demonstrations, where dialogue could take place between visitors and participants. Marie McDonald made an educational experience her definitive Festival anecdote. She remembers a little girl who came to silently watch her make flower *lei*, then came back a week later to tell her that she could do it herself. She had gone home and practiced what she had learned.[53] For McDonald, an educator as well as *lei* maker, this incident proved the ability of her cultural demonstration to extend beyond the Festival.

For many participants unaccustomed to being public figures, thinking of themselves as cultural authorities was daunting and sometimes transformative. The daughter of James Kealakalani He'eu had said her father, a taro farmer from Maui, was a silent man who would not be able to face a crowd of curious onlookers, much less describe what he did for a living. According to Napoka, however, once Mr. He'eu was installed in his miniature taro patch on the Mall, "he blossomed." He loved talking to people and had a sense of the importance of what he did for the first time.[54] His amazed daughter later jokingly asked Kennedy and Napoka, "What have you done to my father? He's a changed man! He never used to talk at all and now he won't stop!"[55]

Although organizers say that overall presenters were delighted with the level of interest and knowledge expressed by visitors,[56] identities were sometimes negotiated against a perceived lack of audience awareness. One presenter claimed that someone in the audience of a talk-story session asked if everyone in Hawai'i lived in grass shacks, to which the annoyed presenter replied, "No, we live in trees!"[57] While it is hard to imagine such a question being serious and impossible to determine anything about its source, the fact that it has been remembered and retold indicates there was some sense of frustration among Hawai'i people with the misinformation of visitors who had not traveled to Hawai'i. Of course, misinformation is understandable given the primitivized tourist industry packaging of Hawai'i and the erasure of non-indigenous populations. Hawai'i participant responses varied from patient instruction to opportunism and self-amusement at the expense of tourists. At the foodways stage, the presenter started several of the demonstration sessions by asking how many people thought that the performers were Americans. She says that there was always a scant show of hands.[58] We might surmise this was because the people onstage did not look like what the audience had expected, but other presenters fielded questions that demonstrated many people still considered Hawai'i a foreign destination. Even parts of the Smithsonian had committed this error, arguing with the OFP that Hawai'i was an international location rather than a domestic one.[59] Occasionally, participant responses to audiences were abrupt simply due to weariness at repetition, as when one participant snapped at a visitor, "Whassa madda, you stupid? I just said that!" Napoka summed up the possibilities for frustration as, "You say something to 250 people, and then you look up and there's another 250 people. How many times can you say the same thing and still be fresh?"[60] Still, given the number of visitors that came through the program in its ten days on the Mall, the general assessment was that most visitors were well informed and sincerely interested in learning from the participants at a level far beyond that of the stereotypical Hawai'i tourist.[61]

The tactics that participants employed to deal with the ethnic labels utilized for the program demonstrate the slippage of such categories within the program and in Hawai'i. Some participants, like the Korean group that had to perform without its teacher, Mary Jo Freshley, due to Festival restrictions that required the group members to all be Korean, were unhappy with what they saw as artificial constraints on ethnic categories and Festival roles, while other Hawai'i participants simply stepped over them. One day a participant was sick, and Napoka, whose designated role was as a presenter, filled in as a performer. His job was to demonstrate how to husk coconuts, something he had seen done many times but had never tried himself.[62] He started a patter with the audience, but when he struck the coconut, nothing happened. He tried repeatedly, but the coconut remained embarrassingly intact. Finally, a Samoan man sprang out of the audience and said, "Gimme me that coconut!" and effortlessly broke it open. He then proceeded to husk several more. Napoka said he felt "really dumb," but the crowd loved the role reversal, and Napoka enjoyed the joke on himself: "He'd been doing it all his life. I had no interest in husking coconuts." Of course, the audience had been fooled as well in this case because they had presumed, based only on Napoka's Native Hawaiian appearance, that the scholar in front of them possessed the requisite traditional skills. Whereas Freshley's racial difference had been cited as a reason to disallow her from performing with her dance troupe, Napoka's assumption that as far as the audience was concerned Native Hawaiians were interchangeable prompted him to transgress invisible boundaries between presenters and presented. His boundary crossing was exposed only by his lack of the appropriate skills for performance.

Other participants amused themselves and each other by playing off the audience's cultural ignorance; for example, one of the *ondotori* (*bon* dance singers), already locally known for singing "Old Susannah" in *bon odori* style, exclaimed during a late-night drinking session, "Listen, tomorrow I'm going to sing 'Old MacDonald Had a Farm,' and no one is going to know!" He did, in fact, just that, to the glee of participants who had witnessed his proposal.[63] The *bon odori* provided ample opportunities for such jokes since the *yagura* was one of the most visible structures and the *bon odori* a daily participatory performance. In more than one style of *bon odori,* a *hayashi* (caller) makes vocal interjections, and Robert Cato, *bon odori* singer from Kaua'i, recalls Reverend Pang playfully interjecting calls in Chinese, "just to throw [him] off."[64] When Chinese participants joined in, they joked that the audience could not tell the difference between Chinese and Japanese anyway.[65]

Category jumpers were not practicing situational ethnicity only to play with the mostly white visitors' ignorance and tendency to generalize about exotic others, although they seem to have enjoyed that aspect immensely; they also crossed ethnic lines in ways that were in accord with practices at home. Lion dances, *hula,* and *bon* dances are familiar to people of various ethnicities, especially in small, rural communities. People of all ethnicities can and do study *hula* and other traditional arts. The temples that host *bon* dances invite outsiders, and some encourage participation in all or some of the dances (Van Zile and Kirchhofer 1981). Also, because many people hail from multiple ancestries, they are more likely to have been exposed to or curious about multiple cultural practices. For example, one Hawaiian *lei* maker who was "a tiny part Chinese" became friends with Reverend Pang and enthusiastically filled in on the gong accompanying the Chinese lion dance.[66] In short, Hawai'i participants enacted the OFP paradigm of multiculturalism onstage while practicing a much more fluid interpretation among themselves. Not all category jumping was ethnic—when Senator Akaka sang at one of the Hawaiian music sessions on the narrative stage, he was stepping out of his official role as politician for Hawai'i and into that of a very different kind of Hawai'i delegate.

The talk story, or narrative, stage, held on the porch of the K. Awa Grocery storefront presented a different kind of informality and intimacy from that of the demonstration areas where visitors could carry on conversations with the participants. Two to several participants at a time sat in folding chairs on the stage/porch and talked with each other and the audience while a presenter stood to one side to introduce and facilitate. The audience would sometimes be addressed and at other times would experience overhearing an impromptu and informal, albeit miked, jam session or conversation. They could also ask questions of the participants.[67] As previously noted, these sessions covered a range of topics that had been selected by the presenters, coordinators, and curator. Although unscripted, the frames and the staging were not exactly spontaneous, since speakers were prompted by their presenters, but the sessions represented a genuine effort on the part of the OFP to invite participants to speak candidly on traditional practices and related issues. Some of these sessions were mini-performances or demonstrations of musical practices or sessions of traditional storytelling. These were overtly directed at the audience. Some became comparative oral history sessions about immigration, plantation life, or learning a craft. A few were reserved for discussions of contemporary issues such as tourism, cultural revival, and access to natural resources. In some cases the talk story stage elicited stories that might otherwise not have been told outside a family circle or at all and validated family and community histories, practices, and values. In other cases, the presentation was treated more formally.

The Festival ideal is to create a place where participants can tell their stories in their own words, in their own terms, to encourage "dialogue, not didacticism" (Kurin 1989, 14–15). The Smithsonian policy has been not to shy away from difficult topics on the narrative stage, and the Hawai'i organizers had included, along with sessions on immigrant histories and traditions, several on tourism in Hawai'i and the Hawaiian renaissance and one session called "Haoles in Hawai'i." Community and academic scholars participated in these sessions. While organizers and presenters seemed quite comfortable raising difficult topics, they were sometimes put on the spot, especially in tourism sessions, by questions that evidenced inside knowledge about Hawai'i issues like Japanese investment and development. This kind of interchange suggests that people from the HSS or even other participants were present in the audience at the time.

These and other topics were discussed quite candidly, but it is clear from the stage recordings that there was a certain amount of editing that took place in spite of attempts to create an open environment for dialogue. In one tourism session, a person in the audience asked about Japanese tourists and a participant responded by saying they are better liked because they spend more money, are more respectful, and do not stay as long. These are comments openly made in Hawai'i, but the Festival audience reacted defensively, and the presenter quickly covered the comment and moved on. In another session, when issues of real estate inflation were raised, someone in the audience shot back with, "Then why do you sell your property?" The presenter responded with, "Money talks" and an admission that if someone offered him a million dollars he might take it. At the "Haoles in Hawai'i" session Puakea Nogelmeier, a European transplant who teaches Hawaiian language at the University of Hawai'i and also performs *hula,* gave an etymology of the term *haole* in which he suggested a connection to white-skinned pigs. When they ended that session, Kennedy and Martin sounded more than a little apologetic in thanking the Hawai'i Visitors Bureau, "who didn't drop any strings on what they said on the stage."

In at least one session on the Hawaiian renaissance, the movement to stop military testing on the island of Kaho'olawe was brought up by someone in the audience and discussed by participants. A presenter, Edward Kanahele, mentioned that one craftsman had used the Festival as his opportunity to tell Governor Waihee, "Stop the bombing, Governor!" The audience laughed, and one of the other presenters said, "That's nice, put the governor on the spot!" Kanahele responded with, "Make him feel comfortable, like he never really left home. Yes, it's even happening over here." He went on to inform any Canadians who might be in the audience that their government was also involved in bomb testing and encouraged them to pressure it to stop participating as well. The audience could laugh about the governor, but the tourism talks apparently hit closer to home for former or future tourists.

More than once an audience member asked why the discussants were so negative and how they could complain about an industry that gives them work and helps the economy. In one session, visitors asked what the solution was, but were clearly not receptive when the answers had to do with limiting visitors. When one session was up and there was still tension in the air, the moderator concluded by saying, "That topic was somewhat disturbing" and trying to smooth it over with a joke about how Spam was traditional in Hawai'i.[68] In that case, both time and the audience were editing factors.

Participants self-edited onstage. McDonald remembered kicking her sister, Irmalee Pomeroy, in a discussion about tourism, saying that she did not agree with her opinions about tourism but making it clear that the dissent was a family matter, not one to be aired in front of a crowd.[69] Some topics were subject to self-editing based on anticipated crowd response. In a session on Japanese in America, a participant talking about her own family mentioned the difference between the "katonks" (insider term for mainland Japanese Americans; a reference to the sound an empty coconut makes when it hits the ground) and "Buddhaheads"

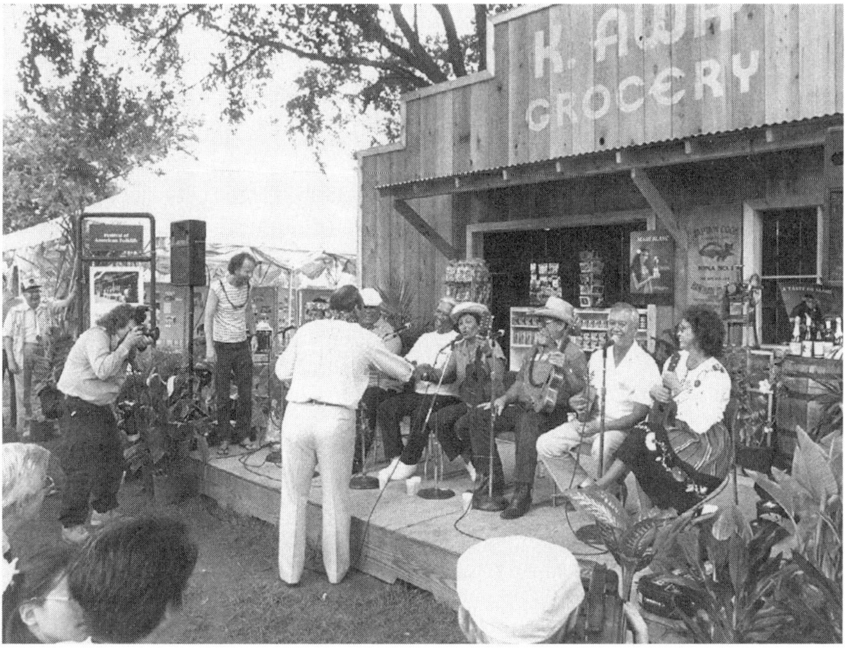

Fig. 4. *'Ukulele* music at narrative stage. Governor Waihee in foreground. From left to right onstage: Jay Junker (presenter), Richard Ho'opi'i, Solomon Ho'opi'i, Faith Ku'ulei Kekiwi, Clyde "Kindy" Sproat, Samuel Kamaka, and Josephine Carriera. (Courtesy of the Center for Folklife and Cultural Heritage, Smithsonian Institution, Washington, D.C.)

(local term for Hawai'i-born Japanese). The speaker, realizing that the terms might be seen as offensive on the mainland, quickly backtracked over what she said. One elderly *lauhala* weaver who worked in a resort doing weaving demonstrations mentioned that she worried constantly that she would end up living on the beach since everything had gotten so expensive, then covered her tracks with a laugh and said that at least she had a job she enjoyed. Others responded to actual reactions. Kindy Sproat, a falsetto singer from the Big Island, made a jovial comment onstage about *paniolo* "working all day and then going home to beat their wives." According to Jay Junker, the stage presenter, "You could see the crowd gasp," and Sproat quickly self-analyzed and self-edited. As Junker said, "I never heard him say *that* again!"[70] What these anecdotes suggest is that for all its seeming informality and invitation to speak freely, in fact, limitations of time, assigned topics, cultural constraints, and a heightened sense of place and occasion made in-depth discussion of controversial topics highly unlikely.

We can only speculate to what extent the tangible and intangible Smithsonian frames influenced the degree to which participants felt they could speak freely. There were many extant reasons for participants not to bring up controversial subjects onstage. Jonathan Okamura argues that the appropriation and constant evocation of "the spirit of *aloha*" by local government and the tourist industry effectively serve to suppress dissent in Hawai'i. Many people in Hawai'i cite a cultural style, based both in Hawaiian and Asian values, in which reticence and indirectness in social situations are highly valued, and many people from elsewhere, especially *haole*, are seen as *maha'oi* (overly probing, direct, and aggressive).[71] Native Hawaiian participants discussed onstage that the traditional way of teaching for Hawaiians was the "shut your mouth school of learning," marking a clear contrast between the direct style of Festival education in which questions are encouraged and the Hawaiian one being discussed. For the majority of performers, being part of such an impressive production was an honor, and they responded to the opportunity for recognition as cordial and cooperative guests, delighted to have their state and ethnic group recognized in the nation's capital, although several asked, "Why did it take so long?"[72]

Program definitions were most contested by musicians who had performed professionally, had a degree of self-confidence about their identities as cultural practitioners, and whose established repertoires did not necessarily fit within Festival parameters. This might also be a reason that Festival organizers prefer to work with musicians who have not performed professionally nor had much public recognition. Musicians who were used to playing a variety of music felt restricted; for example, the Puerto Rican musicians were unhappy that the folklife definitions had made it necessary for them to eliminate their popular *salsa* repertoire.[73] Restrictions opened up spaces for resistance. The Filipino musicians, instructed to play "pure" Filipino music rather than commercialized, performed film songs in Tagalog—traditional as far as non-Tagalog speakers knew.[74] For musicians used to creating and holding audience rapport, the time restraints of the Festival program seemed truncated and arbitrary. Ray Kane, a very talented slack-key guitarist who had recently received a National Heritage Fellowship award, got onstage and refused to get off. The more he was urged by the time-conscious stage managers, the more he ignored them and, as is customary in other stage venues, asked the appreciative crowd, "Do you want to hear one more?" Kane, evidently caught up in the crowd's enthusiasm and proud of his newly acquired status as a national treasure, proclaimed, "I'm a living legend!" Meanwhile, the stage manager/presenter was reprimanded for not clearing the stage according to the strict Festival time schedule.[75]

One incident in particular, which spans the Honolulu and Washington, D.C., locations, illustrates a tension between institutional directives and participant views of acceptable repertoire. Prior to leaving Honolulu, the Hawaiian musicians, a group put together expressly for Festival performance, rehearsed in the University of Hawai'i Department of Theatre and Dance. Because the musicians enjoyed playing together, these sessions could be quite spontaneous and experimental. They were playing "chalangalang" music[76] one day when one of the organizers dropped in and explained to them that the rule for the Festival was to stick to music in Hawaiian and, to be safe, not to play any music after 1924. They smiled and agreed, but Violet Liliko'i (Auntie Vi) was heard to say after she was gone, "I've been playing for sixty years, so don't tell *me* what's Hawaiian and what's not!"[77] In setting such limitations, the organizer may have been concerned that veteran Waikīkī performers like Auntie Vi would veer off into Waikīkī entertainment mode and undermine the program objective of representing traditional rather than commercialized material.

Once in Washington, this rule provided a point of resistance for the Hawaiian musicians from Honolulu, and to protest the arbitrary year that they had been given as a cutoff, they played songs in Hawaiian that had been composed much later. One day they played the popular 1940s *hapa-haole* song "Going to the Hukilau," and their presenter was immediately reprimanded with the "no *hapa-haole* music" rule. According to him, the musicians were quite aware of the rule, but the song had been played in response to a request from a Hawaiian *kumu,* and they responded to what they considered a higher authority than the program coordinators.[78]

What this anecdote illustrates, both in terms of its actual content and its retention as a moral tale a decade and a half later, is that although the actual performance of the program may have appeared seamless to the public, it was in fact a site of contestation and negotiation. In this incident, which moved from Hawai'i pre-performance to D.C. performance, there was dissent not only about what constituted traditionality for a particular community, but also about who could or should define both authenticity in the national arena. Organizers understandably wanted to counteract past cultural compromise by showing America a "Hawaiianness" uncontaminated by the taint of tourism—one that had survived in private and had meaning in local settings. Yet the arbitrary boundaries imposed by the program's culture brokers were not necessarily ones these savvy performers, comfortable in tourist venues as well as informal settings, always found meaningful or valid. In fact, the Honolulu end of this story illustrates that in their own informal "backyard" settings, these musicians find Hawaiianness in a variety of musical genres.

Backstage and Behind the Scenes

The staged cultural displays and demonstrations comprised a spectacle for the public, but for many participants the most memorable part of the Festival happened outside the public eye, in the regions behind and beyond the stage. In a program installation that was primarily composed of "staged back regions," performance areas designed to appear unstructured and accessible, there was minimal backstage on the actual Festival site. There was only one fenced staff and participant area that was off-limits to the public—for the Hawai'i program it was called the *pu'uho'omaha,* or place of rest. Otherwise, the on-site Festival "backstage" could be construed as any place out of hearing, out of view, or beyond the understanding of spectators. Beyond where tourists were made to feel they had entered into real people's lives, there were pockets of reality in the wings to which tourists and even the organizers were not privy.

Occasionally, these moments happened under the noses of OFP officials. One presenter remembers Alan Lomax, a well-known folklorist active in creating many public programs, putting his arm around a musician from Hawai'i and introducing him to another academic as "my slack-key player." According to the presenter, the musician "shuffled his feet and 'yes-sirred' him, but when Lomax walked away, the musician turned and made a derogatory comment about Lomax.[79] This incident strongly suggests a dual consciousness in which the musician chose to comply with, without buying into, official expectations for dealing with institutional representatives.

The most obvious "offstage" arena was the city itself. Considerable preparation time and concern was devoted to making sure that participants could safely and efficiently navigate Washington, D.C., and to minimize culture shock for people coming from radically different environments. To this end, participants were provided with maps and city information, as well as a series of accompanied outings. As Hawai'i coordinator and a friend, Moriarty was especially concerned about the culture shock that the participants from the island of Ni'ihau might experience, since most of them were from a rural and isolated cultural environment and some had never even been to Honolulu. What actually happened when they got to Washington illustrates how resourceful they really were. The women, says Moriarty, were the first to learn how to use the Metro: "They all had these big wide feet, and they found the black part of town and bought all kinds of shoes. They must have gone back with a hundred pairs of shoes!" [80]

The truth is that organizers could not really anticipate how people would operate on their own. Many participants had been to Washington before or had family there. For them, the Festival period was another kind of experience in their off hours, one conducted on their own terms. For instance, Chauncey Pa, a participant from Kaua'i who was demonstrating fishing and net-throwing techniques, decided while he was in town to take his son to visit an old friend. The friend had attended Occidental University with Pa and worked for the U.S. Department of Housing and Urban Development (HUD). Pa, who claimed he was "the most comfortable person on the site" because he performed in swim trunks most of the time, donned an *aloha* shirt, shorts, and rubber slippers to go to the HUD office. Moriarty was horrified and told him he could not go to Washington, D.C., offices dressed like that, but he insisted "Hawai'i casual" was appropriate for visiting an old friend, even if he did work in a government office in Washington.[81]

Offstage, the ethnic categories of the Festival were reconfigured. Participants tended to "hang out" by island rather than ethnic group, and when it was time to go back to the site, they re-sorted themselves back into ethnic categories for the purposes of the Festival.[82] New and old friends were a large part of the offstage scene. People from the HSS arrived at the hotel with coolers filled with food and partied with the participants. Family members from the mainland joined the participants for meals and stayed at the hotel.[83] The number of participants who had family members living in the Washington area underlined a major omission in both the program's demographics and themes, one that was mentioned a few times on the narrative stages: the loss of young people to the mainland due to lack of jobs and the severely inflated cost of living in Hawai'i.[84] Also visible offstage was the Native Hawaiian diaspora. The program focus on "A Sense of Place" rendered the diaspora invisible, along with its causes.[85]

Sometimes the behind-the-scenes situations overtook the front stage, as in the case of the disappearing Spam. In order to make it appear authentic, K. Awa Grocery had been stocked with various local foods such as rice, kimchee, and Spam—the infamous canned ham product that had arrived with American G.I.'s and stayed on to become a favorite island food among the working class.[86] At scheduled times of the day, groups of presenters would appear on the narrative stage to talk-story. Every night the stock of Spam in the "store" went down. Every morning there was a feast at the hotel in the room of the Ho'opi'i brothers, or what became unofficially known as the "Ho'opi'i Café" or "Club Ho'opi'i." When the stage manager was quizzed about this mystery by Festival staff, he shrugged, saying cryptically, "It's a store—stock is supposed to go up and down."[87] Moriarty related how she found out about this.

> By the fifth day, every morning the fire alarm would go on. . . . You'd be up in the morning, getting ready to go downstairs to get started with the Festival . . . and the fire alarm would go on and you'd have to go downstairs, everybody had to vacate the building. . . . And there were a number of high school groups staying in this hotel. . . . I think most of us looked at these high school kids thinking, some little jokester pulled the fire alarm and thinks this is funny. Well, the first day it was one thing, then it happened three or four other times, and I think I complained to the hotel . . . [that] the high school kids are playing around, maybe you should talk to the counselor. . . .Well, as it turns out, the reason the fire alarm was going off was because the Ho'opi'i's and Violet Liliko'i and the Maui group every morning had their two big electric

> skillets that they brought with them. . . . They had their rice cookers and they were frying up Portuguese sausage [and Spam, apparently] with eggs and rice! And you know, Portuguese sausage with all that oil makes a lot of smoke and was setting off the fire alarms![88]

By turning their hotel room into a gathering place, the Ho'opi'is took the national party indoors and re-localized it; the guests of the Smithsonian, who were required to act as hosts to Festival visitors, had set themselves up as hosts to other participants.

Another skirmish began onstage but unfolded offstage. At a *hula* performance, one Hawaiian musician confronted Noenoelani Zuttermeister, a *kumu hula,* asking why they were performing "devil songs" when everyone knew that Hawaiians were all good Christians. This challenge was shocking to other participants, who all respected Zuttermeister and understood this as an infraction of protocol and manners. Soon no one was speaking to either the musician or his wife. Seeing them sitting alone at a meal and picking up on the tension, Kennedy became concerned enough to talk to Papa Auwe, who had become the unofficial *kupuna* among the Hawai'i participants. Papa Auwe, at Kennedy's request, gathered the Hawaiians together and reminded them that in Washington they were all *'ohana* and must act cohesively.[89] In this incident, the imagined community of Hawaiians that had gathered at the Festival acted on principle by shunning someone who had transgressed their unwritten rules; however, an OFP prompt forced them to overlook the behavior they found objectionable and suspend the discipline they had applied in their own move toward group harmony.

As a direct result of participants being "the others" in Washington, there were internal debates about identity and the formation of new alliances, many of which continued past the Smithsonian experience. Reportedly, due to numbers and internal diversity, the majority of these took place among Native Hawaiians. People from different islands, rural and urban environments, political alliances, educational levels, and occupations had come together in a common intensive experience where they were made hyper-aware of ethnic identities, a pressure cooker that was bound to create moments of bonding as well as tension. Debates took place about who was more Hawaiian and more authentic. For example, the *hālau* from Lāna'i wanted to know why everyone from O'ahu and the Big Island were making such a big deal of *hula kahiko* (ancient *hula*) when they, who considered themselves more Hawaiian due to relative isolation, did not perform it themselves.[90]

While the rituals conducted in performance might be seen to secularize sacred practices for the sake of edutainment, there were rituals conducted offstage that served very different purposes. Two of them involved Robert Cato, the Japanese *bon odori* drummer who emerged as a sort of comic genius. Cato is a self-proclaimed heavy drinker whose alcohol consumption became legendary at the Festival. He carried a flask with him on the Festival grounds (he said it was beer, but one of the Japanese dancers present at the interview insisted it was sake) and collected drink tickets from anyone who was not using them. Several people remembered seeing Cato with strings of tickets draped around his neck. Moriarty recalled one night in the hotel ballroom where participants from the four programs gathered, an inebriated Cato became interested in a nearby table full of Native Americans.

> After the first day of the Festival, we all sit down and we're going to have a little program, and this tiny little Japanese man—must be all of 5'4"—with no teeth, goes up to these HUGE Indian guys, who look a bit formidable to us, who've never really seen or had much interaction with Native American Indians—goes up to about seven of them at this big table and they're BIG—and he goes right up to them and he says HOW [fingers raised in a "V"]—and we were looking at them . . . and they said "How! C'mere! Sit down!"

Moriarty said she thought, "Uh oh, there's going to be a racial incident." Instead, she was surprised: "And this Japanese guy and these Indians became the best friends. He got them every day during his time slot when they had the *bon* dances—he got the American Indians to come over and dance around the *yagura* with the *bon* dancers."[91]

Cato's version of this story is slightly different. He claims that a Native American came over to his table and said, "Your drum is bigger than mine," so Cato replied, "It's calling you."[92] Either way, the result was an alliance and Cato being befriended by a group of Native Americans. Later Cato was made an honorary tribal member by a chief and given the name "Walking Eagle." When someone yelled, "Hey, I thought eagles could fly!" the chief's reply was, "Not this eagle!"

Cato was also the subject of a Chinese ritual. Reverend Pang performed a Taoist ritual for Cato's birthday, which occurred over July 4. Cato remembers only that horseflies were biting his legs, and he was told to stand still. When he complained, Pang jokingly told him that the pain was good for him.

Among participants, characters like Cato and the Ho'opi'i brothers emerged as much or more from behind the scenes as they did from the stage. Not everyone stayed up late for jam sessions in the ballroom or dined in the "Ho'opi'i Café." But most drifted through the communal spaces of the hotel, and camaraderie was born of proximity and shared experience. Even some of the oldest members of the group participated. Samuel Kamaka, master *'ukulele* maker and what Moriarty refers to as a "a real gentleman," stayed up late every night with his tape recorder in hand because he was so excited about all the music being informally played. He said he "didn't want to miss anything."[93] Auntie Esther Makua'ole, in her seventies, happily flirted with the men and seemed blithely unconcerned when she became lost in the elevator on more than one occasion.[94] On the other hand, some participants, like *hula* dancers who were busy with costumes and internal protocol, apparently had little time to socialize.[95]

Like the behind-the-scenes regrouping by island, occupational alliances dominated participant exchanges within and between programs. The musicians jammed in the hotel lobby and ballroom and in their rooms. Offstage they could play whatever they wanted, and what they chose was often not the repertoire they played on the Festival site; rather, it included the modern, the popular, and the cross-cultural.[96] Craftspeople discussed their materials and techniques, learning from each other. Ni'ihau shell *lei* makers and Native American beadworkers recognized similarities in each others' fine detail work and gifted each other with shell *lei* and beaded hats, respectively.[97] *Kumu hula* and Voudon priestesses debated traditional beliefs, power, and rituals.[98] Behind the scenes, remedies and advice that could not be shared at the Festival due to health code regulations were freely distributed. Papa Auwe's reputation as a healer quickly spread among the participants of the Hawai'i program and other programs, and soon a line formed at the door to his hotel room. Some of those seeking his help did not speak English, but they came from cultural traditions in other parts of the world that respected herbal healing.[99] Reverence was mixed with irreverence, and sometimes alliances were made through mutual commiseration. A Hawai'i program organizer at one point admonished some of the Hawai'i presenters with, "Go see the Indians. Now that is real culture!" indicating that the Native Americans were successfully representing a spiritual sensibility in their cultural performances, a combination that the organizer apparently saw as a benchmark toward which the Hawai'i program should aspire. Offstage, however, some of the same Native Americans who socialized at

Club Ho'opi'i were reported to be complaining about what they had to do, "saying it was all an act and a load of crap."[100]

Both on and off of the Festival site participants constellated in newly imagined communities that crossed ethnic boundaries. Unlike the program concept, which had divided people by ethnicity and re-clumped them through the alleged historical experience of their ancestors, these constellations formed around similarities in cultural practices and shared personal histories. Although there were certainly aberrations like Cato, reportedly most Asians made their closest alliances with other Asians, while Hawaiians grouped by island and closely associated with the Native Americans. At the pre-Festival meeting of all the participants in 1989, when Rinzler had asked all of the participants to hold hands and sing Woody Guthrie's classic "This Land is Our Land," the Native Americans were overheard singing, "This land was our land, you took it from us. . . ."[101] This kind of covert resistance, along with on- and offstage opportunities to compare similar indigenous issues, must have resonated for politically minded Native Hawaiians.

* * *

When asked in an interview about ideals versus realities of Festival performance, Kurin replied that "ideals have a way of becoming reality."[102] The Hawai'i program performance phase provides glimpses into how the frames of the Festival were contested and appropriated. It illustrates the disjunctions between the Hawai'i program ideals and the actual lived experience of the participants and others, and it illuminates some of the moments in which the ideals did, indeed, become reality. Despite its evocations of lived experience, the Hawai'i program was a utopian experiment in the sense that it compressed Hawai'i pluralism and history into a single site and moment. As a performance of an ideal in public space, it actually constituted the ideal. In speaking about street parades, Susan Davis points out that the notion of public culture is itself based on an ideal.

> The domain in which public performances take place must be viewed as structured and contested terrain, rather than as a neutral field or empty frame for social action, and the public nature of street parades should be analyzed rather than assumed. The institutions, practices, behaviors, space and places we call the public sphere include the very idea that there can and should exist social interaction open and accessible to the widest popular participation and influence. (1986, 12)

The Mall is a nationalized version of the public street, and what happens within it seems democratized precisely because of its privileged location in the ultimate national public space.

Martin reported that one visitor to the 1989 Hawai'i program on the Mall exclaimed, "I've been to Hawai'i many times—but I never saw this. I must have been on the other side of the Island" (1998, 120). Her story has been much repeated by program staff as a useful measure of the program's success in problematizing public views of Hawai'i. Likewise, much analysis of festival/public culture concentrates on what is seen by the public. The stories of participants indicate, however, that this was not the only locus of meaning. In fact, much of what performers found memorable about the Festival happened out of the public eye altogether.

Although the careful orchestrations of the Festival provided convincing illusions of authenticity for audiences, its spatial, logistical, and ideological edges prompted participants to transgress its boundaries and subvert Festival limitations. Carnivalesque spontaneity and inversion did erupt at the Festival, instigated by participants, but in the program's seams much more than onstage. Whereas the fieldwork and production phases had homogenized pluralism into an institutional counter-narrative of cultural harmony expressed as creolization and cultural resurgence, the Festival actually became multi-vocal only in the sum of its parts. In its totality—front, back, and offstage, as well as contexts—it embodied conflict, negotiation, and community in forms that eluded co-optation, for the most part, by either the tourist or the ethnographic gaze. In conceptual form, the program paradigm existed as an abstract ideal that was actually experienced by audience and participants in fragments, never holistically as it was designed; it was, instead, a multi-sited production whose shape morphed moment by moment in relation to its frames as well as in response to human interaction in its various zones.

Nor would it have been possible to experience it as a whole. On the ground, the Festival was filled with chance encounters, cameo appearances, and moments of insight, connection, entertainment, and education. The performance phase raises important questions of what was and was not seen by visitors and participants. Even participants, most of them present on site for a full ten days in 1989, have random memories. Fourteen years later, what they remember are selective moments, like a member of the audience falling into a trance at the voodoo stage, the surprise birth of the buffalo calf, fireworks on the 4th of July.

Audiences were critical to Festival production, but they seem to have been peripheral, in most cases, to participant experiences and meaning-making. The Festival conceptualization, selection, and design processes had been orchestrated to impose harmony on cacophony through thematic linkages, spatial design, and textual productions, but performance takes on a life of its own. When referring to what happens once the plans, the participants, the audience, the site, the weather, and the fates come together and combust, many can find no more appropriate word than "magic." Beyond craft and illusion, the magic that can, and sometimes, does, occur is the ineffability of festiveness, forging of new communities, empowerment of individuals and groups, and creation of understanding. As Cantwell says, "The purposes of the Festival of American Folklife are best achieved, when they are achieved—where the cultural recovery or recontextualization of the folk performance is, if temporary, more than didactic, theoretical, or imaginary" (Baron and Spitzer 1992, 300). For many who were there in the Hawai'i program, ideals did become reality during the Festival.

Many of the participants at the Festival had a new sense of themselves and of their cultural capital. They experienced personal and community gains that cannot be dismissed. What the anecdotal evidence surrounding the Hawai'i program suggests is that the radical juxtapositions of the Festival may provide for redefinitions of community that transgress assigned categories. The OFP prefers to think of the Festival as dialogic rather than didactic; however, the insertion of a dialogic model of ethnographic display into national space is in itself didactic. In addition to serving as an ethical and aesthetic model, the Festival is clearly a contact zone in which multiple discourses collide and coincide. Perhaps "the question that remains at the end of the day is," as Nick Stanley asks in relation to Asia-Pacific performers in cultural theme parks, "who will come to own the script?" (1998, 112).

Chapter 5

Beyond the Festival Afterglow

> The essence of the carnivalesque is that one cannot tell male from female, rich from poor, black from white: those differences, ordinarily so crucial, do not matter for the duration of the carnival. Everything is freer there, everything is possible. But carnivals do not last. And the interpenetration of third and first world is not just festive. Behind the festivities are social and economic facts we should not forget.
>
> —Marianna Torgovnik, *Gone Primitive*

In the summer of 2003 I traveled to Waimea, Kaua'i, to meet some of the surviving members of the Waimea Hawaiian Church Choir who had performed *hīmeni* choral music at the Festival. When I arrived at the house of Miriam Kaleipua Pahulehua, a crowd of relatives was busily tending an *imu* across the dirt road while the elders sat and enjoyed the shade. Soon after I had introduced my husband and myself, Miriam invited us to her grandson's wedding the following day. The wedding was held in the tiny Waimea Hawaiian Church, and the wedding *lū'au* was held down the road in a beach park. It was a huge event with, in addition to an endless spread of food, a performance by Sonny Ching's *hālau hula* from the Big Island, an appearance by a popular local band, and a local radio personality as the master of ceremonies. At the wedding we had noticed two casually dressed *haole* carrying cameras, a tripod, and a microphone. They reappeared at the reception, so we assumed that they had been hired to film the event. However, midway through the feasting, the MC brought them to everyone's attention. "Hey everybody!" he said, "We got folks here from the Smithsonian taking pictures! They're researching *lū'au* all across the nation, so when they come around with the camera, you better smile big! You never know—you might end up in *National Geographic!*" Later we talked to the embarrassed photographers, who explained that they were actually from a nearby town and doing a feature on *lū'au* for a local television station. While our inclusion in the festivities certainly speaks to rural Hawaiian hospitality, the razzing of the would-be ethnographers at the reception and the MC's conflation of the Smithsonian Institution and *National Geographic* magazine say a great deal about the naturalization of the ethnographic gaze within Native Hawaiian cultural activities. On the other hand, I wondered, would he have made this particular joke before the 1989 Smithsonian Folklife Festival had turned its spotlight on this small community's cultural traditions? At least at the level of rhetoric, the Smithsonian had left a legacy.

Although most visitors and scholars focus on the Festival itself, or portions thereof, the Smithsonian envisions the festival-making process as a catalyst, not an end in itself. Advocating cultural preservation, it encourages local sponsorship to pick up where the Festival leaves off. Center for Folklife and Cultural Heritage (CFCH) literature cites successful post-Festival programs at the local level, but CFCH directors admit this outcome is not always predictable. This chapter traces the aftermath of the Hawai'i program to look at its legacy on several levels—local and national, institutional and personal—and at the various forms in which it was transported back into a local context—performance, film, follow-up projects, and memory. Along the way it raises a number of questions about Festival aftereffects. How did the Smithsonian living museum philosophy and methods translate into a Hawai'i socioscape many residents claimed was still operating under "plantation mentality" and where the tourist industry continues to peddle a "soft savagery" image of Native Hawaiian culture for tourist consumption? How did the Smithsonian use its institutional power to negotiate asymmetries of power between Hawai'i's peoples and between Hawai'i and the rest of the nation? What happened in the transference of responsibility from national to state institutions? What effect, if any, did the Festival actually have on cultural preservation programs and policy in Hawai'i, and what are the larger implications of institutional attention to tradition? In the Festival's aftermath, these issues played out on the local level. I argue that beyond its time-bound performance, the Hawai'i program provided an ongoing means of production and reproduction, but that its aftereffects were blunted by local politics and socioeconomic factors.

Local Celebrities and the Festival Afterglow

The Smithsonian's validation created a palpable afterglow for participants. Along with other federally funded cultural agencies like the

NEA, the Festival legitimized and made cultural celebrities of participants, albeit mostly on a small scale. During and immediately after the Festival, local newspapers sported photos and stories about the local residents who had performed on the Mall. Many participants returning to Hawai‘i had a new sense of their cultural capital after their Festival experience.[1] While some tradition bearers were already known within their own communities, most of them had not previously been recognized beyond them, and for other participants the Festival was the first public recognition they had ever experienced for their traditional skills.

Several people from Hawai‘i had previously been recognized by national arts agencies in the nation's capitol. For instance, Kau‘i Zuttermeister, a *kumu hula,* her daughter Noelani, and granddaughter Hao‘oli had danced *hula* in the 1984 Festival program called "The Grand Generation," which had focused on intergenerational transmissions of folklife. Pualani Kanaka‘ole, *kumu hula* and educator, had participated with Lynn Martin in the 1988 Festival program marking the American Folklore Society centennial. She and Martin were part of a Festival experiment in presenting folklorists and the people they study as equal partners in dialogue. Kennedy jokingly referred to it as exhibiting "folklorists and their catch."[2] Four traditional artists from Hawai‘i—Kau‘i Zuttermeister; Meali‘i Kalama, quiltmaker; Raymond Kane, slack-key guitarist; and Kindy Sproat, falsetto singer and *‘ukulele* musician—had previously been recipients of National Heritage Fellowship (NHF) awards, based on recommendations by culture brokers and scholars knowledgeable about particular traditions. By 2006 six more Hawai‘i artists would receive this prestigious award—all of them former Festival participants.[3] At the 1989 Festival, the Hawai‘i NHF award winners were showcased as exemplary cultural practitioners, valorizing their expertise and styles in front of their peers as well as a national audience.

While these artists were indeed deserving of recognition, some local culture brokers and traditional arts practitioners point out that the sort of canonization involved in an NHF award and Festival selection has sometimes had the detrimental effect of elevating personal style in communities that have customarily not prized individual style over community aesthetics. Once recognized as National Heritage Fellows, tradition bearers were assured of being on the permanent "A" list for future Smithsonian appearances that might require Hawai‘i representation. Whether or not celebrity status was merited was sometimes a covert, but contentious, issue in the home environment. As one culture broker in Hawai‘i, who prefers to remain anonymous, stated,

> Culture brokers create situations where opportunity and status is assigned to the cultural practitioners that "market" themselves the best. Once someone gets into the loop, it becomes a self-fulfilling prophecy. . . . Kimo does a workshop for the museum, someone writes an article on it, a teacher sees the article and hires Kimo to do a talk at the school, a TV crew is on hand at the school, a non-profit org. sees Kimo on TV and thinks he's the expert they need for their festival and when someone comes into town and asks who's the best, we all say in unison: "Kimo" da guy does all kine festivals, and workshops. . . . The western world anointed Kimo, when in actuality the museum workshop was the first one he ever did and he was just a newbie. Meanwhile, unbeknownst to the western world, Kimo's teacher's teacher keeps the tradition alive for those who really know. By now Kimo has developed a "shtick" and is quite good—does the culture circuit for a living like those motivational speakers. In his native culture, Kimo's rise to fame would never have happened.

This hypothetical anecdote might be applied to a pivotal irony of the Festival: while folklife is embedded in community values, beliefs, and aesthetics, institutional recognition imposes a system of meritocracy. The complaint against celebritizing individual culture bearers is generally not a judgment that those being recognized are lacking in artistic merit; rather, it asserts that traditional practices, such as *hula* or *paniolo,* vary from place to place and insists that one style is not necessarily superior to another. Some local culture workers point out that the merit system upends the natural horizontal proliferation of cultural practices by legitimizing one lineage over others or crediting certain teachers while overlooking others.[4] At issue is not just the question of whose cultural authority is the final arbiter of excellence, but also whether a merit system fits a community ethos. A related issue is that for the purpose of administering public programs, institutional perspectives tend to flatten many small communities into conglomerates. Hawai'i folklife practices vary over several islands, and although the Festival staff had made a concerted effort to represent the diversity of styles in the islands and to represent Hawai'i as multi-regional as well as multicultural, for budgetary reasons the selection had been limited. Three *hula* variations were represented out of between 150 and 200 *hālau hula*.[5] For other traditions the program had been able to choose representatives of only one community to represent a diverse tradition or one to a few individuals to represent a large group, with the aftereffect that one style was valorized over others. This sort of celebrity making and style validation was bound to leave some individuals and groups disgruntled.

Selective Documentation

Tensions between the linked issues of cultural authority and cultural celebrities were played out in conflicts over visual Festival documentation. Two local firms went to Washington to document the Hawai'i program on video. Juniroa Productions, a Hawai'i-based documentary film company founded by Heather Giugni and Esther Figueroa that has produced an impressive array of local films, contracted with the state of Hawai'i to film the Hawai'i program.[6] Giugni's proposal stated that the principal goal of their film would be to bring the Festival home for the Festival participants and the people of Hawai'i. To this end, Giugni and Lurline MacGregor, her partner on the project, hoped to air the final product on local television while the HSFCA planned to distribute it to participants, schools, and libraries.[7] Juniroa proposed to interview participants before, during, and after the Festival, but when they finally received approval for their proposal, it was too little and too late for such an ambitious plan. Juniroa had to shrink their project to half of the requested budget and a shorter video format that would cover only a portion of the Festival itself.[8] Festival director Diana Parker met with Giugni and stressed that her first imperative should be to devise a way to film all of the participants, despite budget and time constrictions.[9] Juniroa's contract, however, expressly stated that they retained the right to make artistic decisions about format and editing, so they chose to follow their own directives. This choice laid the groundwork for an unpleasant dispute centered on issues of ethnographic authority and control over Festival imaging and historiography.

Based on their filming of the Hawai'i program in 1989, Juniroa produced a twenty-four-minute video titled *Celebrating Hawai'i's Cultures*. It opens with a *lauhala* mat filling the screen, and centered on the mat is what appears to be a photograph held by corner mounts. Along the top and left sides of the photograph, a small graphic is superimposed repeatedly on the mat in single rows. From this image the camera zooms into the central photograph, which becomes a narrated film segment. This sequencing of still shot to film is repeated several times using various photographs surrounded by graphic symbols. Some of the sequences begin with black-and-white historical images while others start with images of the Festival performances and demonstrations.

Within the film, Richard Kurin, Richard Kennedy, and Linda Moriarty are interviewed about Festival philosophy, and various tradition bearers are shown demonstrating their skills in the context of the Festival. Abbreviated histories of immigrant groups begin with historic photographs that were actually exhibited in the Hawai'i program learning center, surrounded by a repeated iconic graphic, such as a *forno* for the Portuguese or an *ipu* for Hawaiian instrument makers. A female voice-over explains pertinent histories, such as the immigrant experience in Hawai'i, and narrativizes the Hawai'i program at the Festival. Although the film had been drastically abridged due to a reduced budget, film time is also devoted to portions of the other three programs concurrent on the Mall in 1989, after-hours jam sessions at the Festival hotel, and even the food concessions—Styrofoam and all (Giugni and MacGregor 1989).

When presented with the finished film, Martin was displeased enough to ask Juniroa to make changes and to request that the governor's office or the HSFCA come up with the funds to facilitate them. Juniroa dug in its heels and cited the original contract agreement that had granted them artistic control.[10] Martin expressed her disapproval to Pat Brandt at the governor's office and to Millicent Kim, president of the HSFCA Board of Commissioners. She cited several objections to the Juniroa film that ranged from credits to content. Chief among them was that the NHF award winners and Hālau o Kekuhi, the prestigious *hālau hula* from the Big Island, had not been depicted, nor had *hula kahiko*. Taking to heart the notion of folklife as anonymously authored and communally owned, Juniroa had deliberately chosen not to focus on celebrities and instead use their shortened film format to focus on cultural practices, not individuals, particularly those practices less well known than performance arts like slack-key guitar and *hula*.

Martin was horrified to learn that due to budgetary and time constrictions and because another Hawai'i film crew was also filming on site, no one had filmed the "artists of stature," to use Martin's words. This meant that even if Juniroa had wished to comply with Martin's demands, the requested footage did not exist. Another problem with the Juniroa film was that subtitles were used to identify officials like Kurin, Kennedy, and Moriarty, but individual program participants who appeared on screen were not identified. Martin's correspondence shows an acute awareness of both political and cultural protocols. She asserted that the choice to represent cultural authorities from the Smithsonian over Hawai'i cultural practitioners misrepresented OFP and HSFCA principles and that it was highly inappropriate to narrate over silenced participants when the Festival mission was to present tradition bearers in their own voices. She deemed the voice-over superimposed on a Hawaiian chant given by Pualani Kanaka'ole as disrespectful, and she was understandably offended that the Hawai'i State Folklorist (herself) had not been mentioned in the final credits. Tactfully stated at all times, her correspondence reveals a particular concern that the omissions and exposures in the film and its distribution as a public record of the program might open up the HSFCA to criticism and affect her careful cultivation of HSFCA relationships with key Native Hawaiian cultural practitioners. Much to Martin's dismay, neither Brandt nor Kim was willing to take on the fight, and in her replies Giugni staunchly defended her position on the grounds that she and MacGregor were both part-Hawaiian and therefore "naturally sensitive to the issues of Hawaiian representation." Giugni argued that she had not felt it appropriate to ask cultural practitioners to explain Festival policy or philosophy, that the names of all participants had been listed in the credits, that the HSFCA was listed (Martin had not been an official member of the Festival crew), and that their understanding was that the emphasis was to be on the traditions, not on individual accomplishments.[11]

Both sides of this altercation raised ethical issues important in the politics of representation. Where they clashed was over their interpretations of institutional versus artistic integrity. On one level, the issues surrounding the Juniroa film were about creative agency, interpretation, and reputation, but on a deeper level they were about *re*-presentation and historicization through selective distillation and narration. Film productions had the power to codify how the empirical and conceptual aspects of the event would enter into public and even participant memory. An interpretation at variance with the institutional view had the potential to give the organizers a permanent black eye.

As part of its *Spectrum* series, Hawai'i Public Broadcasting Service (PBS) set out to make a very different kind of Festival film. The twenty-eight-minute PBS episode was titled simply "The Festival" and directed by Bart Fredo. Contracted by the state of Hawai'i, Juniroa had situated the Festival as a locus from which to examine Festival philosophy, histories of Hawai'i communities, and selected traditional arts. Fredo, on the other hand, chose to locate the Festival as a point on a chronological trajectory that began in Hawai'i, journeyed to Washington, and returned to Hawai'i. The film enters and leaves the Mall from an aerial view that symbolically positions Washington as a destination on the horizon from a Hawai'i geographical perspective. Within this frame, the film features a series of vignettes on Festival participants that are based on interviews conducted in Hawai'i before and after the Festival and on the Festival site.

A female Native Hawaiian voice is employed for voice-overs (Nalani Wilson-Ku), but only as a transitional device to segue between sequences in which individual participants are cameoed. As in the Juniroa film, filmic time limitations allowed only enough space to highlight a few artists. Within that space, both directors chose to portray all nine ethnic groups, but where Juniroa had decided to focus on historical storytelling about major ethnic groups, Fredo focused on contemporary stories about individual tradition bearers. Similarly to Juniroa, Fredo concentrated almost exclusively on people who had not been previously celebritized by the NEA or the Smithsonian. The one exception in "The Festival" is Meali'i Kalama, a quilter who had been the first artist from Hawai'i to receive an NHF award. Fifteen participants from a range of craft and occupational traditions are portrayed, along with two cooking and seven performance traditions. Tradition bearers are identified with subtitles throughout, along with their practices: *lei* making, bulrush sandal making, calligraphy, canoe building, rawhide braiding, doll making, quilting, and *imu* and *forno* cooking. As in the Juniroa film, the high-profile traditions of *hula* and slack-key were omitted in favor of portraying less well-known performance traditions. In the PBS episode, these include Hawaiian falsetto singing and *lū'au* music, Puerto Rican *katchi katchi* music, Filipino *rondalla,* Japanese *bon odori* music and dance, and Korean and Okinawan dance. The Festival experience is characterized through narratives about the Hawai'i program, some in participant voices.

In the PBS show, Henry Silva, a *paniolo* craftsman who had never left Hawai'i prior to the Festival, recounts his initial reluctance to go to Washington, D.C., whereas in the Juniroa film, participant hesitance is recounted by a coordinator speaking for participants. Three moments in the PBS film anchor its multicultural theme. Near the beginning, Marie McDonald talks about herself and Hawai'i diversity as "chop suey." Halfway through, Meali'i Kalama refers to herself as a quilt because of her "mixed race" heritage. In the conclusion to "The Festival" the narrator defines the Hawai'i program as a "symbol of our ability as a nation to celebrate unity in diversity." Displayed prior to the credits is the aforementioned Hawaiian proverb about coming down from the cliffs to get to know those below—the same quote that Kennedy had dispensed with on Nathan Napoka's insistence that its Hawaiian meaning was really a call to war. Here, Fredo uses it in the spirit of Kennedy's misinterpretation—reading it as an invitation to understand difference from up close rather than as a challenge (Fredo 1989). These anchors define a multicultural frame for the film, but unlike the Juniroa production, which stresses ethnic diversity through immigrant histories, there is little mention elsewhere of ethnicity in the PBS show.

Both versions were designed to historicize and bring the Festival home to Hawai'i by creating a definitive account of the performance event, but while the Juniroa film attempted to capture the festive spirit of the Hawai'i program and the effect of Hawai'i on a national audience, the PBS episode was more interested in the effect of the Festival experience on tradition bearers from Hawai'i. Neither features the institutionally legitimized stars, but only one of them was in a position to answer to Festival organizers who were concerned about image and damage control for the Hawai'i program's historic record.

The Hawai'i program was also returned home in the distillations of memory. According to Marita Sturken, "What memories tell us, more than anything, is the stakes held by individuals and institutions in attributing meaning to the past" (1997, 9). Festival memory serves its tellers in various ways, and the personal narratives connected to the Hawai'i program are illustrative of a variety of positionings. Directors tell stories about meetings with officials and stories about outsmarting or eluding rigid institutional limitations. OFP staff narratives tend to reinforce the image of the OFP as a cultural ally to the Hawai'i communities it represented and thus incorporate a body of stories about successful intervention and facilitation, unlikely friendships across cultural and class lines, and their own inclusion in communities of participants. *Haole* presenters from Hawai'i, many of whom operated as midlevel culture workers in fieldwork and performance, reinforce their ally status by stressing intimacy with participants and downplaying their connection to organizers, often relating stories in which they act as witnesses or confidantes to small resistances invisible to directors and others at the upper institutional levels. Although culture worker stories concentrate on relationships with participants, it seems that few participant stories mention culture workers at all. Instead, participant stories tend to focus on relationships formed with other participants and Festival high jinks. In other words, while insider (participant) stories serve to verify an inside and outside to the imagined community of performers, outsiders (culture workers and brokers) tell stories that assert their own inclusion and access while maintaining community exclusivity by differentiating themselves from those with less cultural savvy and sensitivity (tourists). The result is a centrifugal layering in which the narration of memory operates selectively to make meaning of a set of experiences and to reveal and reify (or create) each teller's ideological and social position vis-à-vis the others.

In the same way that the primacy of memory is sometimes difficult to determine once an event has been solidified by technologies of film or print, the recounting of personal narratives raises the question of whether the media simply reflected or actually constituted Festival stories as official Festival memories. All participants and staff members received a copy of the Juniroa film and several wrote to the OFP to say that they had re-lived the Festival experience through its viewing. Most of them probably also saw the PBS special.[12] The interweaving of media encapsulization and memory cannot easily be untangled and serves to illustrate the potential of media to intervene in memory. For example, on a routine survey of former Festival participants years later, McDonald recounted the same story she had told on camera about the little girl who had learned to make *lei*. In the PBS documentary she states that she was the one who overheard Festival visitors observing that they had traveled to Hawai'i but "must have been the other side of the island" since they had never seen the folklife presented on the Mall. This same story was recounted to me by a Festival staff-person as his partner's firsthand experience. In Kurin's book on the Festival it appears as a third-person narrative told by Martin (1998, 120). Whatever the source, the re-circulation of certain Festival narratives that reinforce official Festival rhetoric and the program themes has the effect of legitimizing them as the "correct" memories. Not surprisingly, it is the narratives distilled into official accounts that best exemplify the program as a utopian multicultural experience.

Beyond presenting regional folklife at a national level and American folklife to the world, Festival directors hope that regional participation in the Festival will breed cultural preservation efforts at home. In the production and performance phases of the Festival, a plethora of supplementary materials is produced that extends a Festival program beyond its existence as a performance bound by time and space. For instance, annual Festival books with program-specific articles are sent to institutions and libraries throughout the country. During the Festival, volunteers make audio recordings and handwritten logs at the various performance stages. After the Festival, this documentation, along with fieldwork recordings and reports, is compiled by OFP archivists for future research purposes, one copy to be archived at the OFP and a second set to be presented to the cooperating agency at the local level.

These pre-Festival and Festival materials are presumed to form a valuable database for local researchers and culture workers. For example, although considerable research had previously been conducted into the cultural practices of certain groups in Hawai‘i, such as Native Hawaiians, Filipinos, and *paniolo,* and into particular crafts such as *lauhala* weaving, the Smithsonian project instigated the first and only comprehensive survey of Hawai‘i folklife to look beyond performance and crafts and include such a wide range of ethnicities. The final compilation returned to the state of Hawai‘i consisted of fieldwork reports and interview logs and Festival tapes and stage-recording logs. These materials found a home in the Hawai‘i/Asia/Pacific collection of Hamilton Library at the University of Hawai‘i at Mānoa, where they were lodged after being rejected by the Hawai‘i State Archives.[13] Although the reasons for the Archives declining such a treasure trove of information about Hawai‘i's living cultures are unclear, apparently at that time the Festival was not anticipated to have historical value at a local level, and the documentation of Hawai‘i's living cultures was deemed inappropriate to archive in an institution devoted to social and political history.

Restaging Hawai‘i for Hawai‘i

One splashy way to capitalize on the energy and momentum of the Festival was to restage it in Hawai‘i. Moriarty and Martin both remember that when they were first approached about restaging the Hawai‘i program in Hawai‘i, the Festival production was in progress, and they were horrified that anyone would suggest that they consider undertaking such a project. They were understandably exhausted and relieved to see their year and a half of preparation coming to fruition and considered the 1989 program the final product of their labor. Most accounts attribute the idea to Governor Waihee, who said that he wanted to bring it to Hawai‘i because he strongly felt the people of Hawai‘i should see what was being presented in Washington, D.C.[14]

The idea of a restaging may well have germinated in conversation with OFP directors who were aware there was a precedent in the 1987 Michigan program on the Mall that had generated an in-state folklife festival. However it was instigated, no time was lost in building on Festival momentum, and on August 15, 1989, less than a month after the close of the Festival, Martin sent a memo to Sarah Richards, acting HSFCA director, proposing a six-week planning period in which to consider the project. To accomplish this task, Martin suggested a staff of herself, Moriarty, Kennedy, Lau, and Nahwoosky—the joint creators of the 1989 Hawai'i program.[15] Kennedy was especially keen on the project. In his six-month stay during the fieldwork phase, he had become very attached to the islands, and follow-up projects would enable him to return as more than a tourist. In September the president of the HSFCA Board of Commissioners, Millicent Kim, sent a letter to Waihee that stressed the Smithsonian's enthusiasm for the project and outlined the benefits of restaging the Hawai'i program: it would stand as the first multicultural cultural festival in Hawai'i, and it would become a model for future cultural programs within the state. She estimated a cost of $500,000, half of the state's contribution for the program in 1989.[16] In October Martin called a pre-planning meeting at the HSFCA,[17] and on November 11, 1989, she submitted a formal proposal, co-authored with Moriarty, to the OFP, Governor Waihee, and the HSFCA.

Despite the expense, the proposal for the Hawai'i program restaging argued for a full restaging rather than a more economical partial one in order to avoid any problems of making selections from the original lineup of participants and the risk of offending some groups. In this way the HSFCA could still deflect any local criticism to the Smithsonian's original selection process. The proposal highlighted several ways in which localizing/re-contextualizing the national program incurred subtle reorientations of its educational agenda. Most evident was that despite a state economy deeply enmeshed with tourist promotion and the financial backing of the original version by the Hawai'i Visitors Bureau, this event was being pitched, at least overtly, to local residents. According to the proposal, the stated purposes for the restaging were seven-fold.

1. To highlight folk art traditions in the state of Hawai'i.
2. To provide a highly visible means of focusing public attention on the importance of the HSFCA Folk Arts Program and its impact on identifying and nurturing folklife traditions and artists in Hawai'i.
3. To provide a state sponsored venue, open and free to the public for the honoring and celebrating of the great diversity of folk arts traditions in Hawai'i.
4. To provide a model for the professional presentation of folk

arts traditions for other organizations and ethnic festivals in Hawai'i.

5. To provide an educational opportunity for the residents of the state of Hawai'i to learn more about our multi-cultural community and its localized traditions.
6. To provide an educational opportunity for visitors to experience authentic representations, performance and displays of the folk traditions of Hawai'i.
7. To provide an educational opportunity in the area of festival production and interpretation for local organizations and institutions through the development of an ancillary educational workshop.[18]

On his copy of the proposal, Kennedy added one more handwritten item to the purpose list: "Capitalize on momentum." The Washington program had been geared toward educating or reeducating tourists, but the restaging was overtly directed at educating residents. Tourism benefits appear in the proposal's purpose statement, but near the bottom of the list. However, the need to attract a broad audience is implicit in proposing funding for a state-sponsored venue for folk arts that could serve as a model for future ethnic festivals, since these are generally held in the tourist zones. Also implicit in the purpose statement is the idea that the Smithsonian fieldwork-based model of cultural representation could be interjected into Hawai'i tourism to present a more textured and authentic view, an alternative to primitivism, cultural commodification, and erasures of pluralism.

Ancillary educational opportunities were planned utilizing the skills and advice of OFP educational specialist Betty Belanus. A special festival day would provide docent-led tours for schoolchildren, and Belanus would meet with the Department of Education and private school art programs to offer curriculum suggestions and other information. Workshops on festival production and folklife presentation were planned for professionals and cultural groups, taking advantage of the restaging as a tool and model. Ultimately, the rationale used to sell the restaging proposal was that a single event could be used to maximize educational opportunities for schools, the general public, and community professionals, as well as to increase visibility for the HSFCA and its Folklife Program. Where the Washington, D.C., version of the Hawai'i program had been outreach, transmitting what the OFP felt Hawai'i had to say to the nation about living with diversity, the Hawai'i version was shifted to "inreach," [19] providing a role model for local cultural exhibition and local education about diversity while enhancing the HSFCA's image as a folk arts and ethnic diversity advocate.

Orchestrating the restaging was less demanding in some ways and more in others. The fieldwork had already been done, reducing the program process to planning, production, and performance phases. Production was also simplified because the signage from the Hawai'i program had been donated to the HSFCA, eliminating a major production-phase task. However, presenting the program in Hawai'i also meant it was under new scrutiny, since the organizers were presenting Hawai'i to Hawai'i rather than to a national/international audience.

The restaging also incurred new logistical problems. As an HSFCA-sponsored event, the restaging would not have the benefit of the OFP's large and experienced staff and streamlined infrastructure, although it would have advisory assistance from Nahwoosky and Lau and a small staff from the OFP. Furthermore, using local labor involved dealing with the state of Hawai'i's cumbersome fiscal procedures requiring all state-funded jobs over a nominal amount to be sent out for multiple bids. Faced with the dismal prospect of a process with which she was all too familiar, Martin predicted that it could take years instead of months if a solution was not identified that would skirt the "projected obstacle" of state regulations and fiscal restrictions.[20] Martin recalls that at one official meeting she was frustrated enough to state outright that perhaps the project was impossible. In the silence that followed, alarmed glances were exchanged between state employees. Finally, the spokesperson suggested that maybe they could pull a few strings to get around the rules.[21] This would become the pattern for dealing with the state of Hawai'i throughout the restaging.

The new context shifted program meanings. Although two other time slots were up for consideration, one of them Admissions Day,[22] and one other site, the committee settled on restaging the Hawai'i program, to be called "Folklife Hawai'i," from October 18 to 21, 1990, on Magic Island, a man-made promontory shaped like a foot and located midway between the Waikīkī and downtown areas of Honolulu. Again by happenstance, there was cause for celebration. The year 1989 had marked the thirtieth anniversary of Hawai'i statehood, a symbolic reenactment of Hawai'i's inclusion in the nation. The following year would mark the twenty-fifth anniversary of the HSFCA, a chance to publicly recognize the state agency's commitment to local communities (and not just to fine arts, as HSFCA interests were often characterized) and in particular affirming the importance of the Folk Arts Program, a fledgling addition to the HSFCA.

Surrounded by the ocean on three sides, Magic Island had a decidedly different feel from the landlocked National Mall—an island of green surrounded by the imposing edifices of government buildings and national museums and galleries. Evoking Hawai'i out-of-place had relied heavily on making associations to place through images, language, music, and dance—much of them about the ocean and nature. Implying ocean and tropical ambiance where they were not had been a problem made infinitely easier by the global commodification of Hawai'i as an exotic tourist destination coded into a recognizable tropical iconography of *hula, aloha* shirts, and flower *lei.* These exotic but familiar icons could then be recoded into more ethnographically "accurate" forms through their connection to participant hands and voices and by supplementary captioning. In Hawai'i, the in situ programmatic challenge was to translate the ordinary—everyday people against a familiar backdrop of tropical sea and landscape—into an attraction extraordinary enough to draw crowds.

In Washington, D.C., the geometric grid of the Mall had been organicized through a clever site design that broke up its hard lines with a profusion of plants, lava-rock walls, and circular exhibition spaces. Like the Mall, Magic Island is traversed by walkways that skirt the perimeter and subdivide the interior, but these are meandering and follow the topography of the site. The difference between cityscape and naturescape dictated very different exhibit and performance strategies, with a much looser arrangement on Magic Island than in Washington. Due to the limited space in which to accommodate audiences, the two music stages were located all the way to one side of the park. The *yagura* was erected on the other side of a small hill and within the same walkway-bound area. Asian crafts were arranged around it, as they had been on the Mall. Also within this area were the foodways demonstration area, plantation exhibit, and narrative stage. In an adjacent area on the other side of the peninsula the *hula* stage, occupational areas, and Hawaiian crafts were located. While the ordering of the new site into immigrant and indigenous areas roughly replicated the split arrangement of the original design, it also deviated in some important ways. Hawaiian quilting was placed off by itself and Asian crafts were distanced to a far corner. Overall, the design was loose and sprawling rather than tightly integrated as it had been on the Mall, where the goal had been to present a unified diversity knit together by shared history alongside shared cultural practices. In the Magic Island site map, juxtaposition seemed considerably more accidental. The various groups had coalesced to make the Hawai'i program an imagined island in metropolitan Washington, but on Magic Island, where the cultural and geographical boundaries were again blurred, each cultural group seemed to surface as an island on its own.

Martin and Moriarty made an effort to re-create and even expand the original performance lineup. They augmented the history-bound definitions that had limited the initial selection to nine ethnic groups by adding several groups and traditions that had not been represented in Washington: Laotian music, games, and flower arranging; Vietnamese traditional theater; Southeast Asian weaving traditions; Chinese paper cuts; Japanese stitchery; Portuguese dance; African American gospel music; and Tongan church music. In the process of expanding the roster of traditional practices, they added ethnic groups that had immigrated to Hawai'i after the plantation era: African Americans, Southeast Asians, and Tongans. They also brought in two groups from the contingent 1989 programs: a zydeco group called the Lawtell Playboys and a group of Plains Indians dancers. Moriarty said that as soon as word got out that the restaging was going to happen, she began receiving phone calls from 1989 participants who insisted that those from the other Festival programs should be included so that people in Hawai'i could experience what they had experienced in Washington. She remembered that many of them had felt strongly that Hawai'i residents needed to see cultures from other places. Some of the Hawai'i performers had become particularly friendly with the zydeco musicians and the Native American dancers because of the similarities in their traditions, so they petitioned organizers to include them. Newly savvy about Festival workings, Hawai'i participants argued that if these performers' wives came along they could do cooking demonstrations in the restaging.[23]

Despite efforts to re-create the program in Hawai'i, it was impossible to maintain the same sense of cohesion precisely because much of the sense of community had been predicated upon participants being in a location outside of Hawai'i. As the cultural and geographical others in Washington, D.C., participants had bonded through the joint experiences of liminal time (two weeks of semi-vacation), dislocation (the mainland), and location (the Festival site and hotel). The restaging lasted only four days versus the two-week stretch on the Mall. Off-island participants stayed at the Ramada Renaissance Ala Moana Hotel, while participants from O'ahu went home at night, so there were far fewer opportunities to convene informally. This reinforced the "Honolulu versus the rest" division that had been temporarily bridged during the Festival.[24] The Festival's imagined community was fragmented in its own locale because it lacked the original sense of unity and removal from reality.

As in Washington, day and night performances took place—alongside crafts, occupational, and cooking demonstrations—but with modifications. The K. Awa Grocery narrative stage was reconstructed, and potentially controversial topics such as "Tourism in Hawai'i," "Natural Resources," and "Islands in Transition" were presented along with informational topics like "Asians in Hawai'i," "Cultural Preservation," "Plantation Life," "National Heritage Award Winners," "American Indians," and "Paniolo." Most topics were presented twice in the four days of the restaging, except "Paniolo," which was presented three times. Several of the informational topics were repeated in modified form in the children's area. Perhaps due to time constraints, none of the restaging guests other than Native Americans were given time on the narrative stage. All of the narrative stage presentations remained upbeat—in keeping with a festive ambience.

Folklife Hawai'i presumed an audience comprised mostly of uninformed residents. On the Mall, audiences had included former residents of Hawai'i and diasporic Native Hawaiians, but had been predominantly people unfamiliar with a vision of Hawai'i that existed outside of tourist industry packaging. The restaging was an opportunity to teach local young people from various ethnic groups about the past and to teach local residents about each other. This "inreach" undertaking underscored the utopian program concept given that one of the principal ideas of Hawai'i projected in Washington was of a multicultural society intimately interconnected through generations of shared cultural practices. Local television news coverage featured persons not usually seen on the news; polished urban announcers discussed occupational skills like *poi* making, canoe building, rock-wall building, and *forno* cooking as exotic relics of a past being resuscitated, providing further evidence that these practices were not as widely practiced or known as festival programming suggested.[25] According to staff and participant narratives and news reports about interactions between participants and visitors at Folklife Hawai'i, older visitors remembered the past, younger people remembered stories they had heard from elders, and many youngsters encountered ideas and practices quite new to them because they had not had occasion to see them before. Ninth graders were bused in from throughout the city, and participants became teachers using Folklife Hawai'i as a culture lab in which to educate Hawai'i youth about the importance of keeping traditional practices alive. Kennedy linked the dual cultural preservation goals of education and counter-hegemony in his opening address to the restaging.

> Today some 5,000 kids came here. Kids need heroes. Kids have to see their history, their culture, their art reflected in educational programs. MTV, Indiana Jones, and Bart Simpson are not going to give the children of Hawai'i the confidence, pride and knowledge of self necessary to summon past wisdom and knowledge and to create their own future, here on these grounds today, kids made connections to the older generations, to bearers of artistic, cultural, historical and occupational traditions.[26]

Although the local news clips showed rapt faces and reporters interviewed suitably impressed students, this reconnecting of generations was not always a complete success. Henry Silva, for example, looked down after talking to a group of students about *paniolo* crafts such as rawhide braiding and discovered that his favorite leather-working knife had

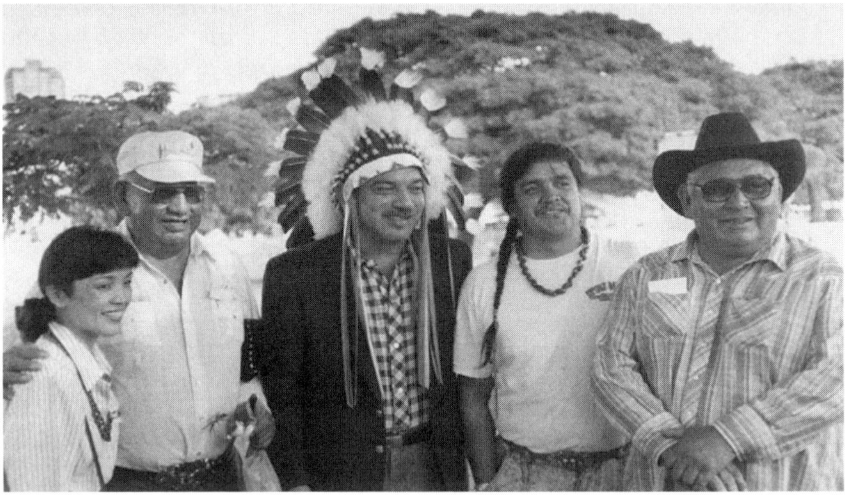

Fig. 5. Governor Waihee posing with Native American participants at restaging. (Photo taken by Lynn Martin Graton. Courtesy of the Hawai'i State Foundation for Culture and the Arts, Honolulu)

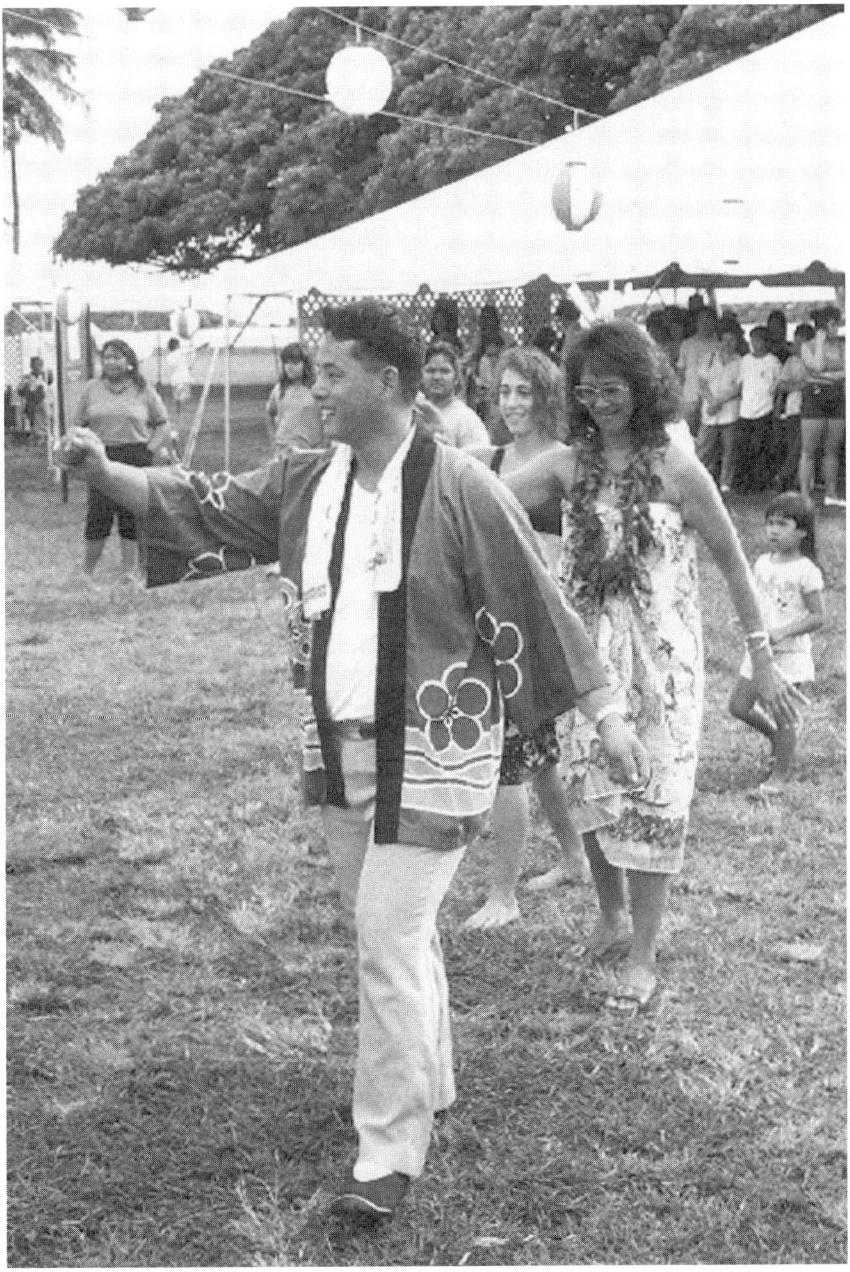

Fig. 6. Reverend Duane Pang, Taoist priest, in Japanese *bon* dance at restaging. (Photo taken by Carl Hefner. Courtesy of the Hawai'i State Foundation for Culture and the Arts, Honolulu)

been stolen.[27] This petty theft, although an isolated incident, suggests that not every young person approached the demonstrations with reverence for elders and tradition. Rather than being a confirmation of living traditions that had been kept alive inter-generationally, the restaging's emphasis on reaching children was an attempt to reinstate a missing generational link by inspiring young people to become interested enough to learn, or at least value, traditional practices. This encouragement and support for transmission of folk arts was already in place as a mission of the HSFCA through its NEA-sponsored Master and Apprentice Pro-

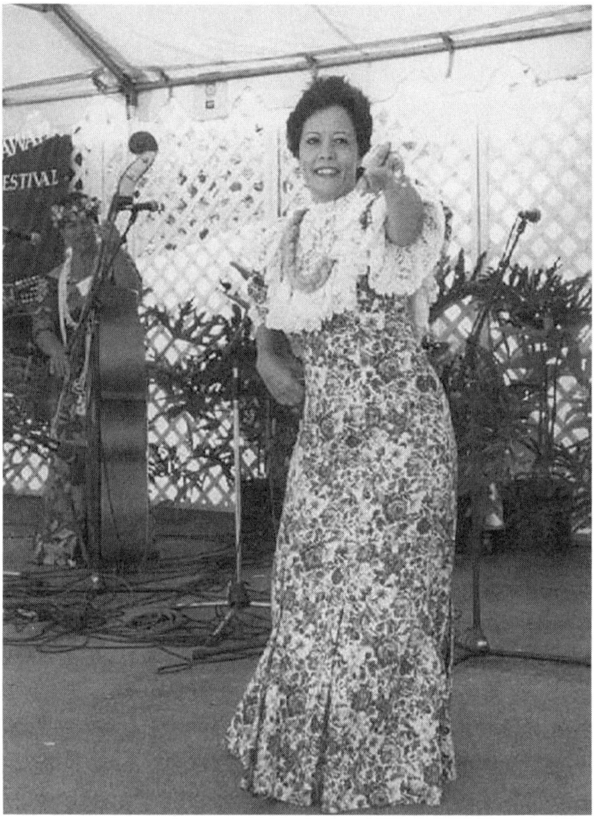

Fig. 7. Noelani Zuttermeister dancing *hula* at restaging. Violet Pahu Liliko'i on bass guitar. (Photo taken by Carl Hefner. Courtesy of the Hawai'i State Foundation for Culture and the Arts, Honolulu)

gram, which encourages tradition bearers to pass on their knowledge and skills. The restaging was a visible impetus for that process on a wider scale.

When I asked former participants about their memories of the restaging, their responses seemed much more ambivalent than their memories of Washington, D.C. They were in agreement that it had felt different from the Mall, but they found it difficult to articulate just how and why. That it was short and lacked the intensity of the original were standard observations, yet participants had still been delighted to reconvene, to renew friendships and mourn lost ones. Emotion had run high at both the opening and the closing. On closing night, those who had worked on the festival were so reluctant to see it end that they started a fund to keep it going. It was a dream not to be realized.[28]

Folklife Hawai'i, the Book

Like the Washington, D.C., program, Folklife Hawai'i was accompanied by a handsome program book that could be donated to libraries and used to provide supplementary information on performances and demonstrations. Graced with a color photograph of mixed flower *lei,* the Folklife Hawai'i book mimicked the OFP production in format, including introductory statements from officials—in this case the governor, the HSFCA Board chairperson, and the chairman of the Department of Land and Natural Resources. This replication is especially pronounced in the opening essay by Marie Strazar, which paraphrases much of Kennedy's essay, "Cosmopolitan Hawai'i," from the 1989 program book. In the Folklife Hawai'i book, however, the Smithsonian's emphasis on culture and change through the processes of creolization was abandoned in favor of a more conventional ethnic categories approach. Where the Smithsonian's program book was organized around "big idea" essays keyed to each of four program themes, the Hawai'i book is devoted almost entirely to profiles of performance genres neatly defined by ethnicity, making it serve as a general Hawai'i folklife reference rather than a festival guide. This privileging of ethnicity over hybridity seems ironic in that the Hawai'i crew had hotly debated such compartmentalization when shaping the Smithsonian program. It also suggests that the assessment of HSFCA organizers was that different interpretive rationales were required in Washington, D.C., and in Hawai'i. Both strategies were Hawai'i-centric. In exporting Hawai'i to the mainland, the goal had been to disrupt mainland notions of racialized multiculturalism that Hawai'i residents did not see as applicable in the islands. Importing the Festival back into Hawai'i, on the other hand, meant aligning Festival categories with local expectations. In Hawai'i, where ethnicity is an open and fluid topic, the solution was to add to the complexity by adding in additional ethnic categories not bound to overarching historical narratives.

Photographs in the Folklife Hawai'i book indirectly compensate for the deficiencies of the Juniroa film by devoting several images to "master artists" that had been recognized by the Smithsonian and/or the NEA. Sixteen articles, many written by fieldworkers for the Festival, conceptually replicate the dual emphasis of the site design and general program concept by allocating half of the main text space to Native Hawaiian folklife and subdividing the remaining space among immigrant groups. A third section is added for the guests from the other programs and the new groups from Hawai'i. The first section, "Profiles of the Festival," is divided into halves, like the Hawai'i program in Washington. One half features articles on Hawaiian topics: performing arts, crafts, and occupation. In the second half, Japanese, Okinawan, Chinese, Korean, and Samoan traditions each have their own headings, but Portuguese, Puerto Rican, and Filipino traditions are lumped together under the single heading of "Music from the Plantation Camps." The final section, "Guests of the Festival," introduces, in abbreviated form, the added local groups and the zydeco and Native American groups. Although the restaging represented folklife in multiple categories—foodways, crafts, and occupational, narrative, and performance traditions—the majority of the articles concentrate on performance arts. In an attempt to give equal weight to each ethnic group, ethnic nomenclature is distributed in nonparallel categories that waver between ethnicity, nationality, and genre: "Music and Art in the Life of Laotian Immigrants in Hawai'i"; "Vietnamese Popular Theater"; "A Gospel Song Is a Sermon Set to Music, Gospel Music in Hawai'i"; "Zydeco Music—the Lawtell Playboys"; "Native American Music—the Plains Indian Ensemble." The confusion between ethnic labels and topic-focused headings suggests that an effort was made to avoid racial terms by not identifying gospel music as African American, but that there was a difficulty in placing this group within ethnic categories construed by country of origin. Inversely, Tongan hymn singing is not directly identified as Tongan, although other practices are labeled by ethnicity. Reserving the "Guests of the Festival" for last has the effect of symbolically othering the later Laotian, Vietnamese, African American, and Tongan communities and marking them as outsiders with regard to "localness" based on shared history, a principal theme of the Smithsonian program (Martin 1990).

In the Washington program *haole* were widely present in the Festival frame as authors, presenters, and organizers, but they were invisible in the restaging programming despite the inclusion of other groups that had not appeared in Washington. Ethnic culture on Magic Island was made visible through its apparent disconnect from the results of white privilege and power. Of course, a perceptive visitor's peripheral vision in at least three directions from Magic Island—within sight of Ala Moana Center (a large shopping mall) and the skyscrapers of downtown Honolulu and Waikīkī—would have encountered traditional culture as enveloped by tourism, development, and consumerism. The Hawai'i evoked on the National Mall, on the other hand, had been uncluttered by the concrete jungle of Honolulu development and traffic.

Spin-Offs

The Hawai'i program ended with the restaging, but a number of other events, programs, and projects emerged from the Festival and restaging afterglow. Local culture workers who had attended the workshops created festivals of their own on a smaller scale but modeled after the Smithsonian example—two on the Big Island.[29] Martin built on the Festival fieldwork to produce a number of projects in her capacity as HSFCA Folk Arts coordinator, including a concert series, two rock-wall builders conferences, and an authoritative and widely used book and audio CD-ROM set called *Musics of Hawai'i* (Martin 1994). These projects manifested the OFP goal of the Festival serving as an impetus for local initiatives.

The Festival experience also blossomed informally in participant communities. Ku'ulei Kekiwi, of the Hawaiian backyard *lū'au* band Ku'ulei's Own, had gone to the Festival against her doctor's orders, proclaiming that if she died there, she'd die happy.[30] When she passed away soon after the Festival, six women from the Waimea Hawaiian Church Choir traveled from Kaua'i to Maui with "tons of coolers full of all kinds of food" and proceeded to stay for a week to cook and take care of her family. Ku'ulei and Merton Kekiwi, whom the women had not known prior to the Festival, had become extended family by way of the Festival experience.[31] Another community that formed in the wake of the Festival was constellated around performance. Some of the Hawaiian musicians—Barney Isaacs, Auntie Vi, Richard and Solomon Hoʻopiʻi, Ledward Kaʻapana—had enjoyed playing together so much that they decided to do an inter-island tour so they could reconnect with former Festival participants as well as perform for new audiences. Jay Junker, their Festival presenter/stage manager, had previous experience as an agent, so he set up their gigs. They called themselves, simply, Da Bunch. In various configurations and with HSFCA support, they performed together off and on for the next four years, up until Isaacs passed away.[32]

Other participants went home to paste together photo albums and settle back into their lives.[33] What did the Festival mean to them in the long run? In some cases the free exhibition created new markets for folk arts labor. For local musicians like Richard and Solomon Hoʻopiʻi and Harry Nakasone, who went on to become National Heritage Fellows, it was an important step toward wider recognition. For some artisans it meant commissions; for example, rock-wall builder Thomas Kamaka Emmsley was soon working on lava-rock walls for wealthy residents of Maui.[34] In the PBS documentary about the Festival, Kenichi Tasaka politely complained that he could not make enough bulrush sandals to keep up with orders he was receiving from the mainland (Fredo 1989). For nonagenarian Tasaka, at least, being plunged into the capitalist market economy was not a Festival benefit.

The intangible effects are more elusive to determine. For many participants, like the women from the Waimea Hawaiian Church Choir and Merton Kekiwi, the Festival forged connections to people in the islands whom they had not previously known. But over time, the Festival afterglow ebbed. As Napoka reflected, "one day somebody is a celebrity on the Mall, but then the next day he is back in his taro patch, and he's nobody and nothing has changed. He can't even talk to anyone at home about his experience because to them it's meaningless."[35] Napoka said he supports the Festival but that he would like to see some of the money that was spent on such a huge production actually make it to real people who could use it. In terms of ongoing social relations, participants who live in the same small towns say hello when they meet, but those from different cultural groups, occupations, and social classes do not seem to seek each other out, and fourteen years later many have not seen each other at all. Robert Ruiz of Kauaʻi, citing rumors of reunions that never happened, probably spoke for many participants when he said that the only disappointment he had about the whole experience was that it never happened again.[36] Without institutional support to sustain or regenerate it, the dynamic imagined community of the Festival faded to personal memories.

Aborted Collaborations

Organizers on both sides of the Pacific had hoped the degree of enthusiasm generated by the Hawai'i program and the restaging would spawn permanent local cultural preservation endeavors. This did not happen in Hawai'i. It is difficult to pinpoint just where and why the breakdowns in institutional support occurred, but the fact that they did illustrates the degree to which the overall effort was contingent on its political and economic contexts. The Hawai'i program and the restaging both came about because Hawai'i had the right critical mass at the right time: Smithsonian interest, like-minded people at the local level (Martin, Trimillos, Waihee, Moriarty), money (Waihee, HVB), and infrastructure (HSFCA, EWC). Without Waihee as governor, Martin as Folk Arts coordinator, and a flush local economy, the initial collaboration would never have come to pass. The importance of these factors was thrown into sharp relief by Smithsonian attempts to collaborate with the state of Hawai'i following the restaging.

There was no lack of vision on the part of the OFP staff; in fact, their vision for Hawai'i surpassed that of the larger Smithsonian establishment. Kennedy, now deputy director of the Festival, had been on soft money at the OFP throughout the Hawai'i project. During the Hawai'i program, Kurin had been acting director of the OFP. Both new to the job, they developed a daring proposal—to establish a Smithsonian Hawai'i and Asia/Pacific Center in Honolulu, to be co-sponsored by the state of Hawai'i. The Smithsonian had begun a number of distal operations designed to take the museum to the people, and the OFP saw a Hawai'i center as a dramatic challenge to established hierarchical and East Coast–based notions of culture. Kennedy's speech at the restaging attests to this vision.

> We at the Smithsonian have learned much from the people of Hawai'i. We have learned that national institutions, if they are properly to do their job, must engage, as partners—and full partners at that—local communities and state organizations. We have learned that local and

> regional culture are part of a Nation's cultural heritage. And we have learned that all wisdom, knowledge, culture, and art does not repose in New York, Boston, and Washington. Hawai'i's culture and history, and that of the Pacific need to be brought to national consciousness.[37]

After exploratory letters, on March 1, 1991, Kurin submitted a proposal to Waihee, Hawai'i's senators, various members of the Hawai'i State Legislature, and to Bob Adams, secretary of the Smithsonian. In it he outlined a rationale for such a research center: "the new center would deal with Hawai'i as a multicultural society closely connected to those of the Pacific Rim. . . .The Center will research and examine the relationship between culture and economic development, culture and environmental preservation."

This proposal acted on the Festival mission to be a catalyst rather than an end in itself and demonstrated OFP recognition that culture is not static, as the performance-based Festival frame can make it appear despite the good intentions of organizers. Rather, it spoke of culture as dynamic, creative, evolving, and embedded in its sociopolitical contexts. Kurin creatively approached the dilemma of tourism's relationship to traditional culture by proposing that the center would investigate questions about the viability of local culture and whether "bearers of local culture" could "appropriate tourism and control its production of images." He also proposed that by becoming an educational center "along the lines of a continuing festival," the center could evolve into an entity effecting cultural policy. In other words, the center would pick up where the Festival left off, moving beyond cultural conservation to culture-based social advocacy.[38]

As a location for the center, Kurin and Kennedy attempted to rescue a contested property in Waikīkī—the historic Waikikian Hotel where Kurin and Parker had stayed when they first visited Hawai'i in the Festival planning phase. This attempt became their introduction to the contentious politics of Pacific development versus cultural preservation in Hawai'i. The Waikikian was a quaint two-story hotel, a remnant of a bygone era in a resort area quickly transitioning to a high-rise concrete jungle. In it was a bar called the Tahitian Lanai that was frequented by local residents and musicians, as well as tourists, and that was locally famous for its spontaneity and warmth—a rare find in a tourist zone that had become almost exclusively corporate owned and operated (Hoover 1990). When a group called People for the Preservation of Hawai'i's Socio-Cultural Resources (PPHSCR) learned that it had been bought by a Japanese developer and was slated for demolition to make room for yet another high-rise hotel, they circulated a petition to have the building designated a historical landmark and garnered over a thousand signatures. They pointed out that the proposed development was breaking with city codes deigned to control additional development and noted that it was the last of a genre of establishments where locals and *malihini*s (newcomers) freely mixed (Thais and Bullard 1991). Joining the effort to preserve the Waikikian, Kurin and Kennedy jumped on the bandwagon, seeking funds to buy the hotel and establish it as a cultural center accessible to locals and tourists alike. Unfortunately, the best efforts of the PPHSCR, who were banking on nostalgia for old Waikīkī and who had Smithsonian backing, lost out to development by a Japanese corporation. One more element of the Hawai‘i past was consigned to memory.

Exploratory correspondence about a research center between the OFP and Senator Inouye and Governor Waihee continued into 1992. Meanwhile, the HSFCA directorship had changed hands, with Sarah Richards replaced by Wendell Silva. Where Richards had dragged her feet, Silva was a strong supporter of the folk arts program and was enthusiastic about the idea. In Hawai‘i, the proposal finally made it to the legislature, only to be hit by a double economic whammy. At the same time that the OFP was asking for $40,000 in matching funds from the state to open a center, Franklin Odo, University of Hawai‘i professor of ethnic studies, was proposing a much more ambitious plan—a museum of Hawai‘i history—and asking for $200,000.[39] When Odo approached Kurin about supporting his proposal, the two parties joined forces, but the timing was not auspicious for a large expenditure in the arts just when the Gulf War had funneled off federal funds. The state of Hawai‘i, which had been riding an economic wave in 1989, was hard hit. In an address to the Hawai‘i State Legislature titled “Staying Ahead,” Waihee, with his usual eloquence, expressed strong dissent with the Bush administration, noting that Hawai‘i residents were paying more for interest on the national debt than they were in Hawai‘i state income tax: “To avoid deeper debt, the federal government is increasing taxes, cutting services and mandating the states do more with less federal help. The reality is that with problems as deep and wide as homelessness and pollution, Washington has no coherent domestic policy. In effect, they are passing us the buck, without giving us the buck to do it.”[40] In an atmosphere of financial crisis, despite the OFP interest and the governor’s ongoing support for expanding the Festival into long-term commitment to cultural preservation, education, and research in Hawai'i, the piggybacked proposals sank.[41]

Mining the Festival

For the Smithsonian, the Hawai'i program articulated the democratic ideals on which the Festival had been founded, and also presented a new paradigm for representing cultural diversity. Kennedy conveyed the OFP's nostalgia for the Hawai'i program in his opening speech at the restaging.

> In 1989, a bit of Hawai'i came to the National Mall in Washington, D.C. There in the midst of the National Museums and Monuments, more than 150 exemplary musicians, artists, crafts people, cooks and others demonstrated the richness and diversity of the many cultures that make up Hawai'i to over 1.5 million visitors. These artists gave a broad American public a sense of Hawai'i that went beyond the naïve stereotypes and notions of sun, sand, and sea. They gave us all a sense of the people of these islands. Most of all, they brought with them and conveyed the spirit of *aloha*. Frankly, in Washington these days we miss the *aloha* spirit, and need it badly.[42]

The "*aloha* spirit" never quite left Washington, D.C., however, because the Hawai'i program was mined by the OFP for useful by-products. Smithsonian Folkways Recordings had produced two audiotapes of Hawai'i music for sale at the Festival, one an anthology of Hawai'i music and one of Puerto Rican music in Hawai'i (Apolionia 1989). The Smithsonian newsletter was renamed "Talk Story." In 1991 a Smithsonian cookbook was produced, and Hawai'i was included in a section called "The Islands," for which Moriarty contributed an article that incorporated foods from several of Hawai'i's ethnic groups and ended with Hawai'i's version of fast food—the plate lunch (Kirlin and Kirlin 1991). The progression of Moriarty's article makes clear that when it comes to food in Hawai'i, it is difficult to sustain any pretense of cultural boundaries.

In the 1990s the Hawai'i program was one of three chosen for the Virtual Smithsonian Festival website. This website features an African (Yoruba) naming ceremony, Borderlands culture (southwestern states and Mexican border), and a Hawaiian *lū'au,* with several related subtopic links under each of the three. In addition to information on typical foods one might find at a Hawaiian *lūʻau,* the Hawaiʻi online presentation offers photographs and information on *hula,* falsetto singing, and *lei* customs. It includes a bibliography of suggested readings on culture and one reference on Hawaiʻi history. On the one hand, this virtual site enacts the educational mission of the OFP, but its informational value is mediated by its circular re-presentation of Festival culture as authentic culture and by the doubled use of recycled and reconstituted cultural performance for educational purposes and institutional promotion. The virtual venue presents visual images and sound bites, bringing the Festival to life but in limited space where tidbits of the Festival are fragmented and de-contextualized. Bits of Native Hawaiian culture have been skimmed out of what the Festival (and Moriarty's cookbook article, which had incorporated immigration and modernization) had presented as a complex, cosmopolitan culture and thus appear to stand in for the whole of Hawaiʻi culture.

The Virtual Festival teeters between museum strategies of collection and action. As many scholars have pointed out, collection and de-contextualization imply possession and facilitate power through the acquisition of knowledge of one group about another. Looking from an opposing direction, MacLeod, in discussing the post-colonial museum of the Pacific, asserts that "treating objects in the context of their local importance restores sovereignty to their owners" and negotiates away "ancient binaries" (1998). The Virtual Festival attempts to perform a post-colonial action by re-contextualizing culture. However, the danger is that, showcased in cyberspace, Hawaiʻi lapses back to the mono-cultural portrayal favored by the tourist industry, and, like flies in amber, the same fragments of indigenous culture that have been exoticized since the Panama Pacific Exposition set off the Hawaiiana craze—*hula, lūʻau, lei,* and Hawaiian music—are again used to interpolate the Hawaiian islands as a primitivized and conflict-free zone.

In addition to being reproduced as products, the Hawaiʻi program became embedded in Smithsonian memory as an institutional epiphany and Festival watershed. According to Kurin, the OFP had been involved in an internal crisis prior to the Hawaiʻi program and was a place where "nobody wanted to go to work."[43] Due to timing and a number of factors, the Hawaiʻi program emerged as the OFP's perfect program. Its transformative power was attributed to genial people, ample funding, enthusiastic reception, and *aloha.* Another reason it was upheld as a model was because it marked a turning point in OFP administration, when Kurin had just stepped into the director's position, Kennedy came on board, and the Festival was reconceptualized. Earlier programs had featured ethnic groups from American states and regions, Native American, and occupational groups, but the OFP had taken new directions with transnational programs such as the Old World/New World programs that began in the late 1970s and continued into the 1980s. The Hawai'i program pointed toward a further transition, this one between American and the international programming that would follow (India, Tibet, the Silk Road, and so on).[44]

The 1989 Festival also laid the groundwork for more introspection. The 1988 Festival had marked the centennial of the American Folklore Association and had brought folklorists to the Mall to discuss their work alongside "the folk." This program implied the beginning of a new self-consciousness and self-reflexivity in the work of culture brokers, akin to post-colonial directions in academic anthropology. However, following the Festival tendency toward education and celebration, sessions were mostly descriptive. The festival-making process in Hawai'i had tested new research processes and blurred previous cultural categorizations, helping to shape a new paradigm for the Festival, one that would recognize the need to be informed by local fieldworkers and inclusive of ever more complex ethnic identities. Small failures of the Hawai'i program, such as the exclusion of Mary Jo Freshley from Korean dance on the grounds of her race, were absorbed as lessons for future programs. Kennedy thoughtfully says that the Hawai'i program was a learning experience and that they would do that and many other things differently now.[45]

Some festival staff attribute personal epiphanies to the Hawai'i program. One OFP staff person attributed a "Buddha-like quality" to the people of Hawai'i. Several made pilgrimages to the islands, and some bought property there so they could return regularly. In 2001 one State Department employee who had worked on the 1989 Festival enthusiastically told me that the Hawai'i program had "changed [his] life." "Look!" he said, and showed off his neo-native armband tattoo as evidence of his "going local." These narratives, while heartfelt, also resonate with the cadences of orientalism and primitivism.[46] While some people involved with the Festival were genuinely moved by their association with people from Hawai'i, others responded to the selective repackaging of Hawai'i by seeing it as a multicultural and inclusive paradise in which they could find themselves.

Hawai'i as National Metaphor

In a Festival promotional film produced in 2002 by the CFCH (formerly the OFP), Hawai'i multiculturalism and cosmopolitanism are showcased in much the same way that Appalachia was presented as a symbol of American heritage in an earlier promotional film. Bracketed within Smithsonian promotional materials, portions of the Hawai'i program re-present Hawai'i as a national asset and as a CFCH tool to expound the textural and spatial dimensions of American diversity. Permanently quoted within the new institutionally produced text, Waihee's address from the 1989 opening ceremony, which focused on what Hawai'i was bringing to the National Mall and the nation, takes on a global dimension and becomes a statement about what the CFCH is contributing to national ideology by way of having represented Hawai'i. The 1984 promotional film that had been presented at the Hawai'i planning meetings in 1988 had a soundtrack dominated by Appalachian fiddle music. The revamped video features an extended Hawai'i program sequence that operates as a fulcrum between state/regional programs and international programs, such as the ones on India and Tibet (also shown). Hawai'i is constructed as both America's past, as a sort of alternative Ellis Island, and as its future, in the form of an American global village.

Utilized within Festival promotion, the Hawai'i program ultimately becomes a calling card for CFCH success in cultural facilitation and interpretation. By extension, the state of Hawai'i is presented as a poster child for a new national paradigm of American multiculturalism that transcends the old melting-pot metaphor and replaces Old World/New World transnationalism with a cultural paradigm that is much more complex: revitalized indigeneity, creolization, and domesticated internationalism. In the video, Hawai'i segues the CFCH into a vision of an American-mediated, peaceful, and colorful globalism.[47]

Changed Contexts

In her study of the colonization of Hawai'i through law, Merry identifies several forms of resistance to hegemonic domination, some confrontational and others operating from within the dominant system and using its own tools to alter its structure (Merry 2000, 12). Some of these might be perceived as operating within the complex relationship of Hawai'i to the tourist industry. Expressing overt resistance, the Ecumenical Council on Tourism in Hawai'i issued a public statement in

1989 about the detrimental effects of tourism: "A state of emergency exists in regard to the survival, the well-being, and the status of the Native Hawaiian people on the one hand and the near extinction of the precious and fragile environment on the other."

This statement received mixed responses from church members. On one end of the spectrum was the view that tourism has created irreparable damage to the environment and indigenous culture. On the other end is a practical recognition that economic viability for the islands relies on tourism. Many traditional arts practitioners work within the tourist industry, and the tourist industry has been responsible for the perpetuation and development of certain traditional arts by generating employment for performers and craftspeople, creating markets, and raising public awareness. Some art forms, such as *hapa-haole* music, *hula auana,* and *pā'ū* parades owe much of their inspiration to performance venues generated by tourism.

The restaging, as the product of a government agency, demonstrated a middle-ground, pragmatic approach to tourism that suggested cultural groups and agencies could use tourism to their advantage rather than being exploited or ignored by it. Operating with state and national funding, the restaging and related projects were an effort to harness government and business interests to support traditional arts preservation projects and to change the terms of tourism from the primitivized, eroticized images of much corporate tourism to images grounded in actual living culture in Hawai'i. The restaging was overtly geared toward education for residents, and its workshops were designed to train local public culture workers in how to stage events on the Smithsonian model. Fieldwork and collaboration were stressed as ways to aspire toward cultural "authenticity." In the context of omnipresent tourist kitsch in Hawai'i, advocating cultural tourism that rejected trite Hawaiiana and replaced it with respectful depictions of community-based culture can be seen as resistance to the appropriations and distortions of traditional culture by corporate tourism.

From another perspective, the restaging workshops also co-opted culture. Hawaiian ideas/customs like *'ohana, aloha,* and *mālama'āina* were utilized as inclusive and abstract concepts that served to link cultural groups and include culture workers by way of institutionally defined Hawaiianness. Comparing the restaging to a community spectacle three years later—the Onipa'a (a Hawaiian word meaning "steadfast")—demonstrates that Hawaiianness in a grassroots context was being construed very differently from the institutionally sanctioned—by the HSFCA in this case—version that presented Hawaiians as hosts and Hawaiian culture as the ambiance and glue for multicultural unity.

Interpreting the Past through Tradition

Based on HSFCA fieldwork and recommendations and as a gesture of compensation and recognition for the indigenous population and their history, the Smithsonian had made Native Hawaiian culture the centerpiece of its representation of Hawai'i, presenting Native Hawaiians as half of the Festival demographics and Native Hawaiian concepts and culture as the thematic frame for the entire program. The HSFCA replicated the Smithsonian interpretation in its Honolulu restaging. That both of these events were staged on official anniversaries brought other contingencies into the picture. The Festival of American Folklife capitalized on its fortuitous scheduling for the thirtieth anniversary of Hawai'i statehood—an event that was not as uncontested as standard historical accounts have claimed. The HSFCA—an agency that had done much to revitalize and shape ethnic culture in the islands—celebrated its own twenty-fifth anniversary with the restaging. The Hawai'i festivals in Washington and Honolulu were envisioned by organizers as a form of resistance against cultural hegemony and hierarchy from within institutions that did (and do) not historically or proportionally privilege traditional arts or the communities in which most of them are practiced. However, official sponsorship had required that the showcased culture be depoliticized to accord with national and state agency imaging. The festivals were tools for public education about traditional culture divorced from political contexts and in harmony with institutional memory.

That the HSFCA/Smithsonian presentation of indigenous culture and island history was a selective interpretation of indigenous culture and the past becomes sharply evident when contrasted with a spectacle staged just three years later in Honolulu called the Onipa'a. This latter event also marked an institutional anniversary and used it as an occasion for public education. In this case, organizers chose to politicize traditional culture, spectacle, and performance to challenge hegemonic historical and cultural narratives. From January 14 to 17, 1993, the Onipa'a Centennial Committee, formed under the auspices of a conglomeration of Native Hawaiian community groups,[48] performed an on-site restaging of the 1893 overthrow, a bloodless coup in which a group of mostly American businessmen had enlisted the U.S. Marines to force the abdication of Queen Lili'uokalani and illegally seize control of the Hawaiian Islands. Twenty thousand people converged at 'Iolani Palace, the residence of the Kalākaua dynasty. The goal of the four-day theatrical event was to honor the queen, use living history to reenact the events surrounding the overthrow, and act as a forum for the growing Hawaiian sovereignty movement. Unlike the festival programs, it was not an effort to "put Hawai'i's best foot forward." *Hula* and chant were used in a sacred context rather than as entertainment. As Elizabeth Pa Martin, a Honolulu lawyer, put it, "The wrong people are making the decisions. Hawaiian and American values are in conflict. They exploit us, use us. We are supposed to dance hula for everybody and smile" (Reinhold 1992, A24).

The restaging and the Onipa'a—both of which utilized staged authenticity in the interests of educating the local public—illustrate different performance and interpretive strategies and raise questions about their resonance as well as perceived veracity in the local context. There were obvious differences in form between the two events. The restaging aimed to present "everyday" culture in ways that would engage tourists; it avoided historical reenactment and invited interaction. The Onipa'a was living history with no pretense of entertainment. In fact, prior to the event, flyers were distributed under doors in Waikīkī hotels informing tourists that the ceremonies were "of a very personal nature to the native Hawaiian community and not intended as visitor attractions" (Cannon 1993, A33). The restaging had showcased real people performing themselves in a present informed by the past. The Onipa'a used actors to reenact the past as a way to inform the present. Most important, the Onipa'a openly articulated the frames of colonization: missionization and political/military/cultural dominance. The restaging had erased them.

Like the Hawai'i program, the Onipa'a utilized rituals, pageantry, procession, and traditional culture to accomplish an educational purpose. Similarly, it began with rituals and became interactive. Although he would be sharply criticized by Senator Inouye and others and even accused of treason by some military personnel, Governor Waihee ordered that the U.S. flag be lowered on downtown buildings for the duration of the events at 'Iolani Palace (Adamski 1993, A1/A8). The palace itself was draped entirely in black bunting, as it had been for the funeral of King Kalākaua. The first day, leaders of Hawaiian organizations entered the palace to give *ho'okupu* (spiritual offerings). On the second day, the overthrow was performed, an event that moved many in the crowd to lose sight of the unreality of the staging and begin weeping or shouting at the actors. The third day a stone *ahu* (altar) was erected and offerings made. On the final day, sixteen thousand people marched on the palace and an apology was given by a representative of the United Church of Christ for the damage its predecessors had wrought against the Hawaiian people (Tanahara 1993, A6). This was followed by a speech by the actress playing the queen in which she told the people, "Onipa'a! Hold fast!" The final ceremony was a torchlight procession.

The Onipa'a captured public as well as media imagination. In January 1993 the *Honolulu Star-Bulletin (HSB)* ran articles about the historical events of 1893 and profiled figures such as Charles Wilson, Robert Wilcox, and James Blount, who had dared to oppose the provisional government set up in the monarchy's stead (*HSB* 1993, insert). The *Honolulu Advertiser (HA),* on the other hand, carried an invective by its president, Thurston Twigg-Smith, the grandson of Lorrin A. Thurston, who had led the overthrow: "Overthrow: No apology needed." The *HSB* juxtaposed historical accounts alongside detailed coverage of the sovereignty movements; health, education, and socioeconomic statistics on Native Hawaiians; and grassroots protests about development and land disputes. The *HA* ran articles criticizing Waihee's policies as well as Waihee's rebuttal to Twigg-Smith's article. Editorials from this period show a public deeply divided, with Native Hawaiians, as well as other ethnic groups, dissenting among themselves over the issues. These debates reveal a level of anger and frustration that had been masked, by framing institutions and by participants, in the Festival productions.

The combination of theater, ritual, and communal observation at the Onipa'a combined culture with politics in what Arnie Saiki identifies as a powerful recuperation of loss.[49] This sense of loss had no place in the Festival/restaging narrative, nor is it at home in festival culture in general. Where the Smithsonian/HSFCA model had presented traditional culture as a way of celebrating adaptation, survival, and unity, the Onipa'a enacted a narrative of disruption and injustice while offering an opportunity for healing. The restaging/Smithsonian productions implied that Hawai'i and Native Hawaiians, along with other ethnic groups, had transcended politics through culture, but the Onipa'a created space for political mobilization. Certainly, not everyone agreed with the tenants of sovereignty, but "there [was] broad agreement even among opponents of sovereignty that the four-day ceremony [did] much to raise awareness about the problems facing the native peoples here" (Cannon 1993, A3). Saiki argues that a cathartic recognition of loss is necessary for healing. If so, the narrative of benign multiculturalism and happy hybridity, along with the obligations incurred through institutional affiliation, blunts the political edge that a single group can hone. Thus far, accounts of the Festival and the Onipa'a seem to have paid no heed to each other, but together they articulate tensions neither can make legible alone. Both had been designed to empower participants and communities. Tellingly, the Onipa'a, which raised both awareness and controversy, seems much better remembered locally.

* * *

There were happy outcomes to federal attention to Hawai'i—some of which may have been attributable to Hawai'i's high visibility vis-à-vis the Festival. In September 1991, Hawai'i received the largest National Heritage Foundation grant ever given to a state, given for summer training of secondary school teachers teaching Hawai'i heritage, and it was the first such grant for Hawai'i. It signaled serious attention to incorporating a history and heritage that had been previously excised. Hawai'i also appeared on federal radar when Congress passed the Native American Graves Protection and Repatriation Act (NAGPRA) in 1990.[50] In 1990 and 1991 the Smithsonian repatriated 209 Hawaiian remains for burial.[51] It is possible that Smithsonian attention to the state of Hawai'i from 1988 to 1990 may have influenced these positive outcomes by putting the state in the federal limelight.

The legacy of the Festival shows that the Hawai'i program in Washington, D.C., helped the OFP to facilitate an expanded national discourse of dynamic cross-culturalism that was simultaneously American and global. It helped the OFP reinvent the Festival from a focus on geographically bounded American folklife to one with more permeable boundaries. In the aftermath, sound, image, and concept bytes mined from the Festival provided materials and justification for future OFP projects. In Hawai'i, the Washington program and the restaging raised the profile of the HSFCA Folk Arts Program and provided fodder for several impressive and valuable projects. Both productions became sites from which the carefully crafted discourse of Hawai'i multiculturalism and framing of traditional culture were reproduced as an alternative to the imaging of Hawai'i by the tourist industry. They also became sites of meaning-making for individual Festival/restaging participants through both the machinations of memory and of media.

The Hawai'i program, which had re-contextualized Hawai'i in a national frame, did not, however, have the same resonance at home that it did at the Smithsonian. In both memory and media, the FAF was as contested a site as it was in production. In the restaging, the contestations lacked impetus. This shift in impact, combined with the contrast between the restaging and the Onipaʻa as opposed to local sites of meaning-making, attests to the existence of multiple narratives of ethnic identity and of divided political loyalties in the islands. Dislocated from long-term collaboration, the Smithsonian/HSFCA festivals and their offshoots became the locus for perpetuating, through a cultural preservation model, a de-politicized version of Hawaiʻi culture, history, and social relations. The proposed research center could have extended and expanded the research begun for the Festival into socially and politically relevant policy issues, but local and national economics conspired against long-term change and collaboration at the institutional level while grassroots organizations sought their own solutions.

Conclusion

In 2002, on my first visit to the Smithsonian Center for Folklife and Cultural Heritage, I asked Diana Parker if she thought the Folklife Festival was subversive. Her immediate reply was, "God, I hope so!" For many reasons, I think she is right. After all, in 1989 one could step out of the Museum of Natural History, where Hawaiians were still portrayed as artifacts of pre-history, or out of the National Portrait Gallery, where art appears as great masters in gilt frames, and see real people from Hawai'i practicing beautiful and meaningful living traditions. I think that qualifies as subversion. My exploration has not been intended as an invalidation of the CFCH mission. Rather, it has been an investigation into how it was applied in relation to the complex sociopolitical reality of Hawai'i and what it meant at the national and local levels for a former sovereign nation and territory to be inserted into national space.

The issues raised in relation to the production and impact of the Hawai'i program at the Smithsonian Folklife Festival are not new ones, nor were they unfamiliar to the directors and staff at the OFP in 1988–1990. In 1978 many of the same questions had been debated by public sector folklorists and scholars in a seminar on festival issues held at Berkeley and sponsored by the National Council on Traditional Arts and the NEA.[1] Central to the discussion were questions about the intent of folklife festivals. Attendees agreed that such festivals are marginally political in that they can serve to reinforce identity and that they support cultural advocacy. They also agreed that there are many tensions and contradictions inherent in festivals, such as issues of cultural authority, enforcement of cultural definitions, and private agendas. They recognized that festivals brought out tensions between conservative aesthetics and liberal politics, between minority and mass culture, and between the celebratory nature of festivals and the social and political problems in society. Where they strongly disagreed was on the function of the festival in the face of these tensions. What impact and responsibility does a festival have? David Whisnant, author of an important study on the politics of folk music festivals in Appalachia, argued that festivals, in divorcing culture from politics, have the effect of artificially soothing audiences rather than stressing the correlations between carriers of traditional culture and contemporary life. Bess Hawes, director of the Folklife Center at the Library of Congress, disagreed, saying that festivals should do what they do best—be festive. She argued that they have only the limited function of celebratizing, socializing, sharing, and healing. Several people agreed that festivals have only a small job to do and should confine themselves to that function, but added that festivals are also instigators and can introduce and start conversations about larger issues. Smithsonian staff took a slightly different perspective, saying that what festivals do *is* political, albeit covertly so. The Hawai'i program crystallized these debates.

On several levels the Hawai'i program successfully re-imaged Hawai'i in relation to the rest of the nation. It brought Hawai'i's peoples and histories to mainland consciousness and pointed to the selective amnesia of mainstream historical accounts about America's relationship with Hawai'i. Ethnic groups that had been effectively erased became both visible and storied. Through captioning and textual support, indigenous practices that had been essentialized as both relics and "timeless" in tourist venues were embodied and informed by the past. The program design employed an interactive, dialogic model that made space for tradition bearers to speak. In performance genres and through demonstrations, appropriated and commodified cultural practices were reconnected to cultural practitioners and sensibilities. Combined, these aspects of the festival-making process were and are revolutionary, particularly when compared to the commercialized practices of corporate-controlled tourism in the Pacific and to the Smithsonian's past role in ethnographic study and spectacle.

If we approach the Hawai'i program through Hawes' perspective on the function of festivals, then the festival truly did what it does best—it celebrated Hawai'i folklife and people. What was not as easy to see was that it also defined them. A close reading of the planning, fieldwork, and production processes reveals that the program paradigm was tightly controlled at all levels, and while this was done to secure the success of the program and to seal out the perceived distortions of tourism, the effect was also to cull dissident voices through careful selection of planners, fieldworkers, and participants and the relegation of conflict to a selectively narrated past and its exclusion from an aestheticized present. In keeping with the rationale of national arts agencies, the Hawai'i program was used to foreground a national narrative of cultural diversity as a counter-narrative to cultural homogeneity. Read in the context of Hawai'i and the Pacific, however, this effort to mythologize Hawai'i as America's global village had other implications. The representation of living traditions in Hawai'i masked living contexts. It symbolically leveled Hawai'i's rich and poor and, by relegating the issues of colonialism to the past, gave the impression that local and federal government and even the tourist industry were fully invested in the best interests of the people.

The Hawai'i program unfolded within national, state, and tourist frames that influenced its form and message. Of course, it behooves an arts agency dependent on federal funding to present itself as politically neutral if it wants to survive. Consequently, the version of Hawai'i that was crafted for representation on the Mall was a conservative view that celebrated intercultural balance without publicly recognizing how it evolved as a means of coping with economic and political disparities. The Festival is a tourist event, and despite its attention to maximizing educational opportunities, it is calibrated to the tourist gaze, and its educational endeavors are tailored to being engaging, entertaining, upbeat, and festive. In their efforts to portray multicultural harmony, the Hawai'i program organizers erased or neutralized any traces of real conflict. This erasure, in turn, erased the causes of conflict in the present by either containing them in the past or making them invisible in the present.

Whisnant has argued that festivals can have the effect of lulling the public into thinking all is well if they present only the bright side of culture and omit the politics that continue to oppress many culture bearers and their communities.[2] In 1989 Hawai'i was rife with public debates over land, socioeconomic disparities, tourism, and development, and while these issues were discussed on the Festival narrative stages, the larger message presented by the program negated them. Homogenizing Hawaiian culture into core program values worked to make the program cohere and reiterated the tourist tropes that use Hawaiian language and traditional culture to sell Hawai'i. The legacy of the Hawai'i program continues to reinforce, through its ongoing reproductions of aestheticized, ethnicized Hawai'i culture, the notion that all is well in Hawai'i and that Hawai'i is America's gift to the rest of the world.

In their efforts to give voice to Festival participants, organizers made themselves and whiteness invisible as well. Disappeared whiteness worked to foreground indigenous and immigrant peoples, but it also deceptively masked the frames of power. Johnson and Underiner stress how forefronting ethnicity and authenticity in cultural exhibition is linked to the erasure of colonialism: "To ignore whiteness—and the privilege it inherits—not only marks the Other as different, ethnic, exotic; it also denies the power, politics, and historical legacy of colonial discourse. This problem for the invisibility of whiteness is caught up in the illusionary search for authenticity in the Other" (2001, 55).

Invisible in the Festival re-imaging of Hawai'i were military and touristic neo-colonialism, the political dominance of *kama'āina haole* and local Japanese, and the economic dominance of American mainland and Japanese corporations. Native Hawaiian resistances were hidden by being aestheticized. *Haole* control over the Hawai'i program concept and production was hidden in plain sight by their non-performance onstage and omnipresence in program administration.

On the other hand, what is missing from all of these views is participant agency. Without the participants there is no Festival, and Hawai'i participants went to Washington voluntarily and came away, for the most part, enriched and empowered by the experience. They chose to work within the parameters of the Festival constructions of ethnicity and traditionality—some of them only temporarily taking on the labels, like the Okinawans, who agreed to be "folk" for the sake of the Festival even though they played court music and considered "folk" a stigmatizing term applied to peasants.[3] In the seams of the Festival some participants resisted covertly as they defined themselves outside of and in spite of program categories. They may have felt constrained by the Festival frames, but they clearly did not feel threatened and had decided that compliance was advantageous for personal and community reasons. In fact, for Hawai'i participants the Festival was, in large part, what Christine Yano coins a spectacle of "emplacement"—"the process of situating oneself within the larger mainstream community" (2006, 5). At the national level, Hawai'i residents were made visible as citizens of the nation while asserting their cultural differences from the mainland and from each other. This sense of emplacement, however, had different implications for immigrant and indigenous groups.

If we step back one more circle from the Hawai'i program as an interactive performance zone in which ideologies of power were encoded and decoded between its frames, staff, and participants, it appears as part of a complex dance between Hawai'i and mainland America—a dance of resistance, compliance, and centricity. Waihee had offered Hawai'i's "spirit of aloha" to the nation in his Festival address, an offering "to the nation of nations from the community of communities." His speech strategically interpolated the well-worn notion of native hospitality. On the surface, this performance beckoned to tourists, yet it also withheld Hawai'i from the rest of the nation by presenting a Hawai'i both within and separate from the nation to which it proffered its gifts. Anthropologist Annette Weiner has argued that the notion of gifting in Polynesian tradition has been misinterpreted by Western scholars and others to mean reciprocity when, in fact, wealth is actually displayed to protect and withhold what is most valued (1992, 150). A more obvious example of this kind of withholding appears in Waihee's speech to the Hawai'i legislature in 1991, a speech that stands in contrast to his 1989 Festival address: "We are used to living with paradox. We call it diversity. Neither east nor west, part of America—yet still an island people looking inward and outward at the same time. Pacific people carving out an international identity, and stubbornly guarding our values, traditions, and quality of life." [4]

At the 1989 Festival Waihee had located Hawai'i as the center of the Pacific. In this local address, he goes a step further and valorizes that center as an international zone, a "crossroads of the Pacific" [5] that is not simply an American frontier. He asserts that people in Hawai'i are tenaciously hanging on to, rather than giving away, their culture.

In 2003 I interviewed former Festival participant and NHF award winner Richard Ho'opi'i in the tiny village of Kahakuloa on Maui. We sat at a picnic table behind the church where he is a lay minister, and he talked about the wonderful times he had at the Festival and how it had launched a career for himself and his brother Solomon. He also talked emotionally about the young people leaving Hawai'i to find jobs and how tourism and development have accelerated change. He summed up the problem of American appropriation of *aloha* by saying, "I think after the Festival, everyone in Washington wanted to come to Hawai'i. It's not that we don't want them to come. We don't mind giving them our *aloha*. But we also want to be able to tell them good-bye." [6]

The Festival and the restaging reinforced the notion that geniality, hospitality, reciprocity, and inclusivity are qualities inherent in Hawai'i lifestyles. For tourism and culture brokering, of course, this is the happiest of solutions, for such an ethos constructs an exotic locale and its wonderful people as ever welcoming to those displaced souls (mostly white, urban, elite) who yearn for a sense of belonging and community. This is not to say that ideals like *aloha* and *'ohana* do not exist. To ask whether or not they are traditional in Hawai'i, however, is the wrong question. At issue is the impact when a nationally sponsored agency redefines and appropriates traditions for national use and they are imported back into the local environment as the officially endorsed status quo. A better question, then, is: to what extent does essentializing selected traditions construe their opposites as un-Hawaiian and bargain away the language of protest, ownership, identity, and recovery for some groups while reifying the entitlement and emplacement of others? A 2007 flyer from the Office of Hawaiian Affairs advertises a Great Hawaiian Folklife Festival as a draw for registering Native Hawaiians as the struggle for federal recognition continues.[7] This re-appropriation of institutional and academic rhetoric turns the tables on culture brokering and reminds us that when the stakes are raised, there may be surprising turns in the negotiation of tradition.

Notes

Introduction

1. Smithsonian Folklife Festival Documentation Collection, 1966–present. http://siris-archives.si.edu/ipac20/ipac?uri+full3100001~!22879!0&term (accessed April 16, 2007).
2. With regards to *hula,* see Stillman 1996, 357–360; and Whitney 2001, 78–83.
3. For an in-depth discussion of Hawai‘i as a contemporary cultural and geographical contact zone, see the preface and chap. 2 of Wilson and Dissanayake 1996.
4. It could also be argued that Hawai‘i serves a similar function for Japan.
5. For an argument about hybridity from this perspective, see Hutynk 1999–2000.
6. This issue is addressed in publications such as Roof and Wiegman 1995.
7. Richard Kurin, interview by author, Washington, D.C., July 25, 2003.

Chapter 1. Cultural Intervention in America's Eden

1. Interestingly, the "E Pluribus Unum" references were edited out when this was reproduced in the CFCH 2002 promotional video. My text comes from the Festival sound recordings made during the 1989 Festival.
2. Kurin interview, 2003.
3. Merry argues, in relation to the colonization of Hawai‘i through law in the territorial period, that "those targeted for reform and rule responded with varying degrees of complicity, resistance, and accommodation" (2000, 12).
4. For a discussion of the devastating effects of disease post-contact, see Stannard 1989.

5. According to Silva, its suppression had economic motivations. She argues that the creation of a labor force for the burgeoning agricultural industries played a part in the suppression of *hula* as a "leisure" activity.
6. Some scholars and Hawaiian speakers argue that the ability to decode multiple metaphorical meanings in Hawaiian poetry was disrupted by the suppression of the language.
7. For an overview of the Royal Hawaiian Band's history, see Kanahele 1979.
8. Adrienne Kaeppler has observed that this split between anthropological and historical representations of Hawai'i is one that continues in twentieth-century museum displays with international exhibits tending toward anthropological contexts. See Kaeppler 1992.
9. See Rydell 1984 on evolutionary theory and the Midway Plaisance.
10. After being held under house arrest in 'Iolani Palace, her former residence, Liliu'okalani spent time in Washington, D.C., trying unsuccessfully to gather support for reinstatement of the monarchy. Political cartoons of this time show the dignified queen depicted as a pickaninny. Similar cartoon strategies were a popular way of infantilizing and devaluing leaders and residents of other territories acquired by the United States in 1898.
11. See Desmond 1999 and Kanahele 1979 for a full list of films and a detailed discussion of their effects of the imaging of Hawaiians.
12. The Bishop Museum was established by Charles Bishop to house the extensive collection of Hawaiian artifacts belonging to his deceased wife, Bernice Pauahi Bishop. Her will also established the Kamehameha Schools.
13. See Imada 2004 for an interesting discussion of native entrepreneurs and Mossman's Leilani Village.
14. See Desmond 1999 for a detailed discussion of the development and impact of the *hapa-haole* image.
15. For more on "soft savagery," see Wood 1999.
16. Imada's reference is to Rosaldo 1989, 69.
17. Much of this material is from the papers of Emma Ahuena Taylor, Hawai'i State Archives. For a discussion of Roberts, see Kanahele 1979, 334–335.
18. Nathan Napoka, interview by author, Honolulu, May 7, 2003.
19. For more on salvage ethnography, see Jackson 1987, 38–39; and Clifford and Marcus 1986, 113.
20. See the official Polynesian Cultural Center website.

21. Marie McDonald, interview by author, Kamuela, HI, May 9, 2003.
22. Trimillos 2001.
23. Third Legislature, General Session 1965, State of Hawai'i, H.B. no. 10. See Hawai'i State Foundation for Culture and the Arts website: http://www.state.hi.us/HSFCA/ (accessed August 7, 2004).
24. Masaru Yokouchi, interview with author, Lahaina, HI, May 24, 2003.
25. Yokouchi interview, 2003.
26. HSFCA, Annual Report, 1965–1966, Hawaii and Asia/Pacific Collection, Hamilton Library, University of Hawai'i at Mānoa, Honolulu, 25–27.
27. Ibid., 1967–1968, 27.
28. Ibid., 1969–1970, 8.
29. Ibid., 1965–1966.
30. Ibid., 1967–1968, 40–57.
31. Ibid., 1969–1970, 29, 40.
32. Ibid., 22.
33. Ibid., 1973–1974, 8.
34. Ibid., 1972–1973, 11.
35. Ibid., 1978–1979, 12.
36. Ibid., 78.
37. Ibid., 1980–1981.
38. Ibid., 3.
39. Napoka interview, 2003.
40. Kurin interview, 2003.
41. Lynn Martin (Graton), telephone interview by author, September 16, 2002.
42. Kurin interview, 2003.
43. Richard Kennedy, interview by author, Washington, D.C., June 17, 2003.
44. Kurin interview, 2003.
45. Richard Kennedy, notes, 1988, Ralph Rinzler Archives and Collections, Center for Folklife and Cultural Heritage Archives, Smithsonian Institution, Washington, D.C.
46. Contract between the state of Hawai'i and the Smithsonian Institution, Ralph Rinzler Archives and Collections, Center for Folklife and Cultural Heritage Archives, Smithsonian Institution, Washington, D.C.
47. "Attendees for Working Meeting," memo from HSFCA director Sarah Richards to governor's office, July 8, 1988, memorandum to Center

for Folklife and Cultural Heritage Archives, Smithsonian Institution, Washington, D.C.

48. Lynn Martin, notes, 1988, Ralph Rinzler Archives and Collections, Center for Folklife and Cultural Heritage Archives, Smithsonian Institution, Washington, D.C.
49. Martin (Graton) telephone interview, 2002.
50. Working Meeting Minutes, 1988, Ralph Rinzler Archives and Collections, Center for Folklife and Cultural Heritage Archives, Smithsonian Institution, Washington, D.C.
51. Martin (Graton) telephone interview, 2002.
52. Kurin interview, 2003.
53. Working Meeting Minutes, 1988.
54. Kurin interview, 2003.

Chapter 2. Finding and Defining Traditional Hawai'i

1. Richard Kennedy, "In House Mid-Term Progress Report on the Hawai'i Program for the 1989 Festival of American Folklife," November 30, 1988. This story was retold on a panel titled "Cultural Representation through Negotiation." Richard Kennedy, "Curator, Community, and the State in the Representation of Hawai'i," paper presented at the American Anthropological Association Conference, 1993.
2. Linda Tuhiwa Smith outlines five models of culturally appropriate research for non-indigenous people researching indigenous people (the first four from Graham Smith): a mentoring model led by indigenous people, an adoption model in which long-term relationships are established, a power-sharing model, an empowering outcomes model in which indigenous people's concerns shape the research, and a bicultural or partnership research.
3. Kennedy, "In House Mid-Term Progress Report."
4. For further discussion of inter-ethnic relations in Hawai'i, see Kirkpatrick 1987 and Okamura 2000.
5. Kurin interview, 2003.
6. For discussions on the changing and politicized uses of the *haole* label, see Ohnuma 2002 and Young 1992.
7. As some local Japanese and Hawaiian activists have pointed out, as a catch-all category, "local" serves to mask power differentials and erase the resistance of Hawaiians. See special issue of *Amerasia Journal* 26 (2) (2000).

8. Memorandum, 1988, Ralph Rinzler Archives and Collections, Center for Folklife and Cultural Heritage Archives, Smithsonian Institution, Washington, D.C.
9. Martin (Graton) telephone interview, 2002.
10. Kennedy interview, 2003.
11. The information that follows comes from two drafts of this report. Lynn Martin, "Overview of Folklife in Hawai'i and Possible Research Topics/Themes," 1988, Ralph Rinzler Archives and Collections, Center for Folklife and Cultural Heritage Archives, Washington, D.C.
12. In Waikīkī there is a line of hotels called Ohana Hotels that are the lower-budget arm of Marriott. The use of *'ohana* as the central theme in Disney's *Lilo and Stitch* is probably the best known media appropriation, where it could be argued it is more respectfully treated.
13. Some ancient games and sports have since been revived on Moloka'i as part of the Makahiki observances in October.
14. For a history of immersion schools in Hawai'i, see Kame'eleihiwa 1992, 109–118.
15. Martin, "Overview of Folklife in Hawai'i," 13.
16. "Portagee" jokes are the Hawai'i equivalent of Polish jokes on the mainland.
17. Martin, "Overview of Folklife in Hawai'i," 22.
18. Kennedy interview, 2003.
19. Lynn Martin, letter, October 6, 1988, Center for Folklife and Cultural Heritage, Smithsonian Institution.
20. Martin letter, 1988.
21. Richard Kennedy, letter, November 23, 1988, Center for Folklife and Cultural Heritage, Smithsonian Institution.
22. Teri Skillman, interview by author, Honolulu, May 3, 2002.
23. Kennedy, notes, Ralph Rinzler Archives and Collections, Center for Folklife and Cultural Heritage Archives.
24. Kennedy, "In House Mid-Term Progress Report."
25. "Fieldwork Guidelines," 1988, Ralph Rinzler Archives and Collections, Center for Folklife and Cultural Heritage Archives, Smithsonian Institution, Washington, D.C.
26. Untitled document, 1988, Ralph Rinzler Archives and Collections, Center for Folklife and Cultural Heritage Archives, Smithsonian Institution, Washington, D.C.
27. The fieldnotes and field recordings are available in the audiovisual section of Sinclair Library, University of Hawai'i at Mānoa. As a

result of this research, recordings have recently been transferred from aging audiotapes to CD-ROM.

28. The following information comes from meeting notes. Hawai‘i Fieldwork Review Meeting, notes, January 25–27, 1989, Ralph Rinzler Archives and Collections, Center for Folklife and Cultural Heritage Archives, Smithsonian Institution, Washington, D.C.
29. Richard Kennedy, “Curator, Community, and State in the Representation of Hawai‘i,” paper presented at the American Anthropological Association Conference, Washington, D.C., November 20, 1993, Ralph Rinzler Archives and Collections, Center for Folklife and Cultural Heritage Archives, Smithsonian Institution, Washington, D.C.
30. Kennedy is very frank about this incident, saying that it was a learning experience and indicative of the times. He is emphatic in saying that they would do this differently now.
31. Kennedy interview, 2003.
32. According to Kyle Ikeda at the University of Hawai‘i, Okinawans in Hawai‘i practice situational ethnicity, identifying as Okinawans in relation to local Japanese in Hawai‘i but as Japanese in relation to mainland Japan, especially if they perceive that they are being seen as second-class citizens.
33. Skillman interview, 2002.
34. This term comes from Helàn Page’s discussion of black men in the media (1997).
35. Linda Moriarty, interview by author, October 29, 2002.
36. Kennedy interview, 2003.
37. Moriarty interview, 2002.
38. *Hīmeni* originated in missionary projects, especially the singing schools set up by Reverend Hiram Bingham, who taught Native Hawaiians European musical structure in order to teach them to sing hymns. It was further developed with the later translations and adaptations of Reverend Lorenzo Lyons, who sought to bring the music into greater accord with Hawaiian sensibilities. According to George Kanahele, the direction of *hīmeni* since 1820 is mostly attributable to Lyons’ “enormous efforts at synthesizing the musical and cultural elements of the Hawaiian encounter with Christian tradition” (1979, 136).
39. English, Mandarin, Cantonese, and Taiwanese.
40. The HSFCA Master and Apprentice Program has long debated this issue but has chosen in many cases to set up master artists with earnest apprentices from different ethnic groups. This kind of crossing

over was raised in the fieldwork selection meetings as a reason not to stick to ethnic categories.

41. "Fieldwork Guidelines," Ralph Rinzler Archives and Collections, Center for Folklife and Cultural Heritage Archives.

Chapter 3. Interpreting an Authentic "Sense of Place"

Earlier versions of portions of this chapter previously appeared in the *Journal of American Folklore* 121 (479) (Winter 2008): 36–59.

1. Richard Kurin, "Special Events during the 1989 Festival of American Folklife," memorandum to Ralph Rinzler, Ralph Rinzler Archives and Collections, Center for Folklife and Cultural Heritage Archives, Smithsonian Institution, Washington, D.C.
2. "Working Meeting Minutes," 1988, Ralph Rinzler Archives and Collections, Center for Folklife and Cultural Heritage Archives, Smithsonian Institution, Washington, D.C., 1988.
3. Barbara Lau, fieldwork review meeting notes, January 25, 1989, Ralph Rinzler Archives and Collections, Center for Folklife and Cultural Heritage Archives, Smithsonian Institution, Washington, D.C.
4. This information is taken from notes on the conceptual phase of the fieldwork review meetings that occurred in January 1989 in Honolulu (see note 3 above). These notes illustrate some confusion. The overview labeled as a three-part presentation is followed by four categories: traditions with continuation, crafts of acculturation, local, and immigrant traditions that have been continued and revived.
5. Shave ice is a popular local version of the snow cone consisting of finely shaved ice in a cone or bowl with flavored syrups poured over the top. Variations include *azuki* beans in the bottom and sweetened condensed milk poured on top.
6. The Festival has included livestock on several occasions.
7. Memorandum, 1989, Ralph Rinzler Archives and Collections, Center for Folklife and Cultural Heritage Archives, Smithsonian Institution, Washington, D.C.
8. Martin, "Overview of Folklife in Hawai'i."
9. Johannes Fabian (1983) discusses the practice of situating some cultural groups in the past as a strategy with colonialist implications.
10. Kyle Ikeda has since pointed out to me (2005) that red roofs are common in Okinawa and that Okinawans in Hawai'i must have tried to re-create a sense of home by having red roofs in their new environment. Kyle Ikeda, interview by author, Honolulu, March 7, 2005.
11. A detailed history of Hawai'i plantations appears in Ronald T. Takaki,

Pau Hana: Plantation Life and Labor in Hawai'i, 1835–1920 (Honolulu: University of Hawai'i Press, 1983).

12. Jonathan Y. Okamura (1998) argues that the "spirit of aloha" model of multiculturalism is politically constructed and motivated and that it functions to effectively suppress dissent in the islands. Another side to this debate appears in Grant and Ogawa 1993.
13. When I talked with him at the 2002 Festival, Ricardo Trimillos expressed surprise to see the tech crew digging holes for structures and said that apparently this rule had changed since 1989. Memories differ about the *imu* solution, but Kennedy claims that they ended up building it aboveground.
14. At least one person told me that there were protests and that as a precautionary measure the slaughtered pigs were brought in early so that they would be safely tucked away in the *imu* before the crowds arrived.
15. It is worth noting that this attention to plant importation is not, however, observed in the reverse, despite overwhelming evidence that Hawai'i's delicate ecosystem continues to be irreversibly damaged by the importation and improper handling of non-indigenous plant and animal species. While declaration forms are required of all persons entering the islands, disclosure is voluntary.
16. Barbara Lau, memorandum to Jackie Dulaney, May 9, 1989, Ralph Rinzler Archives and Collections, Center for Folklife and Cultural Heritage Archives, Smithsonian Institution, Washington, D.C.
17. Linda Moriarty, supply list to Sally Brodie, May 23, 1989, Smithsonian Institution, Washington, D.C.
18. Sallie Brodie, letter to Mr. Bill Theobald, February 28, 1989, Ralph Rinzler Archives and Collections, Center for Folklife and Cultural Heritage Archives, Smithsonian Institution, Washington, D.C.; Brodie, letter to Mr. Joe Aiken, March 23, 1989, Ralph Rinzler Archives and Collections, Center for Folklife and Cultural Heritage Archives, Smithsonian Institution, Washington, D.C.
19. Keahi Allen, "Pā'ū Riders and Parades in Hawai'i," Fieldwork Report, 1988, Ralph Rinzler Archives and Collections, Center for Folklife and Cultural Heritage Archives, Smithsonian Institution, Washington, D.C.
20. Lynn Martin, memorandum to Richard Kennedy, May 17, 1989, Ralph Rinzler Archives and Collections, Center for Folklife and Cultural Heritage Archives, Smithsonian Institution, Washington, D.C.

21. The CFCH now handles the marketplace.
22. Text for all Hawai'i program signs is in the CFCH Archives. The actual signs were returned to the state of Hawai'i and may be at the Lyman Museum in Hilo. I was unable to track them down during my research.
23. Noenoe Silva, in "He Kanawai E Ho'opau Na Hula Kuolo Hawai'i: The Political Economy of Banning the Hula," *Hawaiian Journal of History* (2000), 34 (Ralph Rinzler Archives and Collections, Center for Folklife and Cultural Heritage Archives, Smithsonian Institution, Washington, D.C.), argues that *hula* was never actually banned, although it was certainly discouraged; rather, a stiff system of fees and limitations was imposed that effectively suppressed it in urban areas.
24. Over the years the Festival staff has tried many strategies to determine the effectiveness of signage. When I was there in 2003, interns interviewed visitors who had stopped to read signs as well as simply counted how many people stopped in particular locations and timed how long they stayed. Signs were moved when deemed necessary. Random surveys have also addressed this issue.
25. Mindful of these challenges to its dissemination of information, the CFCH donates copies of the annual Festival book to libraries around the country as well as using it as a tool for garnering future funding by gifting it to policy makers and prospects. Smithsonian Institution 1989.
26. Program book articles were more randomly connected to the programs in Festival books from earlier years.
27. Martin (Graton) telephone interview, 2002.
28. The use of diacriticals is now mandated by the state of Hawai'i for all its official documents. There are debates about this, however. Some Hawaiians who work with translation argue that diacriticals should not be used because they are a university invention and were not used in the past. They feel that dependence on them makes it impossible for readers educated in this system to read older literature. In Samoa, diacriticals were mandated out by the government in the 1970s as a de-colonizing statement.
29. *Merriam Webster* online: http://m-w.com/dictionary/cosmopolitanism (accessed September 18, 2007).
30. Personal communication with Ricardo Trimillos, March 1, 2006.
31. "Hawai'i Program," Washington, D.C.: Smithsonian Institution, 1989.

32. Kennedy interview, 2003. This quote, rejected by Kennedy on the recommendation of Napoka, was reclaimed for use in a book produced by Martin in 1990 on the restaging.

Chapter 4. Performing "The Other Side of the Island"

1. Mark Miller, interview by author, Washington, D.C., June 28, 2003.
2. Martin (Graton) telephone interview, 2002.
3. Pearl Garmon, undated letter to Linda Moriarty, 1989, Ralph Rinzler Archives and Collections, Center for Folklife and Cultural Heritage Archives, Smithsonian Institution, Washington D.C.
4. Martin, "Overview of Folklife in Hawai'i."
5. "Presenter Guidelines," undated, Ralph Rinzler Archives and Collections, Center for Folklife and Cultural Heritage Archives, Smithsonian Institution, Washington, D.C.
6. Jay Junker, interview by author, Honolulu, April 16, 2003.
7. Ni'ihau is a small, privately owned island and the only one that did not prohibit the Hawaiian language, as happened elsewhere in the islands soon after annexation.
8. Officially referred to as Hawaiian Creole English (HCE), Hawai'i pidgin emerged out of the plantation experience in which contract workers from many ethnicities worked in close proximity. Pidgin, like Ebonics, has been at the center of debates in academia. It has recently been embraced by a number of local creative writers in Hawai'i as a reaction to its general condemnation in K–12 schools.
9. Moriarty interview, 2002.
10. "Presenter Guidelines."
11. Martin, notes, Ralph Rinzler Archives and Collections, Center for Folklife and Cultural Heritage Archives.
12. The participant release form is important in that it "grants the Smithsonian the right to make and use recordings, photographs, movies, and videotapes" of participation in the Festival for nonprofit use. In other words, although the agreement serves to protect the usage of Festival performance by mandating that for-profit use would require the permission of participants, Festival performance directly and indirectly becomes the acquired property of the Smithsonian, to be used for the perpetuation of Smithsonian projects.
13. Junker interview, 2003.
14. Robert Ruiz, interview by author, Waimea, HI, May 17, 2003.
15. Kennedy interview, 2003.
16. Adria Imada identifies this same conundrum for dancers on the early

hula circuits who made personal gains by performing in various venues but who were, at the same time, co-opted by territorial and national interests (2004).

17. I borrow the term "big idea" from Beverly Serrell. In her classic manual on museum interpretation, she stresses the importance of an overarching theme in museum exhibitions (1996, 1–8).
18. In 2003, when I was a pre-doctoral fellow at the Smithsonian, several volunteers were awarded pins for fifteen to twenty-five years of service to the Festival.
19. In 2003 one long computer bank section of Festival offices was designated "intern row" during the Festival countdown.
20. This view is supported by a number of people associated with the Festival and my own observations.
21. Napoka interview, 2003.
22. Kurin interview, 2003.
23. "Notes on Today Show Meeting," Ralph Rinzler Archives and Collections, Center for Folklife and Cultural Heritage Archives, Smithsonian Institution, Washington, D.C., 1989.
24. Mary Combs, "Leis of Hawai'i Are Tokens of Love and Aloha," Smithsonian News Service, July 1989. Versions of this article appeared in papers around the country, such as the *Los Angeles Times* (July 30, 1989), *Chicago Tribune* (August 23, 1989), *St. Louis Community News* (August 1, 1989), *Arroyo Grande (CA) Five Cities Times Press Recorder* (October 6, 1989), *Idaho Falls Post* (July 1, 1989), and *Elryia (OH) Chronicle Telegram* (October 8, 1989). The date suggests that this press release may have been intended as a follow-up, and the various dates of publications indicate that many of these papers published the story as cultural information rather than as Festival publicity. In several cases it appeared in weekend editions. General press releases mentioning all of the 1989 programs went out in May 1989.
25. Of course, this precedes the age of digital photography and the endless potential for photograph alteration. "Notes on Press Tent Operations for Participant Orientation," 1989, Ralph Rinzler Archives and Collections, Center for Folklife and Cultural Heritage Archives, Smithsonian Institution, Washington, D.C.
26. Memorandum, June 15, 1989, Ralph Rinzler Archives and Collections, Center for Folklife and Cultural Heritage Archives, Smithsonian Institution, Washington, D.C.
27. Kurin interview, 2003.

28. Invitation, 1989, Ralph Rinzler Archives and Collections, Center for Folklife and Cultural Heritage Archives, Smithsonian Institution, Washington, D.C.
29. Richard Kurin, "Special Events during the 1989 Festival of American Folklife," memorandum to Ralph Rinzler, March 9, 1989, Ralph Rinzler Archives and Collections, Center for Folklife and Cultural Heritage Archives, Smithsonian Institution, Washington, D.C.
30. This depends greatly on the level of the VIPs. When I was there in 2001 for the opening ceremony for the Silk Road program, Secretary of Defense Colin Powell, Senator Ted Kennedy, and Yo-Yo Ma were all in attendance, and there were Secret Service agents posted at locations close to the stage. Festival staff said they hoped never again to have to deal with that level of security, so obviously it was not the norm.
31. It is difficult not to see government officials in expensive suits sweating in a hot, steamy tent as an inversion of power incurred by the organizers, and one in which I suspect they take a secret delight despite concerns for the comfort of officials.
32. If it is true, as I was told by both Kennedy and Martin (Graton), that the juxtaposition of programs is more circumstantial than deliberate, this theme must have been a happy, after-the-fact discovery.
33. It is worth noting here that on one of the Festival narrative stages, a *kumu hula* from Hawai'i discussed this as a disrespectful appropriation and misuse of the *"aloha"* greeting.
34. Since the Hawaiian renaissance, Hawaiian chant is often performed as a ritual at the beginning of events in much the same way Christian prayers are offered to consecrate what follows.
35. The Cubans were not able to arrive in time for the ceremony due to visa difficulties.
36. Festival stage recordings of 1989, Ralph Rinzler Archives and Collections, Center for Folklife and Cultural Heritage Archives, Smithsonian Institution, Washington, D.C. An edited version of Waihee's speech was reproduced in a 2002 Folklife Festival promotional video, *Smithsonian Folklife Festival* (Washington, D.C.).
37. I borrow this term from Stanley's discussion of theme parks (1998, 17).
38. Since the Hawaiian Renaissance of the 1970s, it has become standard procedure at many kinds of public events—political gatherings, symphony concerts, university conferences, etc.—to ask Hawaiian *kumu*

to perform a chant. In most cases, these events are orchestrated by local *haole* who wish to show their respect for the "host culture."

39. Kennedy remembered, "The Samoans did something on their own." Kennedy interview, 2003.
40. Simeamativa M. Aga, letter to the Honorable Patricia Saiki, June 6, 1989, Ralph Rinzler Archives and Collections, Center for Folklife and Cultural Heritage Archives, Smithsonian Institution, Washington, D.C. *Ava,* or kava, is a mildly intoxicating drink made from a root, and its ritual sharing and consumption is used in various locations throughout the Pacific for ceremonial purposes.
41. Lau, memorandum to Dulaney, May 9, 1989.
42. Hobsbawm and Ranger (1983) discuss the use of extant cultural practices to create invented rituals that serve state purposes.
43. *Palaka* shirts were short-sleeved, plaid shirts worn by plantation workers—also *palaka* cloth. Variations of the *palaka* are still worn today.
44. Richard Hoʻopiʻi, interview by author, Kahakuloa, HI, May 21, 2003.
45. McDonald interview, 2003.
46. Moriarty interview, 2002.
47. Kennedy interview, 2003.
48. Jeanette "Benjie" Bennington, interview by author, Honolulu, November 17, 2002.
49. Beverly Simons, interview by author, Washington, D.C., July 17, 1989.
50. Napoka interview, 2003.
51. Ricardo Trimillos, interview by author, Honolulu, October 1, 2003.
52. International programs tend to attract diaspora audiences as well.
53. McDonald interview, 2003. With slight variations, McDonald related this story in a Festival video, in a report she gave to the CFCH, and in the interview I conducted. My text comes from the interview.
54. Napoka interview, 2003.
55. Kennedy interview, 2003.
56. Moriarty interview, 2002.
57. Junker interview, 2003.
58. Bennington interview, 2003.
59. Kennedy interview, 2003.
60. Napoka interview, 2003.
61. Trimillos interview, 2003.

62. Husking is generally done by hitting the coconut against a fixed spike set upright in the ground.
63. Junker interview, 2003.
64. Robert Cato, interview by author, Lā'ie, HI, May 17, 2003.
65. Clayton Lum, interview by author, Waimea, HI, May 19, 2003.
66. Moriarty interview, 2002. According to Moriarty, he enjoyed himself so much that he has continued to help out whenever needed after returning to Hawai'i.
67. The showcasing of narrative is a type of cultural display that is constantly being rethought in folklife festivals. At other festivals, placing informants face-to-face with the audience in an outer circle to the side or behind the conversation has been used as a way of better simulating a conversation as opposed to a performance facing an audience.
68. Festival stage recordings of 1989, Ralph Rinzler Archives and Collections, Center for Folklife and Cultural Heritage Archives.
69. McDonald interview, 2003.
70. Junker interview, 2003.
71. A local culture worker defined it this way to me in an e-mail:

> There's a Hawaiian word *"maha'oi"* which is the opposite of humble, sort of when you go into someone's house as a guest for the first time, unless you're *maha'oi,* most people won't go looking into closets, helping themselves to the fridge and putting your feet up on the sofa etc. You sorta should "behave yourself." Well, use the house as a metaphor for the islands and the guest as the haoles and you got what a *maha'oi* person can be as opposed to a sensitive person.

72. Ruiz interview, 2003.
73. Kennedy, "Curator, Community, and State in the Representation of Hawai'i," 8.
74. Trimillos interview, 2003.
75. Junker interview, 2003.
76. "Chalangalang," according to George Kanahele, refers to the distinctive twangy sound of Hawaiian popular music (1979, xxiv). More details on this kind of music can be found on the website on National Heritage Fellowship winner Auntie Genoa Keawe, Lifetime Honors: 2000 NEA National Heritage Fellowships. http://www.nea.gov/honors/heritage/Heritage00/Keawe.html (accessed March 6, 2007).
77. I have heard two slightly different versions of this story. Mine is a composite. The two accounts vary in terms of the cutoff date. No one is certain whether the rule was said to have come down from

the Smithsonian or from the Hawai'i end. It may have been a case of blaming the Smithsonian, since Kennedy says that it is not the kind of rule the Smithsonian would make. My feeling is that the fact that the story has become part of the Hawai'i program folklore attests to its validity in terms of testing the Festival frames, whatever the truth might be. Junker interview, 2003; Trimillos interview, 2003.

78. Junker interview, 2003.
79. Ibid.
80. Moriarty interview, 2002.
81. Ibid.
82. Trimillos interview, 2003.
83. Moriarty interview, 2002.
84. According to an online source, estimates of where Hawai'i stands in terms of relative cost of living vary from 30 to 60 percent above mainland averages. Alternative Hawai'i 2006, http://www.alternative-hawaii.com/overpop.htm (accessed March 6, 2007).
85. For an in-depth look at Hawaiian diaspora and its identity issues, see Halualani 2002. The largest community of Native Hawaiians outside of Hawai'i is in Las Vegas, often jokingly referred to in Hawai'i as the "eighth island."
86. E.g., Spam *musubi,* a snack made of a block of *sushi* rice and a slab of Spam wrapped with *nori* (seaweed), is ubiquitous in Hawai'i—yet another example of the Hawaiianization of a mainland import, this one from the U.S. military presence. It is worth remembering that imported foods such as white rice and Spam have greatly contributed to the alarming health statistics among the poor in Hawai'i, especially Native Hawaiians.
87. Junker interview, 2003.
88. Moriarty interview, 2002.
89. Versions of this story were told to me in the interviews I conducted with Kennedy and Junker.
90. Trimillos interview, 2003.
91. Moriarty interview, 2002.
92. Cato interview, 2003.
93. Moriarty interview, 2002.
94. Sherlin Beniamina, interview by author, Waimea, HI, May 11, 2003.
95. Kamuela Chun, interview by author, Honolulu, May 1, 2003.
96. Ho'opi'i interview, 2003.
97. Moriarty interview, 2002.
98. Napoka interview, 2003.

99. Ibid.
100. Junker interview, 2003.
101. Ibid.
102. Kurin interview, 2003.

Chapter 5. Beyond the Festival Afterglow

1. Trimillos interview, 2003.
2. Richard Kennedy, notes, Ralph Rinzler Archives and Collections, Center for Folklife and Cultural Heritage, Smithsonian Institution, Washington, D.C., 1988.
3. Marie McDonald, *lei* making (1990); Seisho "Harry" Nakasone, Okinawan music (1991); Pualani Kanako'ole and Nalani Kanako'ole, *hula* (1993); Solomon and Richard Ho'opi'i, Hawaiian music (1994); Genoa "Auntie Genoa" Keawe, Hawaiian music (2000); Kaupena Wong, Jr., Hawaiian chant (2005).
4. This view was expressed to me in several conversations with four different Hawai'i culture workers.
5. Skillman interview, 2002.
6. This meant that although the film was paid for primarily by the Hawai'i Visitor's Bureau, payment had to be cleared through the HSFCA since it had been designated by the state to handle all Festival funds.
7. The film was entered into the 1989 Hawai'i International Film Festival and aired on KGMB-TV on December 2, 1989.
8. Heather Giugni, letter of agreement, July 12, 1989, Ralph Rinzler Archives and Collections, Center for Folklife and Cultural Heritage, Smithsonian Institution, Washington, D.C.
9. Millicent Kim, letter, September 15, 1989, Ralph Rinzler Archives and Collections, Center for Folklife and Cultural Heritage, Smithsonian Institution, Washington, D.C. According to attached memos, this letter was drafted by Lynn Martin, with the help of Dolly Strazar, and reflected Martin's views. It went through at least three drafts.
10. Heather Giugni, letter to Lynn Martin, October 10, 1989, Ralph Rinzler Archives and Collections, Center for Folklife and Cultural Heritage, Smithsonian Institution, Washington, D.C.
11. Heather Giugni and Lurline McGregor, letter to Millicent Kim, October 10, 1989.
12. Several participants with whom I spoke mentioned having seen this on TV.

13. This information was gleaned from conversations with University of Hawai'i librarians.
14. Kurin interview, 2003.
15. Lynn Martin, memorandum, August 15, 1989, Ralph Rinzler Archives and Collections, Center for Folklife and Cultural Heritage, Smithsonian Institution, Washington, D.C.
16. Millicent Kim, letter, undated, Ralph Rinzler Archives and Collections, Center for Folklife and Cultural Heritage, Smithsonian Institution, Washington, D.C.
17. Lynn Martin, memorandum, October 17, 1989, Ralph Rinzler Archives and Collections, Center for Folklife and Cultural Heritage, Smithsonian Institution, Washington, D.C.
18. Lynn Martin and Linda Moriarty, "Proposal for the Possible Re-Staging of the Hawai'i Program, Smithsonian Institution's 23rd Festival of American Folklife," November 11, 1989, Ralph Rinzler Archives and Collections, Center for Folklife and Cultural Heritage, Smithsonian Institution, Washington, D.C.
19. Bess Lomax Hawes came up with this term to refer to connecting a community to itself. Dan Sheehy, "Smithsonian Folkways Recordings," *Talk Story,* spring 2003.
20. Martin and Moriarty, "Proposal for the Possible Re-Staging of the Hawai'i Program."
21. Martin (Graton) telephone interview, 2002.
22. On August 18, 1959, Hawai'i was admitted as the fiftieth state of the United States. Admissions Day, or Statehood Day, is observed as a state holiday.
23. Moriarty interview, 2002.
24. Trimillos interview, 2003.
25. All the local news stations ran clips—some of which were collected at the HSFCA.
26. Richard Kennedy, "Opening Address at Festival," 1990, Ralph Rinzler Archives and Collections, Center for Folklife and Cultural Heritage, Smithsonian Institution, Washington, D.C.
27. Ruiz interview, 2003.
28. Richard Kennedy, letter, November 14, 1990, Ralph Rinzler Archives and Collections, Center for Folklife and Cultural Heritage, Smithsonian Institution, Washington, D.C.
29. Martin (Graton) telephone interview, 2002.
30. Junker interview, 2003.

31. Ibid.; Moriarty interview, 2002.
32. Junker interview, 2003.
33. Several participants mentioned their photo albums, but no one I interviewed was sure where they were anymore.
34. Napoka interview, 2003.
35. Ibid.
36. Ruiz interview, 2003.
37. Kennedy, "Opening Address at Festival."
38. Richard Kurin, memorandum, March 1, 1991, Ralph Rinzler Archives and Collections, Center for Folklife and Cultural Heritage, Smithsonian Institution, Washington, D.C.
39. "Hawai'i/Smithsonian Center for Asian and Pacific Cultures," 1991, Ralph Rinzler Archives and Collections, Center for Folklife and Cultural Heritage, Smithsonian Institution, Washington, D.C.
40. John Waihee, "State of the State Address: 'Staying Ahead,'" Smithsonian Institution, Washington, D.C.: January 22, 1991. [Original source: Office of the Governor, state of Hawai'i.]
41. Reflecting on this effort years later, Kurin said that perhaps if he had not been so green on the job he might have been able to get the proposal through, but this perspective does not take into account that without sympathetic supporters in state government and agencies, many lofty ventures get mired in Hawai'i. As one reply to Kennedy's inquiries warned, people in the islands can also be very protective of their "turf." Kurin interview, 2003.
42. Kennedy, "Opening Address at Festival."
43. Kurin interview, 2003.
44. The winter 2008 special issue of the *Journal of American Folklore,* "Interdisciplinary Perspectives on the Smithsonian Folklife Festival," vol. 121, no. 479, ed. Heather Diamond and Ricardo Trimillos, comprises six articles that focus on this transition and case studies of some international programs.
45. Kennedy interview, 2003.
46. See Torgovnick 1990.
47. See Satterwhite 2008.
48. In 1991 forty Native Hawaiian groups had joined forces under an umbrella organization called Hui Na'auao.
49. Saiki 1993.
50. See Thomas 2001, 214–221.
51. See Gulliford 1996, 119–143.

Conclusion

1. David E. Whisnant, "Folk Festival Issues Report from a Seminar," John Edwards Memorial Foundation at the Folklore and Mythology Center, University of California, Los Angeles, July 31, 1978.
2. David Whisnant, letter to Ralph Rinzler, August 27, 1973.
3. Trimillos interview, 2003.
4. Waihee, "State of the State Address: 'Staying Ahead.'"
5. Wilson 2000.
6. Ho'opi'i interview, 2003.
7. The flyer reads, "We need your help building the Hawaiian Nation. Kau Inoa is the 1st step towards self-determination. Register now to have a say in your future. If you have already registered, bring your 'ohana and friends and visit us at the Great Hawaiian Folklife Festival, Kapiolani Park, March 25 & 26, 2007, 10 a.m.–5 p.m. For more on Kau Inoa see http://www.oha.org/."

Glossary of Foreign Words

NOTE: Unless otherwise specified, these terms are in the Hawaiian language.

ahu	altar
'āina	land
aloha	love, greeting, kindness, compassion
bon odori	music and dance performed during Japanese *Obon* Festival
forno	Portuguese beehive oven
hīmeni	Hawaiian style of hymn singing
hālau hula	hula school or lineage
hale	house
hapa-haole	style of Hawaiian songs with mostly English words
haole	Caucasian; formerly, any foreigner
heiau	ancient temple, pre-Christian place of worship
hula auana	modern *hula*
hula kahiko	*hula* in the traditional style
imu	underground oven
ipu	gourd idiophone used in *hula* dance
kahili	feathered standards associated with Hawaiian royalty
kama'āina haole	Caucasian born in Hawai'i
kapa	cloth made from tree bark
kumu hula	*hula* teacher
lā'au lapa'au	plant-based medicinal lore
lauhala	pandanus leaf, especially used in plaiting
lei	garland or necklace of flowers
lo'i	irrigated terrace for taro and rice
lū'au	a feast or gathering
luna	labor boss
malihini	newcomer, stranger, tourist
mālama'āina	care for the land
'ohana	family

paniolo	cowboy
pāʻū	skirt worn by women horseback riders
poi	cooked taro, pounded and thinned with water
puka kom	western gate
puʻuhoʻomaha	place of refuge
rondalla	Filipino string band
sanshin	Okinawan three-stringed plucked lute
ʻukulele	a small, four-stringed plucked chordophone in Hawaiian music
yagura	tower around which Japanese *bon* dance is performed

References

Adams, Robert McCormick. 1989. "Celebrating Freedom." *Festival of American Folklife Program Book*. Washington, D.C.: Smithsonian Institution.

Adamski, Mary. 2003. "Immigration Roots." *Honolulu Star-Bulletin*. http://starbulletin.com/2003/11/08/features/story1.html (accessed May 23, 2004).

Apoliona, Haunani, et al. 1989. *Musics of Hawai'i*. Sound recording. Washington, D.C.: Smithsonian Institution.

Babcock, Barbara A. 1978. *The Reversible World: Symbolic Inversion in Art and Society*. Ithaca: Cornell University Press.

Bacchilega, Cristina. 2007. *Legendary Hawai'i and the Politics of Place*. Philadelphia: University of Pennsylvania Press.

Baron, Robert, and Nicholas Spitzer, eds. 1992. *Public Folklore*. Washington, D.C.: Smithsonian Institution Press.

Bauman, Richard, ed. 1992. *Folklore, Cultural Performances, and Popular Entertainments: A Communications Centered Handbook*. New York: Oxford University Press.

Bauman, Richard, et al., eds. 1992. *Reflections on the Folklife Festival: An Ethnography of Participant Experience*. Bloomington: Indiana University Press.

Bendix, Regina. 1997. *In Search of Authenticity: The Formation of Folklore Studies*. Madison: University of Wisconsin Press.

Binkiewicz, Donna M. 2004. *Federalizing the Muse: United States Arts Policy and the National Endowment for the Arts 1965–1980*. Chapel Hill: University of North Carolina Press.

Boatright, Mody Coggin. 1958. *The Family Saga and Other Phases of American Folklore*. Urbana: University of Illinois Press.

Brislin, Tom. 1989. "Capital Downpour Unable to Dampen Hawai'i's Big Parade." *Honolulu Advertiser*, June 25, A1, A6.

Bronner, Simon J. 1998. *Following Tradition: Folklore in the Discourse of American Culture*. Logan: Utah State University Press.

———. 2002. *Folk Nation: Folklore in the Creation of American Tradition.* Wilmington, DE: Scholarly Resources.

Buck, Elizabeth. 1993. *Paradise Remade: The Politics of Culture and History in Hawai'i.* Philadelphia: Temple University Press.

Camp, Charles, and Timothy Lloyd. 1980. "Six Reasons Not to Produce a Folklife Festival." *Kentucky Folklife Record* 26 (January–June): 67–74.

Cannon, Lou. 1993. "Waving (and Lowering) Flag in Hawai'i: Pride, Anger Result as Governor Pushes Native People's Cause on Coup's Centennial." *Washington Post,* January 17, 1993.

Cantwell, Robert. 1992. "Feasts of Unnaming: Folk Festival and the Representation of Folklife." In *Public Folklore,* ed. Robert Baron and Nicholas Spitzer. Washington, D.C.: Smithsonian Institution Press, 263–305.

———. 1993. *Ethnomimesis: Folklife and the Representation of Culture.* Chapel Hill: University of North Carolina Press.

Center for Folklife and Cultural Heritage. 1989. *Festival Sound Recordings.* Washington, D.C.: Smithsonian Institution Press.

Chait, Melanie. 1999. "Healing Hawai'i: The Recovery of an Island Identity: A Socio-historical Study of Hawaiian Cultural Resistance from the 1840s to the 1990s." Thesis (D. Phil.), University of Oxford.

Chapin, Helen Geracimos. 1996. *Shaping History: The Role of Newspapers in Hawai'i.* Honolulu: University of Hawai'i Press.

Clifford, James, and George E. Marcus, eds. 1986. *Writing Culture: The Poetics and Politics of Ethnography.* Berkeley: University of California Press.

Davis, Susan G. 1986. *Parades and Power: Street Theatre in Nineteenth-Century Philadelphia.* Philadelphia: Temple University Press.

Delima, Frank. 1991. *The Best of Delima too* (VHS videocassette). Honolulu: Pocholinga Productions.

Desmond, Jane C. 1999. *Staging Tourism: Bodies on Display from Waikiki to Sea World.* Chicago: University of Chicago Press.

Fabian, Johannes. 1983. *Time and the Other: How Anthropology Makes Its Object.* New York: Columbia University Press.

Fairbanks, Robert P. 2003. "A Theoretical Primer on Space." *Critical Social Work* 3 (1): 131–154.

Falassi, Alessandro. 1987. *Time Out of Time: Essays on the Festival.* 1st ed. Albuquerque: University of New Mexico Press.

Ferguson, Kathy, and Phyllis Turnbull. 1999. *Oh, Say, Can You See? The Semiotics of the Military in Hawai'i.* Minneapolis: University of Minnesota Press.

Filene, Benjamin. 2000. *Romancing the Folk: Public Memory and American Roots Music.* Chapel Hill: University of North Carolina Press.

Fredo, Bart. 1989. "The Festival" (VHS videocassette). Honolulu: Hawaii Public Television.

Fuchs, Lawrence H. 1961. *Hawai'i Pono: "Hawai'i the Excellent," a Social and Political History.* Honolulu: Bess Press.

Grant, Glen, and Dennis Ogawa. 1993. "Living Proof: Is Hawai'i the Answer?" *The Annals of the American Academy of Political and Social Science* 530 (November): 137–154.

Giugni, Heather, and Lurline MacGregor. 1989. *Celebrating Hawai'i's Cultures* (video recording)/1989 Festival of American Folklife. Honolulu: Juniroa Productions.

Gulliford, Andrew. 1996. "Bones of Contention: The Repatriation of Native American Human Remains." *The Public Historian* 18 (4), *Representing Native American History* (Autumn): 119–143.

Halualani, Rona Tamiko. 2002. *In the Name of Hawaiians: Native Identities and Cultural Politics.* Minneapolis: University of Minnesota Press.

Hassinger, John A. 1889. *Catalog of the Hawaiian Exhibits at the Exposition Universelle, Paris, 1889.* Honolulu: Hawaiian Gazette Company.

Hawaii and Asia/Pacific Collection, Hamilton Library, University of Hawaii at Mānoa, Honolulu.

Hawai'i Ecumenical Coalition on Tourism. 2004. *The 1989 Hawai'i Declaration of the Hawai'i Ecumenical Coalition on Tourism Conference "Tourism in Hawai'i: Its Impact on Native Hawaiians and Its Challenge to the Churches."* http://members.tripod.com/~MPHAWAII/Tourism/The1989.htm (accessed July 28, 2004).

Hawai'i Exposition. Commission to the Panama-Pacific International. 1916. *Report to Hon. Lucius E. Pinkham, Governor of Hawaii, of the Commissioners for Hawaii to the Panama-Pacific International Exposition.* Honolulu: New Freedom Press. [In Bishop Museum Archives, Honolulu.]

Hawai'i State Foundation for Culture and the Arts. 2004. http://www.state.hi.us/sfca (accessed August 7, 2004).

Hobsbawm, Eric, and Terence Ranger, eds. 1983. *The Invention of Tradition.* New York: Cambridge University Press.

Hooper-Greenhill, Eilean. 2000. *Museums and the Interpretation of Visual Culture, Museum Meanings.* London: Routledge.

Hoover, Will. 1990. "Lanai: The Gang Waxes Nostalgic." *Honolulu Advertiser,* July 25, 1990.

Hufford, Mary. 2002. "American Folklife: A Commonwealth of Cultures (1991) (with text of the Folklife Preservation Act, 1976)." In *Folk Nation: Folklore in the Creation of American Tradition,* ed. Simon Bronner. Wilmington, DE: Scholarly Resources, 237–248.

Hutynk, John. 1999–2000. "Hybridity Saves?" *Amerasia Journal* 25 (3): 39–58.

Imada, Adria. 2002. "'The Naughty Girls from Honolulu Do the Naughty Hula Dance'": Performing Hawai'i in the Imperial U.S." Paper presented at the American Studies Association Annual Meeting, Houston, TX, November 15.

———. 2004. "Hawaiians on Tour: Hula Circuits through the American Empire." *American Quarterly* 56 (1): 111–150.

Jackson, Bruce. 1987. *Fieldwork*. Urbana: University of Illinois Press.

Johnson, Katie N., and Tamara Underiner. 2001. "Command Performances: Staging Native Americans at Tillicum Village." In *Selling the Indian: Commercializing & Appropriating American Indian Cultures*, ed. C. J. Meyer and Diana Royer. Tucson: University of Arizona Press, 44–61.

Jolly, Margaret. 2000. "Specters of Inauthenticity." In *Voyaging Through the Contemporary Pacific*, ed. David Hanlon and Geoffrey White. Lanham, MD: Rowman & Littlefield Publishers, Inc., 274–297.

Kaeppler, Adrienne. 1992. "*Ali'i and Maka'āinana:* The Representation of Hawaiians in Museums at Home and Abroad." In *Museums and Communities: The Politics of Traditional Culture*, ed. Ivan Karp, Christine Kreamer, and Steven Levine. Washington, D.C.: Smithsonian Institution Press, 458–475.

———. 1993. *Hula Pahu: Hawaiian Drum Dances*. Vol. I: *Ha'a and Hula Pahu: Sacred Movements*. Honolulu: Bishop Museum Press.

Kame'eleihiwa, Lilikalāa. 1992. "Kula Kaiapuni: Hawaiian Immersion Schools." *Kamehameha Journal of Education* 3 (2): 109–118.

Kanahele, George S. 1979. *Hawaiian Music and Musicians: An Illustrated History*. Honolulu: University of Hawai'i Press.

Keesing, Roger. 2000. "Creating the Past: Custom and Identity in the Contemporary Pacific." In *Voyaging Through the Contemporary Pacific*, ed. David Hanlon and Geoffrey White. Lanham, MD: Rowman & Littlefield Publishers, Inc., 231–254.

Kennedy, Richard. 1989. "Hawai'i: Cosmopolitan Culture at the Crossroads of the Pacific." In *Festival of American Folklife*, ed. Frank Proschan. Washington, D.C.: Smithsonian Institution, 36–49.

Kent, Noel J. 1983. *Hawai'i: Islands Under the Influence*. New York: Monthly Review Press.

KHET-TV. 1989. *The Festival*. Honolulu, Hawai'i: KHET Television station. Video recording.

Kirkpatrick, John. 1987. "Ethnic Antagonism and Innovation in Hawai'i." In

Ethnic Conflict: International Perspectives, ed. Jerry Boucher, Dan Landis, and Karen Arnold Clark. Beverly Hills: Sage Publications, 298–316.

Kirlin, Katherine S., and Thomas M. Kirlin. 1991. *Smithsonian Folklife Cookbook*. Washington, D.C.: Smithsonian Institution Press.

Kirshenblatt-Gimblett, Barbara. 1998. *Destination Culture: Tourism, Museums, and Culture*. Berkeley: University of California Press.

Kurin, Richard. 1989. "Why Do We Do Festival?" *Festival of American Folklife Program Book*. Washington, D.C.: Smithsonian Institution, 8–21.

———. 1998. *Smithsonian Folklife Festival: Culture Of, By, and For the People*. Washington, D.C.: Smithsonian Institution.

Lippard, Lucy R. 1999. *On the Beaten Track: Tourism, Art, and Place*. New York: New Press.

MacCannell, Dean. 1976. *The Tourist*. New York: Schocken.

MacLeod, Roy. 1998. "Postcolonialism and Museum Knowledge: Revisiting the Museums of the Pacific." *Pacific Science* 52 (4): 308–318.

Martin, Lynn. 1988. *A Guide for Surveying Pacific Island Folk Arts*. Honolulu: Consortium for Pacific Arts and Cultures.

———, ed. 1990. *Folklife Hawai'i: A Restaging of the Hawai'i Program of the Smithsonian Institution's 23rd Annual Festival of American Folklife (1989)*. Honolulu: Hawai'i State Foundation on Culture and the Arts.

———, ed. 1994. *Musics of Hawai'i*. Honolulu: Hawai'i State Foundation on Culture and the Arts.

———. 1998. "Hawai'i, 1989—The Other Side of the Island." In *Smithsonian Folklife Festival: Culture Of, By, and For the People*, ed. Richard Kurin. Washington, D.C.: Smithsonian Institution, 120.

Merriam-Webster Online. http://www.m-w.com/cgi-bin/dictionary?book=Dictionary (accessed 2004–2007).

Merry, Sally Engle. 2000. *Colonizing Hawai'i: The Cultural Power of Law*. Princeton, NJ: Princeton University Press.

Morton, Todd Frank. 1921. *Story of the Exposition: Being the official history of the international celebration held at San Francisco in 1915 to commemorate the discovery of the Pacific Ocean and the construction of the Panama canal*. New York: Published for the Panama-Pacific International Exposition Company by G. P. Putnam's Sons.

Nordyke, Eleanor C. 1989. *The Peopling of Hawai'i*. Honolulu: University of Hawai'i Press.

Nordyke, Eleanor, and Richard Lee. 1989. "The Chinese in Hawai'i: A Historical and Demographic Perspective." *Hawaiian Journal of History* 23: 196–216.

Office of Hawaiian Affairs. Home page. 2007. http://www.oha.org/ (accessed April 13, 2007).

Ohnuma, Keiko. 2002. "Local *Haole*—A Contradiction in Terms? The Dilemma of Being White, Born and Raised in Hawai'i." *Cultural Values* 6 (3): 273–285.

Okamura, Jonathan Y. 1994. "Why There Are No Asian Americans in Hawai'i: The Continuing Significance of Local Identity." *Social Process in Hawai'i* 35: 161–178.

———. 1998. "The Illusion of Paradise: Privileging Multiculturalism in Hawai'i." In *Making Majorities*, ed. Dru Gladney. Stanford, CA: Stanford University Press, 264–340.

———. 2000. "Aloha Kanaka Me Ke Aloha 'Aina: Local Culture and Society in Hawai'i." *Amerasia Journal* 7 (2): 119–137.

"Overthrow Centennial: January 17, 1983–January 17, 1993." 1993. *Honolulu Star-Bulletin,* January 13.

Page, Helàn E. 1997. "'Black Male' Imagery and Media Containment of African American Men." *American Anthropologist* 99 (1): 99–111.

Paradise of the Pacific Press. 1914. *Hawaii a Primer: Panama-Pacific International Exposition.* Bishop Museum Archives, Honolulu.

Polynesian Cultural Center. 2004. Official website. http://www.polynesia.com/dining/aliiluau.html (accessed August 7, 2004).

Polynesian Voyaging Society. 2004. http://pvs.kcc.hawaii.edu/aboutpvs.html (accessed January 28, 2004).

Reinhold, Robert. 1992. "A Century after Queen's Overthrow, Talk of Sovereignty Shakes Hawai'i." *New York Times,* November 8, 1992, A24.

Roof, Judith, and Robyn Wiegman, eds. 1995. *Who Can Speak? Authority and Critical Identity.* Urbana: University of Illinois Press.

Rosa, John P. 2002. "Local Story: The Massie Case Narrative and the Production of Local Identity in Hawai'i." *Amerasia Journal* 26 (2): 93–115.

Rosaldo, Renato. 1989. *Culture and Truth: The Remaking of Social Analysis.* Boston: Beacon Press.

Rydell, Robert W. 1984. *All the World's a Fair: Visions of Empire at the American International Expositions, 1876–1916.* Chicago: University of Chicago Press.

Saiki, Arnie. 2004. *Restoring Loss: Performing Sovereignty in Hawai'i.* http://www.globulab.com/restoring_loss.html (accessed May 10, 2004).

Satterwhite, Emily. 2008. "Imagining Home, Nation, World: Appalachia on the Mall." *Journal of American Folklore* 121 (479) (Winter): 11–35.

Seeger, Anthony. 1988. "Creating and Confronting Cultures: Issues of Editing and Selection in Records and Videotapes of Musical Performances." Unpublished paper.

Serrell, Beverly. 1996. *Exhibit Labels: An Interpretive Approach*. Walnut Creek, CA: AltaMira.

Sheehy, Daniel. 2003. Smithsonian Folkways Recordings. *Talk Story* (Spring): 14.

Silva, Noenoe. 2004. *Aloha Betrayed: Native Hawaiian Resistance to American Colonialism*. Durham, NC: Duke University Press.

Sims, Martha C., and Martine Stephens. 2005. *Living Folklore: An Introduction to the Study of People and Their Traditions*. Logan: Utah State University Press.

Smith, Linda Tuhiwai. 1999. *Decolonizing Methodologies: Research and Indigenous Peoples*. London: University of Otago.

Smithsonian Folklife Festival Documentation Collection. 1966. Ralph Rinzler Archives and Collection, Center for Folklife and Cultural Heritage, Smithsonian Institution, Washington, D.C.

Smithsonian Institution. 1885. Hawaii Exhibit brochure from the World's Industrial and Cotton Centennial Exposition in New Orleans. Washington, D.C.: Archives of the Dibner Library of Science and Technology.

———. 1889. Hawaii Exhibit brochure from the Exposition Universelle in Paris. Washington, D.C.: Archives of the Dibner Library of Science and Technology.

———. 1984. *Festival of American Folklife* (VHS promotional video). Washington, D.C.: Smithsonian Institution.

———. 1989. *Festival of American Folklife Program Book, 1968–1997*. Washington, D.C.: Smithsonian Institution.

———. 2002. *Smithsonian Folklife Festival* (VHS promotional video). Center for Folklife and Cultural Heritage, Smithsonian Institution, Washington, D.C.

———. 2005. Website. http://www.folklife.si.edu/center/festival.html (accessed September 1, 2007).

Solāis, Ted. 1989. *Puerto Rican Music in Hawai'i: Kachi-kachi*. Sound recording. Produced by Smithsonian Folkways Recordings, Washington, D.C., distributed by Rounder Records, Cambridge, MA.

Sommers, Laurie Kay, ed. 1994. *Anatomy of a Festival, a Special Issue of Folklore in Use: Applications in the Real World* 2. Chippenham: Hisarlik Press.

Stanley, Nick. 1998. *Being Ourselves for You: The Global Display of Cultures*. London: Middlesex University Press.

Stannard, David E. 1989. *Before the Horror.* Honolulu: Social Science Research Institute, University of Hawai'i.

———. 2005. *Honor Killing: How the Infamous "Massie Affair" Transformed Hawai'i.* New York: Viking.

Stillman, Amy. 1996. "Hawaiian Hula Competition: Event, Repertoire, Performance, Tradition." *Journal of American Folklore* 109 (434): 357–360.

Stoeltje, Beverley J. 1992. "Festival." In *Folklore, Cultural Performances and Popular Entertainments,* ed. R. Bauman. New York: Oxford University Press, 261–271.

Sturken, Marita. 1997. *Tangled Memories: The Vietnam War, the Aids Epidemic, and the Politics of Remembering.* Berkeley: University of California Press.

Takaki, Ronald T. *Pau Hana: Plantation Life and Labor in Hawai'i, 1835–1920.* Honolulu: University of Hawai'i Press, 1983.

———. 1994. *Raising Cane: The World of Plantation Hawaii.* New York: Chelsea House Publishers.

Tanahara, Kris. 1993. "United Church of Christ Apologizes." *Honolulu Advertiser,* January 18, 1993, A6.

Taylor, Emma Ahuena. Papers. Hawai'i State Archives, Honolulu.

Thais, Bullard, and Eva Robinson. 1991. "Project #1: Tahitian Lanai—Waikikian Property. Honolulu: People for the Preservation of Hawai'i's Socio-cultural Resources," January 28.

Torgovnick, Marianna. 1990. *Gone Primitive: Savage Intellects, Modern Lives.* Chicago: University of Chicago Press.

Trask, Haunani-Kay. 1999. *From a Native Daughter: Colonialism and Sovereignty in Hawai'i.* Honolulu: University of Hawai'i Press.

———. 2000. "Natives and Anthropologists: The Colonial Struggle." In *Voyaging Through the Contemporary Pacific,* ed. David Hanlon and Geoffrey White. Lanham, MD: Rowman & Littlefield Publishers, Inc., 255–263.

Trimillos, Ricardo D. 2001. "'Whose Kine'" Music? The Many Meanings of Music." CD-ROM. Honolulu: Hawai'i's Plantation Village.

Twigg-Smith, Thurston. 1993. "Overthrow: No Apology Needed." *Honolulu Advertiser,* January 24, 1993, B1/B3.

U.S. Department of Agriculture Animal and Plant Inspection Service. June 15, 1980. Suggestions for Applicants for Permits to Import Plant Propagating Material under Quarantine no. 37.

Urry, John. 1990. *The Tourist Gaze: Leisure and Travel in Contemporary Societies.* London: Sage Publications.

Van Zile, Judy, and Damaris A. Kirchhofer. 1981. "Bon Dancing in Hawai'i: A Changing Tradition." *Honolulu* (November): 118–123, 152–159.

Virtual Smithsonian Folklife Festival. 1996. Smithsonian Institution. http://www.folklife.si.edu/hawaii/start.htm (accessed October 1, 2007).

Weiner, Annette B. 1992. *Inalienable Possessions: The Paradox of Keeping-While-Giving*. Berkeley: University of California Press.

Whisnant, David E. 1983. *All That Is Native and Fine: The Politics of Culture in an American Region*. Chapel Hill: University of North Carolina Press.

———. 1988. "Public Sector Folklore as Intervention: Lessons from the Past, Prospects for the Future." In *Conservation of Culture: Folklorists and the Public Sector*, ed. Bert Feintuch. Lexington: University Press of Kentucky.

Whitney, Scott. 2001. "The Not-So Merrie Monarch." *Honolulu* (November): 78–83.

Williams, Raymond. 1983. *Keywords: A Vocabulary of Culture and Society*. Rev. ed. London: Oxford University Press. [Original ed. published 1976.]

Wilson, Rob. 2000. *Reimagining the American Pacific: From South Pacific to Bamboo Ridge, New Americanists*. Durham, NC: Duke University Press.

Wilson, Rob, and Wimal Dissanayake. 1996. *Global/Local: Cultural Production and the Transnational Imaginary*. Durham, NC: Duke University Press.

Wood, Houston. 1999. *Displacing Natives: The Rhetorical Production of Hawaii*. Lanham, MD: Rowman & Littlefield Publishers, Inc.

Yano, Christine Reiko. 2006. *Crowning the Nice Girl: Gender, Ethnicity, and Culture in Hawai'i's Cherry Blossom Festival*. Honolulu: University of Hawai'i Press.

Young, Terry. 1992. "Haole: The Politicization of a Hawaiian Word and its History." *Forward Motion* 11 (3): 157–158.

Index

Numbers in **bold** refer to photographs.

Adams, Robert McCormick, 127, 149
aestheticization, 5, 23, 215, 216
African Americans, 73, 74, 84, 196–197
agency: counter-histories, 128, 130; creative agency, 181; dancers at Columbian Exposition, 20; festival representation, 92; participants, 135, 216
'āina, 60, 103, 111, 129, 206
Akaka, Abraham, 47–48
Akaka, Daniel Kahikina, 43, 148, 152, 161
aloha: appropriation, 69, 76, 164, 206, 217; basis of program success, 203; definition, 75; festival theme, 122, 137, 144, 150; Hawaiian hospitality, 13, 26, 202; ideal, 48, 75, 218; participants as ambassadors, 142; tourist greeting, 148
American Folklife Center, 68, 79, 214. *See also* National Endowment for the Arts (NEA)
anachronism, 112–113
anecdotes, 131–133, 145, 158, 164, 166
animals, 145–146, 173, 226n14
anthropology, 27–28, 30, 64, 204, 217. *See also* Beckwith, Martha; ethnography; Roberts, Helen
Asia/Pacific Research Center, 10, 199–202
audience. *See* visitors
audio recordings, 162, 184–185. *See also* Folkways Recordings
authenticity: absence of children, 157; concerns for folklife festivals, 78; conflicting notions, 7, 9, 88–89, 92, 166; definition, 99; ethics, 78; HSFCA programs, 37, 40; museums, 63; performance, 135, 138, 173; program book, 127; restaging, 187, 206; site design, 98–99, 101–102, 104, 108–116, 119; tourism, 26–27, 100, 208; zones, 155–156. *See also* "staged back regions"
Auwe, Henry "Papa," 117, 156–157, 169, 171

Babcock, Barbara, 148
Bacchilega, Cristina, 27
"backyard" culture, 89, 166
Beckwith, Martha, 27–28, 30
Belanus, Betty, 187
Bendix, Regina, 99
Bennington, Jeanette "Benjie," 83, 156
Big Five, 24, 33
Bishop Museum, 29, 30, 38, 43, 53, 220
bon dance, 1, 82, 88, 117, 147, 160, 170, 182, **193**
boundaries: blurred, 154–155; boundary-crossings, 160–161, 173, 202; permeable, 3, 9
Bowman, Kent, **154**

Brodie, Sally, 114, 118
Buck, Elizabeth, 13, 15
Burns, John, 33–34

canoes, 1, 2, 19, 57, 70–71, 90, 103, 134, **154**
canonization, 178–179. *See also* tradition
Cantwell, Robert, 5, 101, 174
Carriera, Josephine, **163**
Cato, Robert, 160, 170–171, 172
Celebrating Hawai'i's Cultures (Guigni/Juniroa), 179–181, 183
Center for Folklife and Cultural Heritage (CFCH): catalyst for local projects, 176; cultural advocacy, 135; history, 2; mission, 157, 180–181; relationship to Smithsonian, 126. *See also* Smithsonian Institution
Chait, Melanie, 46, 50
chant. *See* Hawaiian music: *mele* and *oli*
Chinese: demonstration kitchen, 156; festival selection, 88, 89, 93–94, 96; fieldwork, 74, 77, 160; pan-identity in signs, 124; program opening ritual, 151; restaging, 190; site design, 112
Christians: Ecumenical Council on Tourism, 205–206; participant selection, 111–112; United Church of Christ, 209. *See also* Koreans; LDS; missionaries; Portuguese
colonialism: influence on tradition, 127; Hawai'i, 15, 129, 208, 215; neo-colonialism, 130, 216; responses, 17. *See also* Hawai'i; military; missionaries
concessions, 119–120, 141, 180
cosmopolitanism, 129, 203, 205
"Cosmopolitan Hawaii: Culture at the Crossroads" (Kennedy with Martin), 195
creolization: Caribbean program, 149; cultural expressions, 32, 85, 139; program theme, 9–10, 83, 127–128, 139, 151, 205. *See also* hybridity; pidgin; tradition: shared
cultural authority: institutional, 58, 64, 127, 144, 178; local, 78; participant voices, 113, 158; performance, 135, 166; questions of who can speak, 9, 213; representations in program videos, 179–183; signs framing performance, 121, 126. *See also* agency
cultural capital, 174, 177–178
cultural conservation. *See* cultural preservation
cultural homogeneity, 5, 10, 94, 215
cultural practitioners. *See* tradition; tradition bearers
cultural preservation: Asia/Pacific research center, 200, 211; countering cultural erosion, 130–131; narrative stage topic, 191; NEA and HSFCA programs, 9, 37–38; SFF mission, 2, 5–6, 14–15, 184, 192
cultural revival: countering cultural loss, 130; crafts, 70–71, 90, 93; grassroots, 39; HSFCA inspired, 42, 45, 81; narrative stage topic, 161; Native Hawaiian, 45–50, 57; political nature, 59. *See also* renaissance
culture bearers. *See* tradition bearers
culture brokers: appeal of inclusivity, 217–218; early figures, 30; ethics, 5, 42; interpretation, 131–132; local, 177–178; narratives of festival, 183–184; self-reflexivity, 11, 204; Smithsonian, 4, 63–64. *See also* cultural authority

Davis, Susan G., 172
Delima, Frank, 61
demographics: Hawai'i, 83–84; Hawai'i program, 105, 112; omissions, 168
demonstrations: performance, 2, 147, **154, 155,** 156, 158, 161, 166; planning, 102, 108; site design,

134. *See also* Hawai'i program; stages
Desmond, Jane, 13, 14, 21, 22, 220
dialogue, SFF model, 3, 9, 11, 121, 155, 158, 161, 174, 178, 214
diaspora, Native Hawaiian, 123, 168, 191, 233n85
diversity. *See* multiculturalism

East-West Center, 67, 76, 82
"embraceable imagery," 88, 96, 112
Emmsley, Thomas Kamaka, 118, 198
ethnic groups (ethnicity): added groups in restaging, 190; ethnic labels in performance, 142, 159; festival representation questions, 55; HSFCA definitions and funding, 9, 42–43, 45, 73; program book divisions, 195–197; representation on signs, 123; selection for festival, 74, 88; SFF categories, 2, 154–155, 216; situational ethnicity, 160. *See also names of individual ethnic groups*
ethnic humor, 61, 66, 89, 223n16
ethnic tension, 9, 33, 34, 65, 75, 76, 81
ethnography: ethnographic authority, 179; ethnographic display, 158; ethnographic gaze, 176; ethnographic history, 4, 5; ethnoscape, 88; representational accuracy, 189; Smithsonian history, 6, 214; tourism, 7, 155

Fairbanks, Robert P., 100
Ferguson, Kathy, and Phyllis Turnbull, 16
"The Festival" (PBS), 181–183
Festival of American Folklife (FAF). *See* Smithsonian Folklife Festival (SFF)
fieldwork: ethics, 5; festival role, 61; fieldworkers, 9, 76, 79; limitations, 96; methodology, 62; process and influence, 77–78; reports, 80–82, 108; review meetings, 82–88
Filipinos: HSFCA data, 74, 185; international expositions, 6; NEA and HSFCA sponsorship, 41, 93; panethnic category, 88; performance, 165; site design, 108; vanishing culture, 94. *See also* ethnic groups; *rondalla*
folklife (folklore): definitions, 7, 68, 70, 71; genres, 69, 71, 79–80; immigrant, 73–76; local, 71–72; Native Hawaiian, 70–71, 99; occupational, 2; SFF genres, 100–101
folklife festivals: authenticity concerns, 78; definition, 5; festival culture, 209; functions and impact, 213–214; politics, 4–5, 11; staging methods, 232n67
Folklife Hawai'i program book, 195–197. *See also* restaging
Folklife Preservation Act, 68
folklorists: cultural conservation, 27; defining tradition, 6; festival debates, 11, 213–214; SFF, 2
Folkways Recordings, 119, 140, 202
food: concessions and health regulations, 120, 156; cooking supplies, 115–116, 141; ethnic traditions, 89, 94, 95; shared traditions, 104, 105; site design, 108
forno, 95, 108, 109, 113, 180
Fredo, Bart, 181–183
Freshley, Mary Jo, 86–87, 159, 204
Fuchs, Lawrence, 47
funding: 1989 program, 52; 1990 restaging, 186

Garmon, Pearl, 135
gates, 112, 151, 157
gaze: ethnographic, 176; tourist, 10, 14, 173, 176, 215
Guigni, Heather, 179–181, 183

Halla Huhm Dance Company, 36–37, 43, 86–87, 92
haole: elite, 16, 25, 26, 30, 34, 35, 46; festival selection process, 56, 67, 78; inclusion in signs, 123; and local identity, 56, 65–66; narra-

tive stage topic, 161, 162; omission from festival representation, 85–86, 96, 197, 216; Portuguese as shifting category, 84, 110; self-representation in memory, 183–184; stereotype, 232n71
hapa-haole; images, 25, 220; music, 25, 27, 89, 99, 122, 165–166, 206
Hawes, Bess Lomax, 44, 214
Hawai'i: in American imagination, 8, 12, 24, 61–62, 129, 214; as crossroads of Pacific, 217; as global village, 204, 215; government, 188, 200–201; as "hot spot," 11, 14, 60; Legends and Folklore Commission, 29; as multi-regional, 178; Organic Act, 18; overthrow and annexation, 18, 20, 28; statehood, 34, 125, 150, 188, 235n22; socio-political factors, 233n84; Territory of, 18; transnational location, 7–8; western contact and colonization, 15–16, 20, 58. *See also* colonialism; demographics; immigrants; military; multiculturalism
"Hawai'i: Cosmopolitan Culture at the Crossroads of the Pacific" (Kennedy with Martin), 128–131, 195
Hawai'i program: absence of children, 157; appearance, 1–2, 134, 148; critical factors, 199; cultural politics, 4, 8; impact, 202, 213; multisited, 158, 173; opening ceremonies, 12, 147, 150–151; production logistics, 114–119; proposal, 51; scheduling, 146–147, 164; SFF poster child, 205; sponsors, 113–114. *See also* demonstrations; funding; participants; presenters; speeches; spin-offs; stages
Hawai'i Promotion Committee (HPC). *See* Hawai'i Visitors Bureau (HVB)
Hawai'i State Foundation for Culture and the Arts (HSFCA): Advisory Board, 45, 67; Cultural Heritage Development, 41–43; defining ethnicity, 43, 69; ethnic improvement programs, 38–41; festival planning, 9, 51; Folk Arts Program, 44–45, 52, 189, 210; founding, 34–35; Master and Apprentice Program, 44, 67, 94, 194–195; mission statements, 34, 37, 40; Model Cities program, 38–41; post-festival projects, 197; restaging, 186–189; State Conference on Hawaiian Dance, 38, 40
Hawai'i State Society, 118–119, 143–144, 162, 168
Hawai'i Visitors Bureau (HVB): festival sponsor, 13, 113, 157, 186, 215; international expositions, 21–22; 1909–1928 promotional campaigns, 24–25, 27; promotion of immigration, 21–22
Hawaiian language, 6, 20, 49, 71, 128, 139, 220n6, 227n28, 228n7
Hawaiian music: chalangalang, 165, 232n76; Da Bunch, 198; *hapa-haole,* 25, 27, 165; *hīmeni,* 91, 175; hybridity, 91–92; *mele* and *oli,* 15, 16, 23, 27, 29, 70, 77, 92, 148, 208, 230n38; musician selection, 87; renaissance, 49; slack-key guitar, 1, 165, 166, 180, 182. See also *'ukulele*
Hawaiiana, 8, 23–24, 203
Hawaiianness, 166, 169, 206, 215
Hawaiians. *See* Native Hawaiians
Hawes, Bess Lomax, 44, 67
He'e, James Kealakalani, 158
hegemony: Christianity, 112; diversity as counter-hegemony, 121, 192; dominant culture, 123, 205; festival as intervention in, 125; institutional, 5; narratives, 207; revealed in Onipa'a, 208
hīmeni, 91, 224n38. *See also* hybridity
historiography, 179, 181, 183
Ho'opi'i, Richard and Solomon, **164,** 168–169, 171, 198, 217

Hōkūle'a, 48–49, 90. *See also* Polynesian Voyaging Society
Honolulu, 188, 191, 197; newspapers, 209
Honolulu Department of Parks and Recreation, 31–33
Hooper-Greenhill, Eilean, 63, 96, 107
"hosts and guests" model: participants as guests of nation, 135–136; participants as hosts, 168–169; program theme, 10, 69, 72, 130, 164, 168; restaging, 207; restaging book, 196; SFF, 3, 105
hotel, Washington, D.C., 146, 168–169, 170–171, 180; restaging, 190–191
hukilau, 31
hula: Beckwith on, 28; canonization, 178–179; debates over forms, 169; early, 228n16; festival media representations, 180, 182, 203; festival performance, 1, 144, 157, 171; HSFCA programs, 39–40, 43, 70; international expositions, 20, 22; and Merrie Monarch Festival, 49; narrative stage topic, 140; Parks Department workshops, 32; revivals, 16–17, 29, 30–31, 90; selection issues, 70, 77, 78, 81, 83, 87; shared tradition, 83, 104, 160; signs, 122; site design, 103, 108, 110, 111; suppression, 15, 16, 17, 20, 25, 220, 227n23; tourism, 14, 25–26, 27, 89, 127, 175, 206, 208. *See also* Native Hawaiians; renaissance; tradition
hybridity, as authenticity in Hawai'i folklife: Christianity, 111–112; cultural expressions, 17, 94; and multiculturalism, 210; program theme, 9, 99; in site design, 104–106, 109–110. *See also* creolization; tradition: shared

identity politics, 7, 8, 45–47, 63, 70, 82. *See also* renaissance
Imada, Adria, 20, 23, 25, 26, 27, 220, 142, 228n16
imagined community, 135, 169, 172, 183–184, 191
immersion schools. *See* Hawaiian language
immigrants: arrival in waves, 55–56, 73, 190; contract labor, 18, 21; erasure in promotional materials, 22; media representation, 180, 183; narrative stage topic, 140; representation in festival signs, 122–123; representation in site design, 104, 108; traditions of, 8, 32, 37, 41–43; transnational affiliations, 8. *See also* ethnic groups; tradition: shared
imu: performance, 1; program videos, 180, 182; site design, 103, 108, 115–116, 143, 226nn113, 114
Inouye, Daniel, 33, 43, 148, 149–150, 201
"inreach," 188, 191, 235n19
international exhibitions: ethnographic displays, 6, 44–45, 158; 1885 New Orleans, 18–19; 1889 Paris, 18–20; 1893 Chicago, 20–21; 1901 New York, 21; 1909 Seattle and 1915 San Francisco, 21–24, 203. *See also* ethnography
intervention: critics, 5, 7; cultivating invisibility, 4, 44–45; and cultural authority, 30; as cultural conservation, 15; disadvantaged groups, 93; ethics, 42; institutional policy, 3, 4, 8, 9; local impact, 10
inversion, 100, 148, 158, 173, 230n31
Iolani Palace, 208–209

Jackson, Bruce, 62, 220
Japanese: festival representation, 87, 96, 112; Hawai'i politics after WWII, 33; investment in Hawai'i, 124, 201, 216; local views of, 81, 163–164; restaging, 190; site design, 108, 112; signs, 124; tour-

ists in Hawai'i, 162; traditions, 71, 74, 90. *See also* bon dance; *yagura*
Johnson, Katie N., and Tamara Underiner, 216
Johnson, Lyndon Baines, 34, 38
Jolly, Margaret, 7, 15
Juniroa Productions. *See* videos
Junker, Jay, **164**, 198

Kaeppler, Adrienne, 16
Kaho'olawe, 46–47, 75, 162
Kalākaua, David, 16–17, 20, 209
Kalama, Meali'i, 177, 182
Kamaka, Samuel, **164**, 171
Kanahele, George, 16, 32, 49
Kanaka'ole, Pualani, 148, 177, 181; Hālau o Kekuhi, 180
Kane, Ray, 87, 148, 165, 177
kapa, 18, 19, 70, 90, 109
katchi katchi music, 2, 91; program videos, 182. *See also* Portuguese
Kekiwi, Faith Ku'ulei, **164**, 197
Kennedy, Richard: Asia/Pacific Research Center proposal, 10, 199–202; background, 63, 65; festival reflection, 11, 204, 224n30; fieldwork process, 78, 80; 1989 program video, 180; participant mediation, 169; planning, 76; program book, 128–131, 132; restaging address, 192, 199–200, 202
Kent, Noel J., 8, 34
Kirshenblatt-Gimblett, Barbara, 78
kitchens. *See* demonstrations
Koreans: Christians, 112; fieldwork selection, 74, 86–87, 92; performance, 1, 115, 159; program videos, 182; representation on signs, 124. *See also* Freshley, Mary Jo; Halla Huhm Dance Company
Kurin, Richard: Asia/Pacific Research Center proposal, 10, 199–202, 236n41; background, 204; festival reflection, 11, 65; Hawai'i program, 14, 114, 145; 1989 program video, 180; planning, 76, 101; program proposal, 50–52; on SFF, 2, 3, 5, 63, 89, 121, 147, 161, 172

lā'au lapa'au, 71, 108, 117, 156, 179
Lau, Barbara, 101, 107
lauhala weaving, 71, 94, 120, 164, 185
LDS (Church of Jesus Christ of the Latter Day Saints), 30–31, 123
learning center: site design, 101, 108, 110, 113, 122–123, 124
lei: concessions, 119, 144; demonstrations, 1, 67, 56, 94, 102, 107, 115, 158; festival theme, 122, 130, 144; international expositions, 18–19; *paniolo*, 91; Parks and Recreation Department, 32; *pā'ū*, 118, 127; program videos, 182, 184; shared tradition, 104; Smithsonian statues, 152; tourist tropes, 14, 26; Vietnam War Memorial, 153; Virtual SFF, 203
Lili'uokalani, Queen, 17, 208–209, 220n10
Liliko'i, Violet, 165, **194**, 198
Lippard, Lucy, 98
living history, 208–209
local: identity, 56, 64–65, 86, 204; origins and shifting meaning of term, 65–66; program representations, 104, 111, 197; traditions, 71–72
Lomax, Alan, 166–167
lū'au: Hawai'i program, 115–116, 144, 147, 156; tourism, 31; traditional, 73, 91, 175; videos, 182; virtual, 202–203
Luahine, Iolani, 39, 40

MacCannell, Dean, 100, 155
MacLeod, Roy, 203
Magic Island, 189–190, 197
Makua'ole, Esther, 171
Martin, Lynn (Graton): background, 44, 65–66, 68–76; film disputes, 180–181; Hawai'i folk arts guide, 68–76; 101, 146; 1988 program, 177; planning, 52–53, 56, 63,

136–137; post-festival projects, 197; restaging proposal, 185–186; signs and program book, 128
Matsunaga,"Spark" Masayuki, 33, 43, 148, 149, 150
McDonald, Marie, 31–32, 144, 152, 158, 163, 183, 184
media: festival mediation, 3, 4; handling press on-site, 144–146; influence on memory, 184, 210–211; local coverage of festival programs, 176, 191–192; local coverage of Onipa'a, 209; program press releases, 139, 229n24. *See also* videos
mele. *See* Hawaiian music
memory: function of retelling, 158–159; institutional, 203–204, 207; local, 10, 173, 183, 210–211; nostalgia, 100; restaging, 195; shaped by media, 181, 184
Merrie Monarch Festival, 49, 127
Merry, Sally Engle, 17, 76, 205, 219
military: exclusion from fieldwork, 85; 442nd regiment, 33; inclusion in signs, 123; Kaho'olawe bomb testing, 47, 162; neo-colonialism, 216; presence in Hawai'i, 15, 18, 21, 26
mimesis, 101, 112, 153
missionaries, 15–16, 111, 122, 208. *See also* Christians; *hula;* LDS
Moriarty, Linda, HSFCA, 44; background, 67; offstage, 167–169; participant preparation, 140; planning, 83, 88, 101; restaging, 186; SFF cookbook, 202; site design issues, 115–116
Mormons. *See* LDS
Mossman's Hawaiian Village, 25, 27
multiculturalism: discourse of harmonious diversity, 76, 136, 173, 191, 210, 215; in Hawai'i, 59, 61, 73, 83–84, 142, 178; Hawai'i program theme, 9, 10–11; and "local," 111; paradigms, 63, 72, 104, 154–155; performance, 160–161; program videos, 183–184; restaging as model, 186–187; SFF model, 2, 3; site design, 100, 110, 122, 150; U.S. vs. Hawai'i, 8, 86, 89, 196, 205. *See also* ethnic groups; narratives
museums: "big idea," 142, 195; map as metaphor, 107; methodologies, 63, 96, 101, 203, 220; museumization, 132–133; national, 2, 3, 63, 106, 146, 189; and tourism, 3, 64, 153. *See also* Bishop Museum; Smithsonian Institution

Nahwooskey, Fred, 82, 101, 107, 186
Nakasone, Seisho Harry, 84, 198
Napoka, Nathan, 83, 112, 132, 156, 158, 159–160, 183–184, 198
narrative stage. *See* stages: narrative
narratives: benign multiculturalism, 210; catharsis in Onipa'a, 209; counter-narrative, 10, 173, 215; festival, 52, 56, 59, 66, 74, 99, 110, 120; Hawai'i program film, 180–183; historical, 10, 82, 122–125, 207, 214–215; indicative of relative positions, 183–184; master, 6, 9, 63, 97, 131; multiple narratives of ethnic identity, 211; multicultural vs. post-colonial, 131; in museums, 96; national, 125, 131; "rags to riches," 124; renaissance, 47–50; traditional Hawaiian, 27, 28, 29, 30. *See also* anecdotes
National Endowment for the Arts (NEA): Model Cities program, 38–41; 1980s culture wars, 5; sponsored programs in Hawai'i, 9, 34, 36–37; State Conference on Hawaiian Dance, 38, 40; state resource, 44–45. *See also* Hawai'i State Foundation for the Arts
National Heritage Fellows: creation, 40; from Hawai'i, 82, 87–88, 165, 182, 198, 217, 234n3; local effects, 191

National Mall: layout and features, 107, 110, 189; national public street, 173; 1989 festival site, 1–2, 12, 59, 63, 99, 101, 107, 117, 146, 197; restrictions, 116, 119; sacred ground, 3, 147; symbolic epicenter, 63, 100
National Park Service, 2, 107, 116, 119, 127, 131, 148, 152
nationalism, 5, 148
Native Americans: performance, 6, 148, 149, 170, 171–172; restaging, 190, 191, **192**; restaging program book, 196
Native Hawaiians: activists, 7, 59, 76, 123–124, 172; Civic Clubs, 39, 45, 47; early images of, 22, 25–26, 220, 218; endangered by tourism, 206; Homelands, 29; HSFCA data, 69–71, 185; identity politics, 45–47, 63; internal conflicts, 81, 209; museumization, 132; "Native Hawaiian" label, 46; 1920 Rehabilitation Act, 28–29; Office of Hawaiian Affairs, 47, 218, 237n7; performance, 159–160; program opening ritual, 151–152; "shut your mouth school of learning," 164; signs about, 123; socio-economic status, 70, 93; traditions, 70–71, 99. *See also* Hawaiian language; *hula; Onipa'a;* renaissance
Nogelmeier, Puakea, 162

offstage, 167–172
OFP (Office of Folklife Programs). *See* Center for Folklife and Cultural Heritage
'ohana: appropriations, 69, 206, 223n12; in Hawai'i, 217–218; participant bonding, 75, 136, 169; program concept, 6, 137, 142, 157; program signs, 122
Okamura, Jonathan Y., 65, 66, 76, 164
Okinawans: agreeing to be folk, 216; program videos, 182; selection process, 78, 84; self-identification, 87, 224n32; site design, 108, 109, 225n10
Onipa'a, 7, 10–11, 206, 207–210
opening ceremonies, 12, 147,150–151
"other side of the island" theme, 173, 184

pā'ū riders: program book cover, 206; SFF performance, 1, 127, 144; signs, 122; tradition, 73, 118–119; Vietnam War Memorial, 153
Pa, Chauncey, **155**, 167
Page, Helàn, 112
Pang, Duane, 151, 160, 170–171, **192**
paniolo: demonstrations, 1, 141, 147, 192–194; HSFCA data, 185; hybrid folklife, 91, 92; narrative stage topic, 191; planning, 57, 77, 81; program videos, 182; site design, 105, 108, 110; variations, 179
parade: festival parade, 1, 118, 152–153; and power, 172
Parker, Diana, 52–56, 101, 179
participants: as educators, 157; handling press, 144–145, 146; honored in opening ceremonies, 148–149; as local celebrities, 177–179; missing children in program, 157; narrative stage, 162–164; need for presenters, 138–140; new alliances, 167–168, 169–171, 190; Ni'ihau participants, 167, 171; performance considerations, 95–96; pre-departure preparation, 135–137, pre-performance preparation, 140–142; program videos, 182; selection, 84–88, 136; SFF rhetoric, 121. *See also* ethnic groups; tradition bearers
performance, 4, 9–10; performance zones, 100, 217; performativity, 72, 80, 82, 102, 140, 154; site of contestation, 135, 166
pidgin, 32, 65, 139, 228n8. *See also* creolization; plantation

planning meetings, 9, 52–59
plantation: festival theme, 85, 88, 105, 109, 142, 151; history and experience, 65, 74, 124–125; mentality, 176; narrative stage topic, 140; organizing principle in restaging program book, 196; system, 32, 33
pluralism. *See* multiculturalism
politicians, 3, 147–148, 161, 200. *See also* Akaka, Daniel Kahikina; Burns, John; Inouye, Daniel
Polynesian Cultural Center (PCC), 31
Polynesian Voyaging Society, 43. *See also* Hawai'i State Foundation on Culture and the Arts
Pomeroy, Irmalee, 163
Portuguese: census categories, 84; ethnic humor, 74; HSFCA sponsorship, 42, 93; Holy Ghost Festival, 94–95; identification as non-haole, 86; restaging, 190; signs, 125; site design, 108, 109, 110. *See also* ethnic groups; *forno*
post-colonialism, 7, 64, 131, 152, 203, 204
Preis, Alfred, 34, 35, 43
presenters: festival narratives, 183–184; pre-festival preparation, 137–140, 161–162, 165
primitivism: Beckwith, 28; festival concerns, 90; festival programming, 109, 187; international expositions, 19–20; missionaries, 15; racial stereotypes, 21; SFF, 203, 204; "soft savagery," 26, 176; tourism, 8, 159
program books, 184; 1989 program book, 126–131; restaging program book, 195–197; SFF outreach, 3, 184
public sector culture workers (folklorists). *See* culture brokers
Puerto Ricans, 74, 84, 85, 91, 165. See also *katchi katchi* music

quilting, Hawai'i program, 1, 104, 115, 119, 182

racism (American), 20, 21, 220
renaissance: in festival narrative, 92; influence on fieldwork, 77; multiple narratives, 47–50; narrative stage topic, 161, 162; political protests, 46; signs, 121, 123. *See also* Hawaiian music; *hula;* Native Hawaiians
representation: ethics, 181; institutional, 135; politics, 4–5, 7, 64, 91
resistance: colonial era, 20; covert forms, 76, 205; 1989 neighbor program themes, 149–150; participant, 216–217; performance, 135, 164–166; renaissance, 46, 49; to SFF, 54–55; to tourism productions, 206–207. *See also* Native Hawaiians; renaissance
restaging: children as target audience, 192, 194; cultural appropriation, 206; educational workshops, 187; logistics, 189–190; media and memory, 191–195; narrative stage, 191; participants, 190–191; proposal, 185–188; SFF model for local cultural presentation, 206, 207; site design, 189–190, 196. *See also* Folklife Hawai'i program book
Rinzler, Ralph, 2, 101, 148, 149
ritual: in 1989 program, 147, 150–151, 153, 170–171; in Onipa'a, 208–209
Roberts, Helen, 29–30, 35, 220
rondalla, 40, 41, 74, 94,182
Rosaldo, Renato, 200
Royal Hawaiian Band, 18, 220. *See also* Hawaiian music
Ruiz, Robert, 141, 198–199

Saiki, Arnie, 209
Samoans: in audience, 159; demographics, 84; festival themes, 105; HSFCA and NEA sponsorship, 41, 42, 85; LDS link on sign, 123; opening ritual, 151–152; traditions, 90, 231n40

"Sense of Place" theme: erasure of diaspora, 168; informing performance, 137; planning phase, 57, 60, 62, 66, 69; site design, 84, 100, 102, 108, 128–129, 131. *See also* narratives: festival
shipping, 116–117
signage: as interpretation, 3; textual representation, 121–126; visitor interaction, 227n24
Silva, Henry, 182, 192–194
Silva, Noenoe, 16, 220, 227n23
Simons, Beverly, 156
site design: Big Island inspiration, 107; effects on performance, 131; design phases, 108–113; interactivity, 106, 107; learning center, 101, 108, 110, 113; plants, 102, 105, 112; representing shared traditions, 102–106; standard components, 106. *See also* restaging; stages
"Six Reasons Not to Produce a Folklife Festival" (Camp and Lloyd), 4–5
Skillman, Teri, 78, 81, 87
Smith, Barbara, 55, 73
Smith, Linda Tuhiwai, 64, 222n2
Smithsonian Folklife Festival (SFF): benefits to Hawai'i, 210; changed programming, 204; cookbook, 202–203; as discursive field, 121, 133, 211; festival data, 184–185; festival frames, 136, 142, 146, 164, 172; hierarchy, 127, 146; ideology, 11, 80, 88, 100, 122, 176; local impact, 177–179; magic, 174; 1988 SFF program, 177, 204; 1989 neighbor programs, 1, 107, 126, 145, 147–149; overview and mission, 2–3, 6, 96, 106; political neutrality, 145–146, 147–149; promotional videos, 203, 205; spontaneity, 10, 121, 141–142. *See also* Center for Folklife and Cultural Heritage; Hawai'i program
Smithsonian Folklife Festival: Culture Of, By, and For the People (Kurin), 5, 184
Smithsonian Institution: Asia/Pacific Research Center, 10, 199–202, 211; authority, 144, 148; discursive field, 126; ideology, 70; local reactions, 55, 64, 175–176; newsletter, 202; 19th century ethnographic spectacles, 6
sovereignty movement, 7, 47, 208–209
space: mediated, 158; spatial logic 103, 131; theory, 100
Spam, 168, 233n86
speeches: Hawai'i Legislature, 201, 217; 1989 program opening, 12, 148–149, 140, 205; 1990 restaging, 192, 199–200, 202
spin-offs, 197–198
Sproat, Clyde "Kindy," 81–82, 87, 91, **164,** 177
"staged back regions," 100, 155, 166
stages: cross-cultural workshops, 147; narrative stage (store), 75, 104, 108, 110, 113, 115, 134, 140, 156, 161–164, **164,** 168, 215; performance stages, 103, 108, 109, 111, 113, 115, 118, 134. *See also* site design
Stanley, Nick, 174
Stannard, David E., 65, 219n4
store. *See* stages: narrative
Strazar, Marie D., 56, 83, 195
Strickland, Barbara, 114
Sturken, Marita, 183
subversion: in arts, 18, 20, 213; SFF, 3
sugar industry: history, 13, 25, 33; signage, 124–125. *See also* plantation
supplies, 114–115; horses, 118–119; *imu,* 115–117; lava, 118; participant needs, 141

talk story, 140, 161, 202
taro, 71, 101, 116, 117, 134, 158
Tasaka, Kenichi, 90, 198
Tong, June, 89, 156
Torgovnik, Maria, 175
tourism: airport greeters, 112; colonialism, 13; economy, 150; Ecumenical Council on Tourism protest,

205–206; imagery, 10, 14, 25; inclusivity, 217–218; museums, 3; narrative stage topic, 140, 161–162, 191; opposed to fake, 99; Polynesian Cultural Center, 31; restaging, 186–187; SFF, 4, 121, 215; signs, 124; tourist desire, 24, 100, 155; tradition as medium, 13–14, 200; tropes, 55, 57, 59, 100, 103, 127, 131, 176, 189, 203. *See also* Hawai'i Visitors Bureau
tradition: definitions, 6, 7, 8, 9, 79–81; endangered, 9, 94; medium for power negotiations, 14–15; national appropriation, 218; politics, 4, 5–7, 11, 59, 88 (*see also* canonization); shared, 65, 89, 91, 94, 99, 102–106, 108, 110–111, 142, 154–155, 160–161, 224n40 (*see also* creolization; ethnic groups; hybridity; plantation); and tourism, 13–14, 200; traditionality, 8, 9, 70, 85, 89, 91, 119, 123, 166, 216
tradition bearers: agents of cultural preservation, 121; identification, 76, 78, 80, 88, 95; linked to contemporary life, 214; as participants, 121, 131, 138–140; SFF representation, 2, 5, 61–62. *See also* participants; tradition
Trask, Haunani-Kay, 7, 13
Trimillos, Ricardo, 44, 67, 76, 83, 89
Twigg-Smith, Thurston, 209

'ukulele: Hawai'i program, 1, **164;** at international expositions, 22, 25; Portuguese origins, 17, 74; in schools, 35; and tourist industry, 14, 25–26. *See also* Hawaiian music
UNESCO, 64
United States Department of Agriculture, 117, 226n15
Urry, John, 14

Van Zile, Judy, 82, 92, 103
Velasco, Gordon, 107, 143
videos: 1984 SFF promotion, 205; 1989 program videos, 179–183, 184; 2000 SFF promotion, 203, 205
Virtual Smithsonian website, 202–203
visitors: interacting with performance and signs, 100–101, 120, 125–126; interchanges at narrative stage, 161–164; misinformation, 158–159; missing demographics, 157; peripheral in memory, 173–174; SFF rhetoric, 121
volunteers, 134, 143–144, 147, 184

Waihee, John: conflict over Onipa'a, 208–209; election, 47; 1989 program on-site, 156, 152–153, 162, **164;** 1989 program proposal, 50–52; 1989 program speech, 12, 219, 149–150, 205, 217; 1991 speech to state legislature, 201; restaging, **192;** restaging proposal, 185–186; support for SFF program, 199
Waikikian Hotel, 53, 200–201
Waikīkī, 24, 26, 27, 165, 188, 197, 208
Waimea Hawaiian Church Choir, **153,** 197, 198. See also *hīmeni*
Weiner, Annette B., 217
Whisnant, David E., 5, 6, 214, 215
"Why We Do the Festival" (Kurin), 127
World's Fairs. *See* international exhibitions

yagura, 57, 106, 111, 112, 117–118, 134, 144, 170, 190
Yano, Christine, 216
Yokouchi, Masaru, 34–35

Zuttermeister, Kau'i, 43, 87, 157, 177
Zuttermeister, Noelani, 157, 169, 177, **194**
zydeco, 190, 196

About the Author

Heather A. Diamond received her Ph.D. in American studies from the University of Hawai'i at Mānoa, where she is currently a lecturer in the departments of English and American studies. She was a graduate fellow at the East-West Center in Honolulu, Hawai'i, and a pre-doctoral fellow at the Center for Folklife and Cultural Heritage at the Smithsonian Institution.

Production Notes for *Diamond / American Aloha*

Designed by University of Hawai'i production staff
with Sabon text and display in Senator

Composition by Josie Herr

Printed on 55# Glat Offset B18, 360 ppi